OING BY THE
BOOK

Past and Present Tragedies of Biblical Authority

GOING BY THE BOOK

Past and Present Tragedies of Biblical Authority

ERNIE BRINGAS

HAMPTON ROADS
PUBLISHING COMPANY, INC.

Cover design by Matthew and Jonathan Friedman
Cover photo by Jonathan Friedman

For information write:

Hampton Roads Publishing Company, Inc.
134 Burgess Lane
Charlottesville, VA 22902

Or call: (804)296-2772
FAX: (804) 296-5046

If you are unable to order this book from your local
bookseller, you may order directly from the publisher.
Quantity discounts for organizations are available.
Call 1-800-766-8009, toll-free.

ISBN 1-57174-022-8

10 9 8 7 6 5 4 3 2 1

Printed on acid-free paper in Canada

For my Loving Mother
Ruth

Ignoring knowledge is sickness.

—Lao Tzu*

---

* The Lao Tzu ("old master") is a small book of wise sayings. Tradition-alists hold that the book was composed in the sixth century B.C. and its author was of the same name, Lao Tzu, a senior contemporary of Confu-cius. Others believe the author is unknown. They view this Chinese writing as an anthology of wise sayings dating back to the sixth century, collected and edited between 350-275 B.C. Whatever the case, these sayings serve as the basis for the religion of Taoism ("the teaching of the way"). The Lao Tzu is sometimes called the Tao Té Ching ("the way and its power").

CONTENTS

With Gratitude

I have had suggestions of how to improve this work from a few people who saw preliminary versions, including a fellow seminary graduate friend, Dave Bourquin. Dave was especially helpful in directing me to the writings of some important scholars such as Bruce Metzger and Martin Hengel.

Another phase of this writing was helped along by my nephew, Tim Robbins (an English major), who grammatically corrected my manuscript. He also sent me numerous comments and queries about matters he felt needed improvement. I'm sure that it is a better book as a result of his pertinent comments.

The final polishing phase was accomplished with the helpful suggestions of two good friends, Rev. Lee Neish and Dr. Robert Erickson (Bob and I also graduated together from seminary). As a result of their comments, minor adjustments brought this work to its present form.

Overall, I am also indebted to my special friend Teena Brown for her keen insights and for her perceptive analysis of the early versions of this book. Her constructive criticism was supportive and helpful.

A final thank you is directed to Hampton Roads Publishing, but for which this work would not have entered the public arena.

Prologue

As a young boy, I attended the Evangelical United Brethren (EUB) church which was basically conservative (at least in my Los Angeles neighborhood). In my formative years, church and home provided the loving atmosphere in which I came to understand the basis of Christian faith. In retrospect, I would never trade the nurturing warmth of this experience, although I must admit to its less enlightened side: there were no alternatives to an infallible Bible and a one-wayism Gospel. I did not know, even during my teenage years, of such distinctions.

Beyond the local church, I reveled in Billy Graham crusades and the newly released cinema spectacles of *The Robe, The Ten Commandments*, and *Ben-Hur*. These epics played well against my simplistic understanding of Bible and Church. It all made perfect sense: Jesus, salvation, miracles, and, equally so, an unquestionable source of authority, the Bible.

I realized, of course, that Christians were somewhat at odds with each other in their theological viewpoints and therefore were labeled conservative, liberal, moderate, and so forth. Such variations in faith are natural and expected. But on my way to becoming a United Methodist minister, and during numerous years of higher education, I discovered a significantly different portrayal of Christianity, a Christianity that bore little resemblance to what was being taught at the local level. This was more than just the usual skirmish between conservative and liberal viewpoints. What I sensed was a Christianity transformed—transformed by the collective knowledge of humankind (both secular and religious) and it appeared to be out of sync with traditional Christian beliefs.

At the beginning of my postgraduate studies at United Theological Seminary (Dayton, Ohio), I was baffled by this peculiarity. I found it almost inconceivable that a "parallel" Christianity could have existed without my knowledge. Even worse, it was obvious that most people were (and still are) unaware of its existence. Apparently, in academic circles, Christianity had metamorphosed into a new equation and, for reasons I will discuss later, in most cases it failed to become fishers of congregants. How could this be, and why? Certainly, ministers who had previously traversed this educational ground were aware of this dichotomous situation.

Inevitably, my belief in the Hollywood version of Christianity came to an end. In so doing it created a great deal of personal and professional pain: personal in that it separated me from friends and family roots, and professional in that I had acquired knowledge that, in many respects, conflicted with what most believers held to be sacred. Within the boundaries of this tension I have tried to fulfill my ministerial and Christian responsibilities. Of course, whether one is a minister or layperson, it is not essential to be theologically "correct" in order to love or be loved. Still, to embrace beliefs which are incorrect can serve only to obstruct our evolving human ascent. For these and other reasons, the pursuit of truth must become germane to our spiritual development.

Obviously, my restricted portrayal of the Church is not absolute. Many churches, ministers, and lay people do not resemble what I suggest to be the majority position. Even so, the troublesome characteristics explored in this writing seem to permeate most levels of religious expression. And when progressive churches— even entire denominations—strive to balance new knowledge against traditional dogmatism, adamant resistance generally obstructs the process.

Owing to the candid nature of this work, I know there will be many Christians who will not, or cannot, assimilate this information. I can understand the reluctance to question religious convictions, since only a few years ago I had this same resistance. For most of us, information that conflicts with our basic religious beliefs is rejected, ignored, and considered a sacrilege. But for the sake of our personal development and the continued progress of the human family, it is well to remember that the only real self-deception—regardless of what one does or does not believe—is the denial of truth.

Admittedly, portions of this material will appear as an assault against Christianity and therefore this might be construed as an anti-Christian work. But even seen in that perspective, *the reader must never lose sight of the acknowledgement that any rational comparison of negative and positive aspects of Christianity overwhelmingly favors the positive. The point is, however, that this work does not seek such a comparison. Its function is to expose a theological malignancy which adversely affects people everywhere.*

I stress that my desire is not to shock the reader or misrepresent the facts, but rather to strike at the heart of the matter so as to expose the internal forces which propelled Christianity into a collision course with reality. You need not accept the conclusions reached herein. But if you examine and weigh the facts presented, I believe you will see the numerous fallacies and self-destructive attitudes with which many of us approach our faith. I hope such reevaluation will enable us to develop greater maturity and unity in our *search for truth.*

There is no pretense here to cover up the fact that the treatment of various topics is not comprehensive in scope. There is always the temptation to expand the work, to replace the unfinished blueprints of research with something more visually concrete. I am confident, however, that future writings will dispel any clouds of confusion arising from my limited perspective and opportunity to address all the issues. But please keep in mind that, in the final analysis, I seek only to provide a beginning framework of study. It is up to you, and every reader, to add the flesh and perception that will give it substance and meaning.

Thesis and Clarification

After evolving through its primitive beginnings (magic, fetish-ism, ancestor worship, human sacrifice), religion in the "civilized" countries came to be regarded as one of the noblest pursuits. Today, many believe that to be religious is to be good or moral, if not in practice at least in intention. Thus, religion is generally considered to be a positive influence on society, and there is ample evidence to support this view.

But suppose this religious soup of theology contains an unde-tected ingredient that ultimately sours the flavor of its message. Worse yet, suppose it harbors a poison that destroys the sensibilities of those who consume it. If religion promoted among its followers a mind-set that not only was misguided but also drove them to abhorrent behavior, then it could be regarded (at least in part) as a detriment to humankind—a retrogressive influence on us all. Is it possible that *Christianity* contains such an additive? It does. The basic thesis of this work proposes that Christianity, like many other religions, suffers from an exaggerated claim for the posses-sion of truth. This presumption is clearly prompted by a crucial misunderstanding of the nature of biblical revelation. Herein is the cyanide element of theological brew—a self-imposed notion which, if not neutralized, will eventually destroy the credibility and essence of Christianity.

The assumption of possessing sacred knowledge is woven into the fabric of Christian thought and, for that matter, all belief systems that claim special knowledge. This blind adherence to so-called sacred revelation is the Trojan Horse of well-intentioned but misguided believers.

What I am suggesting as the "enemy within" may not sound impressive, and certainly not ominous, but history tells us a different story. Over the past centuries, bibliolatry has led Chris-tians to bigotry, the persecution of Jews and other non-Christians, murder and terrorism, the oppression of women, the suppression of sexuality, censorship, cult mentality, and other aberrations. These destructive behavior patterns can be easily traced to the unchallenged authority accorded biblical writing.

One readily acknowledges that Christians have made enormous contributions to the social and spiritual progress of humankind. But that is what makes this story so bizarre. Christianity, in spite of all its magnificent contributions, has left an appalling trail of misery and death as recorded in the bloodstained pages of history. And the cruel, grotesque events they record are prime examples of misguided faith, perpetrated under the delusion (sometimes pretext) of divine guidance. Simplistic trust in the Bible as the word of God has given our faith a Jekyll-and-Hyde personality: it kindles love but ignites hate, engenders understanding but breeds intolerance, gives rise to education but reinforces ignorance and dogmatism. A never-ending paradox.

Today, bibliolatry has led us to another social and personal catastrophe—a catastrophe of such grave proportions that only through our willingness to see and acknowledge it can we move toward meaningful solutions. This work will demonstrate that the vast majority of Christians—and, for that matter, non-Christians— are victims of a knowledge gap which places them at a level of religious understanding much more appropriate to the seventeenth century!*

Ignorance of this knowledge gap has led us to one of the most deplorable conditions of our time. This aberration is the direct result of faulty assumptions about the Bible, assumptions which foster the belief that the sacred scrolls are to be honored above all other viewpoints. The reverence accorded biblical writing has trapped most of us, albeit unknowingly, within the religious mental framework of the seventeenth century. The upshot is that we are collectively moving into the twenty-first century with an antiquated mind-set which I shall hereinafter refer to as the *astrolabe mind* (or astrolabe mentality).

An astrolabe is an ancient navigational instrument formerly used for measuring the altitude of the sun and other stars. It was used until the invention in the eighteenth century of the sextant, a more efficient instrument. Today the astrolabe serves primarily as a museum piece.

The science of navigating ships, aircraft, or spacecraft is serious and technical. It demands radar, sonar, and computer guidance. It

---

* *This theme originates from a passing comment made by the late James D. Smart, theologian and professor at Union Theological seminary, in his book* The Strange Silence of the Bible in the Church.

would be preposterous and dangerous if, in place of our modern technology, navigators and pilots insisted on using the astrolabe. At best, they would be considered eccentric. Illustrating my premise of arrested knowledge, the obsolete seventeenth-century astrolabe will serve as the graphic symbol of our present religious mind-set; hence, the term *astrolabe mind.*

What I have expressed may, at first glance, seem absurd. Even so, what I offer here is not opinion but knowledge—knowledge that remains unknown to the majority. The truth of this matter will be supported by evidence to a degree that puts it far beyond reasonable doubt, or at least gives it predominance over contrary views.

In the pages that follow it will become evident that our religious beliefs are significantly out of line with what has been discovered about the Bible and Christianity through historical and biblical scholarship along with the natural and social sciences during the past few hundred years. We must close the chasmic gap between what the world of scholars know about Christianity and what most Christians believe about Christianity. The attempt is not novel. For more than three centuries, the clarion call has been sounded by numerous writers, ministers, and educational institutions world-wide. And yet, the disparity between scholar and layperson remains.

It is essential to remember that the Bible is *not* the venomous problem within Christianity—the problem centers on how most adherents *view* the Bible: with an all-accepting assumption that the message is God-given and, therefore, the indisputable truth.

The belief that the Bible was *inspired* by God has been and still is uppermost in the minds of Christians. Unfortunately, many followers equate the term *inspiration* with *perfection.* Their thinking is as follows: (1) God is perfect! (2) Biblical revelation comes from God! (3) Therefore, biblical revelation is perfect!

This simple formula appears logical, but, among other things, it fails to consider the human dimension in which the biblical writing developed. This oversight reflects a grave misunderstanding. It has led to the belief that the entire Bible is faultless—a collection of sacred messages that are considered unfailing, timeless, and universally valid. This belief has come to be known as the doctrine of inerrancy (or infallibility) and represents the majority view in the Christian community. Although such an approach to the Bible is sterile and superficial, a 1991 Gallup Poll shows that 32 percent of adult Americans believe the Bible is the actual word of God, and is to be taken literally word for word. For these people, all biblical writing is viewed as irrefutable authority. This belief is part of our religious heritage. But even though this viewpoint has been championed by apostles, Church fathers, popes, and present believers, it deserves serious criticism.

Of course, many Christians view the doctrine of inerrancy as unrealistic and simply a form of bibliolatry. They would be more inclined to say that the Bible *contains* the word of God rather than *is* the word of God: a subtle but important distinction. Even so, most of them have not escaped the overbearing influence of biblical authority owing to the belief that God has played a major role in its creation. It may not be perfect because of its entry through the human channel, but the assumption of God's signature on the text is central to all Christians. This conviction drives them to accept the overall truth of biblical writ while simultaneously acknowledging the imperfections caused by its human contributors. While this view of the Bible does not demand perfection, as does the doctrine of inerrancy, it nevertheless fails to engender a realistic understanding of biblical shortcomings. Viewing the Bible as God-given does not permit anyone the natural freedom to challenge or seriously question its content.

It is apparent that this view of the Bible is little more than a smoke screen to hide the perplexing fact that non-conservative believers are only superficially advanced in their comprehension of this issue. In truth, bibliolatry is not restricted, as many believe, to those fundamentalist denominations whose dogmatic doctrine of biblical inerrancy places them on the conservative right. The problem is much more inclusive. The claim for infallibility is merely the flagrant extreme of Bible worship, but the mesmerizing effect of biblical *authority* engulfs most Christians today, regardless of their doctrinal persuasion. In other words, while not every believer accepts the doctrine of inerrancy, almost everyone does take the Bible's authority for granted. This unchallenged assumption has created havoc.

Before we can comprehend the magnitude of this problem, especially in terms of the astrolabe mind and other present-day anomalies, we must first examine the historical repercussions resulting from viewing the Bible as ultimate authority. This investigative journey is not simply informative but essential. Consider the words of Roman orator Marcus Tullius Cicero (106-43 B.C.):

> Not to know what has been transacted in former times
> is to be always a child. If no use is made of the labors of

past ages, the world must remain always in the infancy of knowledge.

To remain in the infancy of knowledge, of course, drives us to think and behave as children, but children with adult power. As we shall discover through the experience of past and present believers, such an intermix can be disastrous. Objectively stated, Christians have always been confronted by a first danger—the assumption of biblical truth; they have always been confronted by a second danger—the failure to recognize the first danger.

Chapter I

Absolute Authority—Tyrannical Religion

The attribution of absolute authority to the Bible by early Christians carried the writings and teachings of Christianity far beyond their original intentions. Going by the Book has led to misunderstanding, intolerance, mayhem, and death.

Paul and other New Testament (NT) writers probably never perceived how great an impact their writings would have on future generations. They could not know their works would be compiled into the official books of the Church and elevated to the same status as Old Testament (OT) literature. When Paul wrote "All Scripture is inspired by God . . ." he was not referring to his own writings. Nor could he have been referring to other segments of the NT, since much of it had not yet been written, and those portions that did exist were not officially proclaimed sacred by the Church until the end of the fourth century. As these early documents became the official books—the *canon**—of the Church and were accorded sacred status, they were indiscriminately viewed as absolute authority. As a result they, along with the OT, had enormous influence on their readers. Unfortunately, some of these writings were contrary and detrimental to the human spirit.

Slavery

The NT is quite explicit in denouncing women who pray with their heads unveiled, but it is virtually silent on exploiting human life through slavery. In fact, it distinctly dictates that slaves be obedient to their masters and suggests that masters are entitled to their slaves.

---

* *The canon is the official list of books of the Bible accepted by the Christian church as genuine and inspired.*

Titus 2:9: Bid slaves to be submissive to their masters and to give satisfaction in every respect . . .

1 Tim. 6:1: Let all who are under the yoke of slavery regard their masters as worthy of all honor.

Eph. 6:5: Slaves, be obedient to those who are your earthly masters, with fear and trembling, in singleness of heart, as to Christ.

Col. 3:22: Slaves, obey in everything those who are your earthly masters.

Col. 4:1: Masters, treat your slaves justly and fairly, knowing you also have a Master in heaven.

The unquestioned authority attributed to these verses becomes apparent when we view their effect upon later generations. The teachings of the early Church, based on the NT, clearly confirm that it upheld slavery. Bishop Ignatius of Antioch, one of the most distinguished clerics of that time, wrote in a letter to Bishop Polycarp: "Do not treat slaves and slave girls contemptuously. Neither must they grow insolent. But for God's glory they must give more devoted service, so that they may obtain from God a better freedom."[1] Similarly, an early text, commonly called the *Didache* or the *Teaching of the Twelve Apostles*, advised: "You slaves, for your part, must obey your masters with reverence and fear, as if they represented God.[2]

Clearly, these examples indicate that the NT Epistles conveyed the approval of slavery. Thereafter, many Christians failed to perceive its fallacy and degradation, and for the next nineteen centuries Christianity openly accepted and supported the marketing of human flesh. During the Middle Ages (from about A.D. 500 to about 1450), slavery was defended by such noted persons as Albert the Great,* Thomas Aquinas,† and Dun Scotus.‡

---

* *Albert the Great (1193?-1280) was a philosopher and scientist who strongly influenced Thomas Acquinas, his favorite pupil.*

† *Thomas Aquinas (1225-1274), Italian philosopher and doctor of the Church, is the greatest figure of scholasticism and one of the principal saints of the Roman Catholic Church. He was declared by Pope Leo XIII to represent the official Catholic Philosophy.*

‡ *John Dun Scotus (1266-1308) was a scholastic philosopher and theologian who had considerable influence on Catholic thought.*

Under the direction of popes, bishops, and other high-ranking clergymen, thousands of male and female slaves labored at cultivating vast farmlands owned by the Church. Slaves who ran away were relentlessly pursued. Those who were caught and brought back were branded as fugitives. They were forced to wear around their necks heavy iron rings embellished with Christian symbols. Church law categorized slaves as "material objects" and "Church property."[3]

Christian slaves were doubly jeopardized by the Holy Writ. Over the centuries they were taught to accept their terrible plight as a natural consequence of God's will, rather than become aware of their right to freedom and self-determination.

> Col. 3:22a, 24: Slaves, obey in everything those who are your earthly masters . . . knowing that from the Lord you will receive the inheritance as your reward; you are serving the Lord Christ.

Such teachings psychologically conditioned slaves to submit to the harshness and injustice of their situation; they also conditioned them to concentrate on the *afterlife*. This pie-in-the-sky promise is an all-too-familiar theme that even found its way into American slavery, where it subdued Blacks into accepting their deplorable existence. One song writer wrote: "This world is not my home, I'm just a passin' thru." The emphasis was on a reward in heaven. What else was there? Here we see Christianity trying to pacify those who "labor and are heavy laden," instead of helping them shake off the yoke of oppression.

To be sure, anti-slavery sentiments did exist within some American church bodies, chiefly among the Quakers. But the majority of churches, including Methodists, Baptists, Congregationalists, and Presbyterians, remained deeply divided on the issue. In 1843, according to Paul Johnson's* *A History of Christianity*, 1,200 Methodist ministers owned slaves, and 25,000 church members collectively owned more than 200,000.

---

* Paul Emanuel Johnson (1898-1974) was a United Methodist minister, author, and professor of philosophy and religion and psychology of religion and the Daniel Professor of psychology and pastoral counseling at Boston University School of Theology and a visiting professor at Duke, USC, and Union Theological Seminary.

The Lutherans, Episcopalians, and Catholics avoided public debates and voting, but they were also split on the issue. In all fairness, it should be noted that some Christians (primarily in the North) rallied hard against the immorality of slavery. Even so, it is evident that many Christians justified slavery on the basis of Scripture.

Some people contend that Paul was attacking the practice of slave-keeping when he wrote, "There is neither Jew nor Greek, there is neither slave nor free, there is neither male nor female; for you are all one in Christ Jesus" (Gal. 3:28). But Paul is referring here to religious equality and not social or political equality.[4] This theme is echoed in 1 Corinthians 12:13; Colossians 3:11; and Philemon 15-16. Moreover, Paul made no effort to translate this spiritual model into a functional, earthly solution to human degradation. Paul's writings do advise masters to treat their slaves justly and fairly since they too have a master in heaven (Col. 4:1). On first reading, this statement sounds humane and compassionate, but this is what makes it particularly insidious. What Paul's words serve to do is justify slavery, or at least condone it. They suggest that one may possess slaves as long as they are treated fairly. Obviously, slaves would rather be treated fairly than unfairly. But Paul's statement overlooks the real issues of freedom, human dignity, and self-determination. Where is the "love your neighbor as yourself" ethic in Paul's statement? It ignores the real meaning of love and justice. This is not to question the magnificent literary and spiritual insights he registered, but there is no doubt that he also reflected the biased beliefs of his time.

While it would be tempting to point an accusing finger at Paul and even blame him for what eventually transpired, this would be unfair for two reasons. First, research indicates that some of the NT writings attributed to Paul might not have been written by him. Second, it does not matter who produced these works—Paul or someone else—since the real issue is not the authorship or even the writings, but how they came to be elevated to the heights of divine authority and regarded as the unquestionable word of God. The responsibility for this must be born by numerous generations of Christians.

Clearly the moral issue surrounding slavery is now a decided one. But just 150 years ago, such was not the case. Here is only one example where Christians followed biblical teaching which was totally out of step with what we now hold to be morally self-evident!

Anti-Semitism

It is no secret that many atrocities committed against the Jews over the past 2,000 years can be traced to the seeds of suspicion and distrust sown in the NT. Since the very beginning of Christianity, believers have regarded the Jews as the wayward children of God and the enemies of Jesus. These anti-Jewish sentiments are clearly reflected in the Book of Acts. Jews are variously called "stiff-necked," "betrayers," and "murderous people" (Acts 7:51-53). This theme is reinforced in Paul's first letter to the Thessalonians (2:15-16) in which he blames the Jews for the death of Jesus. He portrays them as being opposed to all others and displeasing to God. Also, following Pilate's release of Jesus to the Jews while stating that he was innocent of this man's blood, the Book of Matthew (27:25) describes the Jews as pronouncing a curse upon themselves: "His blood be on us and our children!" Although this statement is now considered by most scholars to have been fabricated by the author of Matthew,[5] throughout the centuries it served to excuse and justify the killing of Jews.

Perhaps the strongest anti-Jewish emotion is registered in the Gospel of John. It is ironic that here, in what many Christians call the "love book," are statements vilifying and damning the Jews. They are called the "children of the Devil," who seek to do their father's will—their father, of course, being the father of lies and a murderer (John 8:44). It was only a matter of time until these and other derogatory biblical sentiments fueled the fires of bigotry. The Jews became the targets of distorted theology based on ignorance, bias, and the overwhelming authority associated with biblical writing.

The early Church fathers such as Barnabas,* Justin Martyr,† Origin,‡ and Tertullian§ used violent, abusive language against the

---

* *Barnabas was a prominent member of the early Jerusalem church who, with Paul, was a first pioneer of the missionary apostles outside of Palestine and Syria.*

† *Justin Martyr (A.D. ? -165) was a Christian philosopher and writer.*

‡ *Origin (A.D. ca. 184-254) was the principal theologian of the early Greek church.*

§ *Tertullian (A.D. ca. 160-220) was an outstanding third-century theologian and writer.*

Jews. This anti-Semitic theme gathered full orchestration under the oratory of pastor St. John Chrysostom (A.D. 347-407). In a series of eight sermons, he invoked an arsenal of hateful speech, in which are found all the verbal weapons used against the Jews down to the present day. He called them greedy wealth-seeking misers, demonic, obscene, drunkards, harlots, criminals, devil worshippers, and murderers of the prophets, Christ and God.[6] Although some scholars have suggested that Chrysostom's burning comments were aimed primarily at Jews who had converted to Christianity yet practiced Jewish customs, his remarks are patently anti-Semitic and cannot be excused as anything less.

Early on, Christians looked upon the Jews as "Christ killers" and enemies of Christianity. These venomous attitudes spread quickly from the Christian community to every sector of society and eventually led to the vicious persecution of Jews, especially after Christianity became the official religion of Rome under Constantine in the fourth century.

The Christian clergy encouraged Roman emperors to deal harshly with the Jews. Pagans were forbidden to convert to Judaism and many restrictions were placed on Jewish life.[7] Marriages between Jews and Christians were punished by death. The Roman Emperor Theodosius II (A.D. 408-450) forbade Jews to hold public office or to build synagogues.[8] The Emperor Justinian (A.D. 483-565) went further: He condemned the Jews as heretics and ordered their synagogues to be confiscated by the state and transformed into churches. Justinian also legalized the pillaging and burning of synagogues by Christian bishops and monks.[9]

The anti-Jewish laws set down in Spain were even harsher. In 694 the seventh Council of Toledo declared all Jews to be slaves, and ordered their property and possessions confiscated. The Council also decreed that Jewish children were to be taken from their parents at age seven to be raised by the clergy and later married to Christians.[10]

By the eleventh century, popes exerted more influence than any royal or political rulers of the day. Pope Urban II called for a crusade to take the land of Palestine back from the Moslems. When the Christians of Europe learned that Moslems possessed the tomb of Jesus, their zeal for conquest was ignited. They swarmed to the "army of the Lord" by the thousands. Serfs and peasants alike joined the tremendous emotional movement, though some were nothing more than fortune hunters.[11]

The First Crusade was poorly organized. Armies of peasants

marched off with little or no supervision. While in progress they rationalized that it was pointless to conquer godless people in a distant land when the Jews, equally opposed to Christianity, were at hand. Soon the cry rang out: "Kill a Jew, and save your soul!"[12] It didn't help that the ranks of the crusaders also included *priests* who proclaimed that the Crusade must begin by converting or exterminating the Jews.[13] Some Christian leaders such as Bernard of Clarivaux*and Peter the Venerable† sought to restrain the fanatics from their savage rampage, but with little success. Noted historian Solomon Grayzel‡ estimates that 10,000 Jews were slain in Central Europe during this First Crusade.[14] The prolonged and hideous massacre of Moslems and Jews—men, women and children—when Jerusalem fell added to the number of victims.[15] Many Jews were burned to death in their synagogues.[16]

In 1215, during the reign of Pope Innocent III, it was decreed that all Jewish males older than thirteen and Jewish females older than eleven must wear a yellow patch on the front and back of their garments.[17] This "badge" was regarded as a mark of shame, symbolizing the continuing hostile division between Christians and the so-called murderers of Christ.

This prejudiced attitude was intensified through modification of the Church's ceremonies. The Good Friday and Easter services were uniquely marked with new anti-Jewish emphasis. During these rites, the Jews were referred to as perfidious (faithless, treacherous) and the word "perfidious" was not deleted from Catholic services until 1959.[18] The popular mystery plays, passion plays, and other semi-religious entertainments of the day also mocked and vilified the Jews. In medieval art, the devil often was portrayed with Jewish stereotyped features.

---

* *Bernard of Clarivaux (1090?-1153) led a holy life, had unusual eloquence and a reputation for miraculous cures. His influence on Roman Catholic spirituality is felt today.*

† *Peter the Venerable (1092-1156) was abbot of the monastery of Cluny for thirty-five years. He exerted powerful influence for good.*

‡ *Solomon Grayzel (1896-1980) was professor of history at Dropsie University, Philadelphia, 1966-1978. Rabbi Grayzel received the Frank L. Weil Award of The National Jewish Welfare Board for contribution to the development of American Jewish culture. He was born in Russia and died in Englewood, New Jersey.*

During the fourteenth century, a widespread calamity gripped Europe. Beginning in 1334 the Black Death raced rampantly through France, Germany, Hungary, and England. No part of Europe was spared from the plague and millions perished. One-fourth of the population was lost. Modern medical science has diagnosed the Black Death as bubonic plague and believe it was carried by rats aboard the ships bound for Europe from the East. But the concept of germ-caused disease was unknown to people then; they had no knowledge of the scientific causes of disease. The consequences of this ignorance were most severe for the Jews, since Christians believed the Jews were somehow responsible for the onslaught of this pestilence. After all, Christians were primed through centuries of prejudicial indoctrination that the Jews were diabolical. Was that not the proclamation of Scripture itself? (John 8:44) Rumors began to circulate that the Jews poisoned the water wells. This allegation was nothing more than the revival of an untrue story told in 1321, when a leper said that Jews had instigated a plot to poison the drinking water of Christians.[19] As a result, many Jews were murdered. But the resurgence of this rumor during the spread of the Black Death caused a much heavier loss of Jewish life. Crazed with anger and fear, Christians embarked on a cold-blooded rampage which resulted in the slaughter of thousands of Jews.

Still, some Christians knew that the Jews could not possibly have caused the plague since they were dying in like manner. Pope Clement VI wrote letters urging the protection of the Jews and declaring them innocent, but to no avail.[20] The seeds of biblical prejudice long ago sown in the minds of people by the Church now exploded with fiery wrath. Throughout Europe, Jews were tortured and butchered unmercifully. More than 15,000 German men, women, and children died in Bavaria and at Erfurt alone.[21] According to Grayzel, 50 percent of the German Jewish population was annihilated![22]

This murderous persecution of Jews continued throughout the Middle Ages. On June 4, 1391, the Archdeacon of Ecija incited a riot in Seville, Spain, which resulted in the killing of 4,000 Jews. That same summer, in city after city across Europe, Jews were burned out of their homes and synagogues. The number of Jewish deaths is placed at 50,000.[23]

From its very beginning, Protestantism was as anti-Semitic as Catholicism. Martin Luther, founder and leader of the Protestant Reformation (1517), persecuted the Jews vehemently. His treatise,

"On the Jews and their Lies" (1543), advocates:

> . . . their synagogues or schools should be set on fire
> . . . their houses may also be broken down and destroyed
> . . . their prayer books and their talmudists may be taken
> away from them . . . that their rabbis may at all costs be
> prevented from teaching . . . that they may be prevented
> from praising and thanking God and from praying and
> teaching publicly here among us and among our Christian
> people, on punishment of life . . . that they may be pre-
> vented from uttering the name of God in our presence . . .
> We Christians can hardly believe that a Jew's foul mouth
> is worthy to speak the name of God in our presence, and
> if any one of us should hear a Jew speak that name, he
> should at once inform the authorities or else throw pig shit
> at him . . .[24]

Is it any wonder that during his military trial at Nuremberg in 1946 Julius Streicher, the editor of the Nazi newspaper *Der Stürmer*, cited the teachings of Martin Luther as a justification for his own actions against the Jews?[25]

This brings us to what is perhaps the most appalling epoch of anti-Semitism the world has witnessed. The mass extermination of millions of Jews by the Nazi forces during World War II was the result of many social, political, cultural, psychological, and religious factors; cause and effect remains blurred. Christianity, however, must bear partial liability. While the degree of its accountability is debatable, there can be little doubt that the influence of Scripture and, indeed, of certain Christian leaders contributed to the Holocaust. Lucy Dawidowicz* wrote in *The War Against the Jews, 1933-1945*:

> A line of anti-Semitic descent from Martin Luther to
> Adolf Hitler is easy to draw. Both Luther and Hitler were
> obsessed by a demonologized universe inhabited by Jews.
> "Know, Christian," wrote Luther, "that next to the Devil

Lucy S. Dawidowicz (1915-1990) was associate professor of Modern Jewish History at Yeshiva University (NY), 1969-1974, and visiting professor, Jewish Civilization, Stanford University, 1981. She was awarded the Ansfield-Wolf prize in 1976 for The War Against the Jews, 1933-1945.

thou hast no enemy more cruel, more venomous, and violent than a true Jew".[26]

Adolf Hitler was a Catholic. He never left the Church, nor was he excommunicated. In his discussion with Bishop Berning of Osnabrük in April 1933, Hitler remarked: "As for the Jews, I am carrying on with the same policy which the Catholic Church has adopted for 1,500 years."[27] Hitler claimed to be following the Church's lead, planning to do what Christians had done throughout history—namely, murder Jews!

There is no doubt that Nazi anti-Semitism was derived, at least in part, from Christian anti-Semitism, which grew out of the foundation laid by the Catholic Church and the later teachings of Luther. The Nazi credo was equally a part of German nationalism. Together, Christian bigotry and German nationalism spawned the insanity that murdered 6,000,000 Jews.[28]

This is not to suggest that Hitler embraced the teachings of Christianity. Quite the opposite is true. Early in the development of the Nazi party, Hitler openly declared his scorn for Christianity. Many anti-Christian books were published by the party, disavowing God as portrayed in the Bible and ridiculing the ethics of the NT as fit only for morons and idiots. According to Gustavus Myers,* translations of many of these anti-Christian books can be found in *Watchman, What of the Night?, Can Christianity Survive?* and *A Compilation of Original German Documents*, all by Stanley High.[29]† It becomes obvious that Hitler merely adopted those mutations of Christian thought (such as anti-Semitism) which promoted his diabolic scheme. Inevitably, under his master plan, Christians might have faced the same horrors of carnage which he visited upon the Jews.

Unfortunately, most Christians of that day did not realize Hitler's anti-Christian attitudes, and many church officials believed him to be quite pious and friendly to the faith. This illusion was created by false reports, the gullibility of church leaders, and Hitler's deceitful nature. It is not surprising, then, that the German Evangelical Church fell into line behind the Third Reich. (The German

---

Gustavus Myers (1872-1942) was an American economic historian.
†*Stanley H. High (1895-1961) was the author of religion-oriented books; he worked for many years as senior editor of* Reader's Digest.

Evangelical Church was a federation formed in 1933 of Lutheran, Reformed, and united territorial churches.)

The most notable Christian resistance to Hitler came from the Confessing Church, a German Protestant movement founded in 1933 by Martin Niemoeller* and under the substantial influence of Karl Barth.† The opposition was prompted by Hitler's attempt to purge the German Evangelical Church of converted Jews and make it subservient to the state. The justification for this breakaway by the newly-formed Confessing Church was soon realized as the German Evangelical Church condoned and openly supported the Nazi doctrine. On December 17, 1941, it published the following declaration:

> The . . . leaders of Germany have provided indisputable documentary evidence that the Jews are responsible for this war in its worldwide magnitude . . .
>
> . . . the Jews are the enemies of the nation and of the world . . . the severest measures should be taken against the Jews and [they] should be expelled from all German countries.
>
> . . . Christian baptism does not change in any way the Jew's racial character, his membership of the Jewish people and his biological nature . . . Christians who are Jews by race have no place in that church and no right to a place.[30]
>
> [One must wonder if any of these Christians remembered that Jesus was Jewish!]

On the other hand, the Confessing Church mustered its resistance against Nazi perversion: ". . . during the Third Reich 3,000 pastors were arrested, at least 125 were sent to concentration camps and 22 are known to have been executed for their beliefs."[31] But this does not mean that the Christian community actively opposed the Third Reich. Although some Christians openly opposed the Nazis,

---

Martin Niemoeller (1892-1948) was a German Lutheran pastor who was confined in concentration camps from 1937 to 1945. In 1945 he organized the "Declaration of Guilt" in which German churches admitted their failure to resist the Nazis.

† Karl Barth (1886-1968) was a significant Swiss theologian, a prolific writer, and one of the most influential voices of twentieth-century Protestantism.

the majority of Christians did nothing. The heroic resistance of clergymen such as Dietrich Bonhoeffer* was more the exception than the rule. In the words of Ernst Helmreich:†

> The Confessing Church never made a point of being a political opposition movement . . . it seems clear that the motivation and driving force within the Confessing Church was religious, a desire to maintain the purity of the Gospel message . . .[32]

It also should be noted that any Christian support for the Jews was extended primarily to those who had converted to Christianity, not Jews in general. Thus it is clear that most German Christians could not outdistance their anti-Semitic attitudes—at least not to the point of risking their lives. In short, Hitler's henchmen committed the sin of commission, while the Christian majority committed the sin of omission.

Notable exceptions in the general population did occur. We must acknowledge the courage and kindness displayed by many Christian (and non-Christian) families, who, at their own peril, succeeded in rescuing 100,000 Jewish children from the death camps by passing them off as their own. A 1991 CBS report referred to these fortunate youngsters as "the hidden children."

Since the end of World War II—partly from a sense of guilt—both Catholics and Protestants have tried to reverse the prevalent anti-Jewish sentiments. They have also sought to soften their discrimination against other non-Christians. But though these negative feelings can be somewhat controlled, how can they ultimately be contained if Christians are taught to view the "non-believer" as outside the "true" faith? Consider the following words ascribed to Jesus:

> . . . I am the way, and the truth, and the life; no one comes to the father, but by me (John 14:6).

---

* *Dietrich Bonhoeffer (1906-1945) was an influential Lutheran pastor and theologian involved in an assassination attempt on Hitler. He was hanged April 9, 1945, as an opponent of Nazism. His sister and two brothers-in-law were also executed.*

† *Ernst Helmreich (1902-), Ph.D., Harvard University 1932, is the Thomas Brackett Reed Professor of History and Political Science (1959-), Bowdoin College, Brunswick, Maine.*

Although there are theological maneuvers that can help us skirt around the literal interpretation of this verse, the NT is replete with statements that encourage absolutism and condemn doctrinal divergence. Take for example:

> ...men who will not acknowledge the coming of Jesus Christ in the flesh; such a one is a deceiver and the antichrist (2 John 7).

> Any one who goes ahead and does not abide in the doctrine of Christ does not have God...(2 John 9)

As we see in the morbid lessons of history, the belief that one possesses absolute truth invariably leads to arrogance that breeds intolerance and disdain toward others—attitudes that erupt in verbal and physical hostility. Arrogance is the forerunner of depravity. In his book *The Ascent of Man,* the late Jacob Bronowski* said of the infamous Nazi concentration camp at Auschwitz:

> This is where people were turned into numbers. Into this pond were flushed the ashes of some four million people. And that was not done by gas. It was done by dogma. It was done by arrogance. When people believe that they have absolute knowledge, with no test in reality, this is how they behave. This is what men do when they aspire to the knowledge of gods.[33]

This phenomenon is doubly dangerous in the area of religion because the claim that certain writings are "God-given" assigns them ultimate authority; the belief that one possesses absolute, irrefutable knowledge must inevitably follow. This leads to presumption, intolerance, and fanaticism. Since the NT portrays Jews as evil and as the enemies of God, it is not difficult to see why Christians throughout history have turned against the Jews with such hostility or have failed to speak on their behalf, as was the case in Hitler's Germany. One does not question the sincerity of

---

Jacob Bronowski (1908-1974) was a mathematician by training. He began writing about science and human values following World War II. The Ascent of Man was probably his most popular achievement—his last and greatest creation.

followers who embrace their faith wholeheartedly; but as history clearly demonstrates, they can be extremely dangerous.

The Inflexible Mind-Set

Nowhere are the consequences of sacred authority more apparent than within Christianity itself. Again and again, zealous believers will turn against each other; the lambs of love will become the rabid, snarling, ferocious wolves of destruction.

The first recorded account of a Christian being murdered by other Christians involved a Spaniard named Priscillian, a Church member who was decapitated in A.D. 385 on the orders of Emperor Maximus. Because Priscillian disputed the doctrines of the Trinity and Resurrection, he, along with six of his followers, was tortured and put to death. Many Christians were shocked and outraged at this murderous act, and pressure was brought to bear upon the two bishops who prosecuted the case. As a result, one was expelled from the episcopate and the other resigned.[34] But prudent judgment did not last.

It was only sixty-two years after the execution of Priscillian and his followers that Pope Leo I spoke out in justification of their murders. He said, "If the followers of heresy so damnable were allowed to live there would be an end of human and divine law."[35] Pope Innocent III (served 1198-1216) said heresy was treason against God and more shockingly evil than treason against a king.[36] No one thereafter was allowed to question the *divine word* or the *teaching of the Church*, and anyone who did risked severe punishment and even death.

The Inquisition

Efforts to prosecute heresy cases remained lax and unorganized until the thirteenth century. Then in 1231 the Inquisition was instituted by Pope Gregory IX. Courts were established to hear heresy cases and mete out punishment to persons found guilty. The Inquisition quickly became a ghastly instrument of terror, especially after Pope Innocent IV in 1252 authorized the use of torture to extract confessions from accused heretics.[37] The monstrous legal machinery of the Inquisition was set in motion and became unstoppable throughout Europe for the next *500 years.*

The following summary of the Inquisition's procedures is based in part on the writings of Charles H. Lea, Walter Nigg, John A.

O'Brien, Henry Kamen, Joachim Kahl, Edward Peters, and John Tedeschi.

The accused heretics first were arrested and isolated from the outside world. They were considered guilty from the outset, and it was regarded as the God-given obligation of the inquisitor to shake loose confessions. Only in this way, it was believed, could the accuseds' souls be saved from the clutches of the devil. Defense lawyers were not allowed; the accused had to rely on their own resources.

In contrast, the prosecution was authorized to produce any number of witnesses, including blood relatives. Testimony and hearsay by even the most unreliable witnesses, including children, were accepted as conclusive evidence of guilt. The accused was not allowed to challenge witnesses or even know who they were. The accused, however, was permitted to testify.

Not surprisingly, torture was the quickest and most effective method of obtaining a confession. The heretics first were dragged into the torture chamber and shown all the instruments of torment. If they did not confess their alleged guilt, torture was applied slowly with increasing intensity. These sessions usually lasted two to four hours, leaving the victims violated and shattered.

Often the torture instruments used in these interrogations were first sprinkled with holy water (water blessed by a priest). These numerous devices included:

> **The Thumbscrew.** The accused's fingers were placed between clamps. The screws were turned until blood spurted and the bones were crushed.
>
> **The Boots.** This effective device was used to crush the shinbones.
>
> **The Rack.** The accused was stretched across a triangular frame, bound hand and foot to prevent movement. Wrists and ankles were secured by cords affixed to a jackscrew. When the screw was turned, the limbs were stretched excruciatingly until the wrists and ankles were pulled from their sockets.
>
> **The Strappado (Vertical Rack).** The accused's hands were tied behind his or her back and raised by a rope attached to a pulley to the top of the gallows or to the ceiling. The prisoner was then dropped repeatedly with a jerk to within a few inches of the floor. On occasion, weights were tied to the victim's feet to increase the shock and agony of the fall.

The Toca (Water Torture). The accused was tied to a rack, the mouth was kept forcibly open, and a linen cloth put down the throat to conduct water poured slowly from a vessel. The severity of this torture depended on the amount of water released.

In general, the Inquisition tried to prevent the unrestrained abuse of prisoners by forbidding the breaking of bones or the taking of life during torture—regulations that were not always observed. Whatever the experience, the pain was excruciating. In the words of survivor William Lithgow, an Englishmen who was racked in 1620 by the Spanish Inquisition:

> I was brought to the rack, then mounted on the top of it. My legs were drawn through the two sides of the three-planked rack. A cord was tied about my ankles. As the levers bent forward, the main force of my knees against the two planks burst asunder the sinews of my hams, and the lids of my knees were crushed. My eyes began to startle, my mouth to foam and froth, and my teeth to chatter like the doubling of a drummer's sticks. My lips were shivering, my groans were vehement, and blood sprang from my arms, broken [torn] sinews, hands and knees. Being [freed] from these pinnacles of pain, I was hand-fast set on the floor, with the incessant imploration: "Confess! Confess!"[38]

The only way to stop or avoid torture was to confess (repent), and obviously most accused heretics did. Penalties varied to extremes: Imprisonment ranged from a few months or years to life, depending on the case. Some prisoners were confined to small, dark, solitary cells devoid of adequate ventilation and subjected to violence, brutal treatment by jailers, squalor, and generally inhumane conditions. Heavy iron cuffs were placed around their ankles and sometimes linked by chains to the walls. Their diet consisted of bread and water.

In contrast, some prisoners were confined in hospitals or convents where conditions were somewhat benign. Still others were placed under house arrest and enjoyed considerable comfort and freedom. But even those prisoners who were not mistreated or received only brief sentences, in almost all cases, faced a life of beggary and hunger upon their release, since all their worldly possessions were confiscated. They also faced the added burden of shame, ridicule, and loss of respect.

Some convicted heretics were exiled or sent below decks of ships to the galleys. Others were whipped—a very popular punishment. The penitents were stripped to the waist and often mounted on an ass. They rode through the streets being flogged by the public executioner as onlookers showed their contempt by hurling stones at the victims. Girls and women of all ages were whipped in like manner. No more than 200 lashes were applied and sentences of 100 lashes were common.[39]

The ultimate penalty was death at the stake. This was reserved only for the unrepentant or backsliding heretic. It was not uncommon for such martyrs to be tormented brutally before their final, fiery end. Some were prevented from protesting by having their tongues screwed tightly between two iron clamps. The tip of the tongue was then scorched with a red-hot iron, causing it to swell so it could not be drawn back.[40] Still other unfortunates, while en route to the stake, were prodded with red-hot tongs or had their hands severed. There was no end to the imaginative forms of agony that were inflicted. If the victims repented before the ceremony climaxed, they were "mercifully" strangled before the fires were lit. If not, they were agonizingly roasted alive as the onlookers cheered and sang hymns such as "Great God, We Praise Thee."[41]

The justification cited for this ruthless system was in part the authority of Scripture. Church leaders pointed to the OT as condoning even the most brutal actions against heretics. "He who blasphemes the name of the Lord shall be put to death; all the congregation shall stone him . . ." (Lev. 24:16a). And from the NT, this statement by Paul: "But even if we, or an angel from heaven, should preach to you a gospel contrary to that which we preached to you, let him be accursed" (Gal. 1:8). The support for this condemnation, according to Paul, is the divine nature of the revelation, which he obviously takes for granted:

> For I would have you know, brethren, that the gospel which was preached by me is not man's gospel. For I did not receive it from man, nor was I taught it, but it came through a revelation of Jesus Christ (Gal. 1:11-12).

Some people regarded these verses as a direct call to take merciless action against heretics. It became a fanatical battle against those who dared to challenge the purity of religious teaching. It was a moral crisis which no "self-respecting" Christian could allow to go unchallenged. Thomas Aquinas, the most powerful Christian of his time, declared that heretics must not be tolerated. Heresy, he said, is infidelity to God and is more abominable to God than all other sins. Since it is the gravest of sins, he reasoned, it should be punished more severely than any other.[42]

The cruel and heartless methods used to punish persons accused of heresy indicates the depth of madness and misguided religious passion perpetrated by those who claimed to be doing God's will. Perversities of thought abounded: Setting a torch to the stake of an unrepentant heretic was considered an honor; those who brought wood to the stake were said to be forgiven of their sins. These public burnings were usually held on Sundays and feast days to draw the largest crowds. High prices were paid for positions with the best view. These burnings of heretics were justified sometimes by interpretations such as that of John 15:6:

> If a man does not abide in me, he is cast forth as a branch and withers; and the branches are gathered, thrown into the fire and burned.

Clergymen themselves became the victims of the Church's misguided suppression. John Hus, for example, was ordained as a priest in 1400 and was eventually burned at the stake (July 6, 1415) because, among other reasons, he denied the supreme authority of popes and councils. The same tragedy befell Bishop Ridley and preacher Hugh Latimer, who together were martyred at the stake on October 16, 1555. It is impractical to name all the numerous martyrs and explain the events that led to their demise. Ample sources prevail on this subject.

It must be noted that the Church did not perform the tortures or executions of heretics. This was contrary to Church law. The accused were tried by the Inquisition, an instrument of the Church, but the sentences were carried out by civil authorities and administered, in most instances, by public executioners who worked for the secular courts. But of course, the Church was so powerful that civil authorities had no choice but to carry out its wishes. In short, the Church committed murder by proxy.

Some historians argue that the sentences levied by the Inquisition were far less harsh than those of secular courts. Others contend that the Inquisition has been blown out of proportion by writers and novelists for the purpose of sensationalism. Both contentions are partly true.

By comparison, most of the sentences levied against heretics by the Inquisition were indeed less barbaric than the sentences passed by the secular courts against the common criminal. The Spanish Criminal Code of Charles V, for example, issued in 1530, is a catalog of hideous punishments ranging from blinding and mutilation to tearing of the flesh with hot pincers. Similarly, in England, some criminals were boiled to death. And, in France, women convicted of simple felonies were buried alive, while Jews found guilty of crimes were hung by their feet between ravenous dogs.[43] Skinning convicts alive and tearing them apart between wild horses was not uncommon. These punishments prescribed by criminal law in the Middle Ages were often more ghastly than those of the Inquisition.

Yet can we accept the notion that the Inquisition was less vile because its methods of torture and execution were generally less barbaric than those of the criminal courts? One could argue that the Inquisition was more monstrous since it ordered the suffering and killing of thousands of innocent people, *all in God's name.* What could be more contradictory to the human spirit? From this perspective, one certainly can concur with the noted world historian Walter Nigg,* who said, "Yes, it was bad, it was so bad that it could not have been worse."[44]

Although we cannot accurately measure the magnitude of this tragedy, we have some solid facts of its costs in human misery. Thomas Torquemada, known as the Grand Inquisitor of Spain, sent 10,220 people to the stake and 97,371 to the galleys.[45] These figures are but a minor fraction of the numbers of victims tortured and slain over 500 years. Although certain writers and novelists might have sensationalized the events of the Inquisition, these grim statistics are irrefutable.

It may seem difficult to understand how the Church, in the name of Jesus and love, created, perpetuated, and participated in such madness. There are several factors which may help to explain.

We must understand that the Church was considered both perfect

---

Walter G. Nigg (1903-), a Swiss ordained minister, served as associate professor at the University of Zurich, Switzerland.

and sovereign, charged with the sacred responsibility of teaching what it considered divinely-revealed religious truth. This body of "truth" and the faith to believe it was regarded by Christians of the Middle Ages as the most precious of God's gifts. Thus, anyone who embraced a different view was considered an enemy of God, a heretic to be destroyed at all costs. No one was allowed to publicly repudiate the teachings of Bible or the Church.

We must also realize that during this time the Church and state were inseparable. The state, like the Church, assumed responsibility for the spiritual welfare of its people and closely followed the dictates of the Church. The relatively modern concept of "separation of Church and state" would have been shocking to our medieval counterparts. The freedom to believe what we choose, guaranteed to Americans under the Bill of Rights, would have been considered heresy and treason during the Middle Ages. An enemy of the Church was clearly an enemy of the state.

Further Reflection

Historical distance provides us with nearly 20/20 hindsight. We are shocked and disgusted by the extremities to which the absolute trust in biblical writing carried its most zealous proponents. People who regarded the Scriptures as absolute truth developed arrogant, inflexible mind-sets, rendering them capable of revolting, even inhumane actions.

These heartbreaking events are recounted *not to demean Christianity,* but to expose the depravity that grew out of elevating the Bible to a position of unquestionable authority. It is this misguided attitude that is at fault, and not the basic teachings of our faith. The problem clearly derives from a misunderstanding of biblical revelation. When we view the Bible (or the Church) as the infallible instrument of God, we surrender our reason and intelligence. This all-accepting assumption toward "divine" knowledge (be it of Christ, Bible, Mohammed or the Koran) breeds misconception and fosters the mentality that compels followers to embrace everything within their belief system as the overriding authority for dealing with all the contingencies of life. In this frame of mind, Christians of the Middle Ages wrought havoc and death while fervently believing they were doing the will of God.

Unfortunately, we have uncovered only the first of several tragedies resulting from mindless devotion to the Holy Word.

Scattered throughout the Bible are sexist verses which, taken as God's decree, led Christians in one of the most devastating anti-female movements the world has seen.

Religion and philosophy have their
vestments covered with blood.

—Xavier Doudan (1800-1872)
French author

Chapter II
Absolute Authority—Continued Chaos

The Subordination and Dehumanization of Women

During the time of Jesus, women were treated with little regard. They were considered barely more than property to be owned. The OT, for example, implied that a man could divorce his wife at any time, any place, simply by handing her a written declaration of his intent to divorce (Deut. 24:1). The abuse and misuse of this teaching placed the marriage bond in great peril and threatened the stability of the home. In this setting Jesus took a firm stand against divorce, reflecting an earnest desire to strengthen the woman's role and the Jewish family. Women were now protected by Jesus' unusually forthright statements about the sanctity of marriage.[1]

Furthermore, his respect and compassion for women are reflected in various NT stories, such as those which tell of his encounters with Jairus' daughter and the woman who had hemorrhaged for twelve years, as well as the woman who anointed him and the adulteress at the well. At its inception, then, Christianity appeared to regard women with greater respect. Husbands were urged to look upon their wives with the same reverence that Christ accorded to his "bride" the Church. But Jesus' followers never delivered what his teachings promised. Through the eyes of Paul, another image of womanhood soon emerged.

In writing about women, Paul had two choices. He could either advocate the new attitudes in Jesus' teachings and actions or adhere to the earlier views of the OT and Jewish tradition. He apparently chose the latter. But this might not have been an informed choice. There are strong indications that Paul did not have access to many of Jesus' teachings—an issue widely debated among NT scholars. While specific quotes prove Paul was familiar with some of Jesus' teachings, the sparsity of his direct references to them indicates his knowledge was limited.[2] It is likely that Paul knew little, if anything, about Jesus' view on women, especially when one considers that the Gospel accounts of Jesus' life and teachings were written after most of Paul's writings. Whatever the case, aside from the Gospels (Matthew, Mark, Luke, and John), the remaining NT (with few exceptions) does not reflect the earlier attitudes of Jesus toward women. Instead, they appear biased and insensitive:

> But I am afraid that as the serpent deceived Eve by his cunning . . .(2 Cor. 11:3a).

Paul blames Eve for what took place in the Garden of Eden. This erroneous logic originates from Paul's literal interpretation of Genesis—a natural interpretation in his time since modern knowledge about the parabolic nature of Genesis was not yet known. This type of misinterpretation of Scripture remains today and is a subject for discussion in later chapters. Paul also wrote:

> But I want you to understand that the head of every man is Christ, the head of every woman is her husband, and the head of Christ is God (1 Cor. 11:3).

This verse sets forth an established order of importance, from the greatest to the least. God is highest, then Christ, then man, and, at the bottom, woman.

> For a man ought not to cover his head, since he is the image and glory of God; but woman is the glory of man. (For man was not made from woman, but woman from man. Neither was man created for woman, but woman for man) (1 Cor. 11:7-9).

In other words, woman is not the image and glory of God, as is man; woman is merely the glory of man.

Not all of Paul's comments are discriminatory:

> Nevertheless, in the Lord, woman is not independent of man nor man of woman; for as woman was made from man, so man is now born of woman. All things are from God (1 Cor. 11:11-12).

Unfortunately, this unique theological formula, along with the equality implied by Galatians 3:28 (". . . there is neither male nor female"), went largely unheeded by the Church.³ Such statements were viewed as pertaining to the spiritual world.

Be that as it may, other NT verses also promoted sexist opinions. Again, we have:

> Let a woman learn in silence with all submissiveness. I permit no woman to teach or to have authority over men; she is to keep silent (1 Tim. 2:11-12).

Here the author (unknown) supports the status quo regarding women's noninvolvement in worship. His statements closely reflect and promote the Jewish view of the day which held that women had no business conducting religious worship. Rather, they were required to sit within a segregated area of the synagogue and remain silent throughout the service.⁴ Even today, the imprint of this sexist decree causes great friction in many churches, especially when women seek leadership roles traditionally held by men. The ordination of women, for example, is not allowed in the Catholic Church and a number of conservative Protestant churches.

It is ironic that the early Church fathers and those who followed through the centuries virtually ignored the positive implications of Jesus' encounters with women in favor of the biased words of Paul and other NT authors. One reason may be that Jesus never clearly stated his position on the equality of women except on unfair divorce practices. One can only *assume* Jesus' views and attitudes from his positive treatment of women as portrayed in the Gospels. In contrast, Paul's writings are blatantly prejudiced, repeatedly emphasizing man's "superior" position.

As we have noted, the NT conveyed great authority to the early Christians, especially after the third century when the books of the Bible were canonized—made official, holy and sovereign—by the Church. And there, from the very beginning, was set forth in black and white the subordination and dehumanization of women; the die was cast for women, just as it had been for slaves, Jews, and heretics.

The Church fathers who inherited the imperfect writings of the Old and New Testaments accepted them as sacred knowledge. They in turn continued to echo and instill in their writings the same negative themes toward women.

Tertullian was the son of a centurion and was thoroughly educated. He converted to Christianity in A.D. 197 and became a formidable defender of the faith. This noted theologian wrote about women:

> You are the one who opened the door to the Devil, you
> are the one who first plucked the fruit of the forbidden
> tree, you are the first who deserted the divine law; you are
> the one who persuaded him whom the Devil was not
> strong enough to attack. All too easily you destroyed the
> image of God, man. Because of your desert, that is, death,
> even the son of God had to die.[5]

We can see that Tertullian considered women the sole blame
for the origin and growth of sin and death in the world and even
the death of Jesus. In another writing, he sided with the author
of 1 Timothy by forcefully asserting that women should not have
any ministerial function.[6]

St. Jerome (A.D. 347-420) was another giant of the early Church.
His work was the basis for the important Bible translation called
the Vulgate. Regarding women, he wrote:

> Woman is the gate of the Devil, the way of evil, the
> sting of the scorpion, in a word, a dangerous thing.[7]

St. Ambrose (A.D. 340-397) was Bishop of Milan. St. Ambrose
consistently relied on the NT to support his discriminating views
on women. In one instance, he cited 1 Corinthians 11:14 to show
it degrades a man to wear his hair long, inferring that he would
be imitating the female sex. In another writing he portrayed men
as superior to women:

> The custom prevailed in Greece for women to wear men's
> tunics because they were shorter. Let it be their custom to
> appear to imitate the nature of the better sex, but why should
> men want to assume the appearance of the inferior sex?[8]

St. Augustine (A.D. 354-430) is regarded by many people as
second only to Paul in his influence upon Christianity (possible
exceptions being Thomas Aquinas and Martin Luther). Numerous
Roman Catholic and Protestant scholars look upon Augustine as
the founder of theology. His teachings were a foundation to
theologians in the Church's later development.

Positive contributions aside, he was most instrumental in de-
faming the female image by continuing to support the concept of
her "inferior" nature. With a theological twist he also managed
to portray sex as the conduit by which sin was transmitted.

Augustine's basic assertion was that sin was inherited biologically, from parent to child, by way of intercourse. This is why Jesus, he believed, was born of a virgin—to be free from sin.

Sex and sin soon became synonymous in Christian theology. This eventually led the Catholic Church to proclaim the doctrine of the Immaculate Conception, declared by Pope Pius IX in 1854. This doctrine holds that Mary was conceived and born without original sin. So, not only did Jesus have to be born of a virgin to be sinless, but he had to be born of a *sinless* virgin to ensure the fact! In the final analysis, and contrary to what many believe, this doctrine had a very negative impact on women (see Appendix V).

We cannot blame notions such as these entirely on the Church. It was influenced by several outside forces such as the sexual and cultural taboos common to many civilizations and the moral and philosophical influences of various countries in which Christianity was nurtured. In early Greek society, for example, the Platonic philosophers regarded sex as a hindrance to the spirit and women were looked upon as sirens.[9] The imprint of Greek thought on the Church is deeply ingrained.

The centuries after Augustine were marked by a growing hostility toward women. The bishops attending a convention in Macon (Gual) during the sixth century fervently debated whether a woman was really a human being! This negative attitude escalated through the Middle Ages, along with a growing condemnation of sex. According to Church decree, sex was expressly forbidden on all Sundays, Wednesdays, and Fridays, which comprises nearly half the year. Also, sex was prohibited during the forty days of Lent, forty days prior to Christmas, and three days before receiving Communion. Even the posture of lovemaking was prescribed by the Church, which set forth punishments for any who deviated. Intercourse was to be performed as impersonally and uninterestingly as possible. Long, heavy nightclothes were worn with an opening at the proper place, so the couple could procreate without touching too closely.[10]

St. Thomas Aquinas (1225-1274) was a brilliant philosopher and theologian who had considerable influence on the Church. Considered one of the greatest figures and principal saints of the Roman Catholic Church, he formulated a unique philosophy declared by Pope Leo XIII in the encyclical*Aeterni Patris in 1879

---

*An encyclical is a letter from the Pope to his bishops, stating the position of the Church on important questions; it is intended for wide circulation.

to be the official Catholic belief. But Aquinas' views on women were less enlightened. Like Aristotle, he believed men were meant to pursue knowledge and noble activity, while women were created solely to reproduce and thereby help preserve the species. He also upheld Aristotle's view that a female child was biologically defective.[11]

Martin Luther (1483-1546) was the German priest who founded and led the Protestant Reformation. Luther ranks as one of the most influential religious leaders—he reshaped the Church's destiny and affected the lives of millions of people. But in regard to women, Martin Luther adopted the narrow and often misguided views of his Church predecessors. He wrote:

> Men have broad shoulders and narrow hips, and accordingly they possess intelligence. Women have narrow shoulders and broad hips. Women ought to stay home: the way they were created indicates this, for they have broad hips and a wide fundament to sit upon, keep house and bear and raise children.
>
> . . .
>
> God made Adam master over all creatures, to rule over all living things, but when Eve persuaded him that he was lord even over God she spoiled everything. We have you women to thank for that! With tricks and cunning women deceive men, as I too, have experienced.[12]

Like others, Luther cited the Bible as the final authority for his opinions. In his words:

> I simply point to the Scriptures. There it is written. Read it for yourselves.[13]

Too, we may wonder what motivated statements such as those in the letter to Martin Luther from Cardinal Albrecht, Archbishop of Mainz, who wrote that he ". . . was irritated by no annoyances more than by the stinking, putrid, private parts of women.[14]

From the very beginning of Christianity and through the centuries, biblically-inspired hostility toward women continued to ferment like the pressure in an active volcano that, in its own time, erupts and spills its fiery molten lava across the landscape. We earlier discussed the grim brutality of the Inquisition, which was established to combat heresy. Its prime directive soon changed, and the most common conviction that brought people to the dungeon or to be burned alive at the stake was witchcraft.[15] The most frequent victims were women.

Witchcraft Hysteria

Religious persecution of supposed witches began early in the fourteenth century. Trials and executions were common throughout Europe, peaking during the sixteenth and seventeenth centuries. The wanton humiliation, torture, and slaughter that grew out of these maniacal witch-hunts arose only because certain vital factors were present. A hostile climate toward women had to exist, belief in the existence of demons, sorcerers and witches would have to be the norm, and justification for punishing these evil spirits would have to come from an authoritative source. *All three of these factors were fostered and supported by the indisputable word—the Bible!*

Biblical bias against women and the subsequent rise of hostility toward them have already been noted. Now let us focus on how the Bible was used to support the existence of witches and how these witches should be punished.

Within the primitive beginnings of almost all world cultures, we find deep-seated beliefs in angels, demons, and evil spirits. Some of these occult concepts can be found in biblical writings. They derived not only from early Jewish and Christian beliefs, but from the influences of surrounding pagan cultures, including early Greek mythology.[16]*

One recurring mythical theme had an important impact on later Christian thought. It is in the Old and New Testaments—Genesis 6:1-4, 2 Peter 2:4, Jude 1:6, Revelation 12:9—and in certain non-biblical Jewish writings compiled by sects on the fringes of Judaism (*Book of Enoch*). This theme told of a certain number of heavenly angels who fell from glory when they lusted after the daughters of men and sinned with them. The offspring of these unnatural encounters were called "mighty men," "demons," or

---

* The Devil, Demonology and Witchcraft *by Henry Ansgar Kelly is an excellent source of information on how Christian belief in evil spirits evolved. Kelly (1934-   ) is a Roman Catholic professor of English and Medieval Renaissance studies at the University of California, Los Angeles (UCLA).*

"giant spirits." Virtually all of the early Church leaders accepted this theme literally. Justin Martyr was one of the most significant Christian thinkers of the second century and his writings were especially important in advancing such concepts. He wrote, "But the angels transgressed this appointment, and were captivated by love of women, and begat children who are those that are called 'demons.'"[17]

Likewise, Athenagoras, another Christian leader of the second century, wrote, "These latter angels fell into lusting after virgins and became slaves of the flesh . . . From those who had intercourse with virgins were begotten the so-called 'giants'". St. Irenaeus (A.D. 125-202), who became Bishop of Lyons in Gaul, also wrote about the spiritual powers of wickedness and the angels who transgressed and fell from God's grace.[18]

These are but a few of the many Church fathers who literally and earnestly believed in "giants" or "demons." These men laid the foundation of thought upon which future generations would build.

During the fifth century, Augustine, in his best known work, *City of God*, affirmed the biblical account of the fallen angels' copulation with mortal women. For the next ten centuries his declaration gave added credence to belief in the earthly existence of demons who assumed the forms of men and women; disguised as mortals they sexually molested their victims.[19] These beliefs were adopted by some of the later prominent Christian philosophers and theologians, such as St. Thomas Aquinas and St. Bonaventure.*

Unfortunately, these superstitious beliefs were sanctioned by Pope Innocent VII in his papal bull† *Summis Desiderantes* of December 5, 1484, the first decree to recognize witchcraft and urge its extermination at all costs. In 1486 this papal proclamation became the preface of a book titled *Malleus Maleficarum (The Hammer of Witches)*, published by two inquisitors named Heinrich Kramer and Jakob Sprenger. Major segments of this book supported the existence of witchcraft as described in the Bible, as well as its nature, practices, and rituals, and ways to eliminate it. A monument of superstition, this work abounds with ingenious lies about the existence of witches, their evil deeds, and how to detect

---

* St. Bonaventure (1221-1274) was a theologian and cardinal bishop of the Roman Catholic Church. He taught at the University of Paris with St. Thomas Aquinas.

† A papal bull is a formal announcement or official order from a pope.

their presence. A witch, the authors said, could cause a pregnant woman to suffer an abortion or dry up the milk of a nursing mother just by laying a hand on her. Witches could render women barren and men impotent, cause infants to die by thrusting needles beneath their nails then sucking their blood, cause horses to grow suddenly mad and bolt beneath their riders, and bring plagues of locusts and caterpillars to destroy whole crops then escape detection by transforming themselves into animals.[20]

This unprecedented book also contained a statement declaring approval and support by the theology faculty at the University of Cologne (Germany). Add to this respected authority the fact that the work was printed on a press—at a time when printed works were rare—and we can see why this book exerted such widespread influence on public opinion.[21]

Ignorance soon became the catalyst for disaster. Spring was late in 1586 Germany, and the cold weather continued until June. The people interpreted this strange phenomenon as the work of witches, and so the Church initiated a witch-hunt. On the order of the Archbishop of Treves, 118 women and 2 men were tortured until they confessed to prolonging winter, after which they were burned at the stake.[22]

In some countries the very frequency of execution was appalling. During a three-month period, the Bishop of Geneva (Switzerland) ordered 500 such persons burned to death; a bishop of Bamburg (England) 600; and a bishop of Wurzburg (Bavaria) 900. The senate of Savoy (France), apparently in one meeting, condemned 800 persons accused of witchcraft. Under the Spanish Inquisition alone, in a single month, as many as 3,000 persons were burned as witches.[23]

The final ingredient needed for this holocaust to occur was some high authority to justify punishing these "evil spirits." Obviously, the ultimate authority for reprisal was the same one that fostered belief in evil spirits in the first place—the Bible. Church leaders cited Scripture to justify their sentencing women to execution for witchcraft:

You shall not permit a sorceress to live (Exodus 22:18).

A man or a woman who is a medium or wizard shall be put to death; they shall be stoned, their blood shall be upon them (Lev. 20:27).

Martin Luther, upholding the Bible as the supreme authority, had no reservations about burning witches. He sanctioned four executions at Wittenburg.[24] "I should have no compassion on these witches," he wrote. "I would burn all of them."[25]

Similarly, in 1545, John Calvin, French theologian and influential reformer in the Protestant Reformation whose teaching spread throughout the Western world, personally led a campaign in Geneva against thirty-one persons accused of witchcraft. They all were executed.[26] Calvin declared, "The Bible teaches us that there are witches and that they must be slain . . . this law of God is a universal law."[27] He also wrote, "The fact that the Word of God has been declared by men's lips in no way lessens its nature; it is still the Word of Christ, of God."[28]

These fanatical witch-hunts lasted from the fourteenth to the eighteenth century. The American colonies shared the madness, notably in Salem, Massachusetts, where in 1692 nineteen people were hanged as witches. (150 were imprisoned.)

Why did these distorted views about witchcraft prevail for 400 years? There are three basic reasons. First was the continued sanctioning of these beliefs and "solutions" by Church and state, which were influenced by the Bible's overwhelming sacred authority. Second were mass confessions. Once the torture of accused heretics was approved by Pope Innocent IV in 1252, people were bound to "confess" to anything. Under torture (or threat of torture) women variously admitted to having intercourse with the devil, casting spells, brewing poisonous potions with parts of human and other animal corpses, causing persons to die, making pacts with Satan, destroying crops, and eating corpses of kidnapped newborns.[29] These are some of the bizarre confessions people made in a desperate effort to escape unbearable pain. Their confessions, of course, served only to substantiate everyone's belief that witches actually existed.

The severity of the torture depended on the charge(s) against the accused, the time and place of the trial, the attitude of the prosecutor, and the obstinacy of the accused. We certainly can conclude it must have taken a good deal of pain for victims to confess to these absurdities, especially since many of these confessions led to further torture and possibly death. These tortures included binding the victims with cords tightened to cut through skin and muscle to their bones, tearing of flesh, severing toes and fingers, and dislocating or fracturing bones to cripple the victim for life. Even pregnant women were not spared, though many were tortured in a sitting position.

Many who were convicted perished at the stake. Some were slowly roasted over a fire so they would suffer the maximum agony. Another practice was to bury women alive.[30] According to some historians, however, these latter two punishments were more the exception than the rule.[31]

Ironically, the final reason this incredible witch-hunt lasted four centuries was that there *weren't any real witches.* Universal innocence led people into a false sense of security. Imagine you are a woman living during the height of this madness. You know you are not a witch, so you think you have nothing to fear from the authorities. After all, they arrest only witches. What you don't realize, being a person of that time, is that there aren't any witches! You believe they exist because all the major authorities say witches exist; philosophers, theologians, kings, the Church, and even the God-given Scriptures attest to their existence. You have no reason to question such formidable sources and so you accept the existence of witches as readily as you do the existence of God.

Still, you are surprised by some of the arrests. You never would have suspected the elderly woman living nearby, or the thirteen-year-old girl who seemed so innocent. But a short time later, they both confess and you realize the authorities were right. This causes you to reflect on what you have been taught about witches: how easily they disguise themselves as saints, ordinary people, or even animals. You can't be too careful. But even if you suspect the persons being tortured and executed as witches are innocent victims of a misguided belief system, there is no hope in challenging the powers that be. Were you to do so, chances are you yourself would be accused and eventually convicted of witchcraft.

Then one day the inconceivable happens. Inquisitors pound on your door and formally charge *you* with witchery, ordering you to come with them for trial. A contemporary parallel of how you would feel at this point can be drawn from Aleksandr Solzhenitsyn's *The Gulag Archipelago.** In describing how the former NKVD (People's Commissariat of Internal Affairs) arrested the Soviet people in mass, Solzhenitsyn writes, "Universal innocence also gave rise to the universal failure to act." He then elaborates:

Aleksandr Solzhenitsyn (1918-) is a Russian novelist who won the 1970 Nobel Prize for literature. He was expelled from the former Soviet Union in 1974.

Why then should you run away? And how can you resist right then? After all, you'll only make your situation worse; you'll make it more difficult for them to sort out the mistake.[32]

Clearly, these are some of your thoughts as the authorities order you to come with them. You comply peaceably. After all, you are not a witch.

Soon you discover gross inequities in your trial. You are not allowed to challenge your accusers; they will not even tell you who they are. You are denied a lawyer or aid or the right to appeal. When asked how you plead, you of course answer, "Innocent." But since you are considered guilty until proven innocent, strong arms drag you from the courtroom to the torture chamber. Your person is thoroughly searched for some evil hidden charm. Since such a charm might even be hidden in the body cavities, you are quickly shaved and subjected to the most indecent probings. As this startling, painful, and unjust interrogation continues, you realize the only way out is to "confess." But confess what, you question through your pain? I am not a witch; I have done nothing!

You continue to resist but the intensity of the process escalates. It is only when you are crazed with pain and/or fear that you finally blurt out whatever confession they desire. You do so to avoid further abuse. If you cooperate, you will escape the stake or life imprisonment. Still, the sentence will not be easy; much will depend on you. As the self-incriminating confession passes through your lips, you are ordered to give the names of other witches who are in league with you. To save yourself further abuse you implicate others, suddenly realizing that this must be how you came to be accused. The circle of deception is now complete.

You want to expose this madness. You want to shout to the whole world that this is a tragic mistake being perpetrated on innocent people! But you painfully realize no one will listen to a witch. After all, witches are cunning and they'll say anything to deceive you. Besides, if you speak your views, you will be tied to a stake and incinerated. So you say nothing; you do nothing.

In spite of the risk, there were a few brave individuals who spoke out against the lunacy of the witch-hunt. Giordano Bruno (1548-1600), an Italian philosopher, was burned at the stake as a heretic for suggesting that many women being condemned as witches were nothing more than senile or disordered old people. Is it any wonder that people were reluctant to question the organized butchery they witnessed, even though they might have recognized how contrary it was to the will of God that the Church claimed to be serving? Let us pause to take stock of the words issued by the Church historian Walter Nigg:

> ... one has the feeling that one will never again be able to emerge from one's sadness and be normally happy again. Even today, a fearful nightmare presses down on one's mind as soon as one attempts to describe what this burning of witches was like ... It is such an oppressive burden to bear that it calls both Catholic and Protestant Churches fundamentally into question.[33]

Further Reflection

Christians today are inclined to view these gruesome facts as an unfortunate and tragic detour from what Jesus taught. They also contend that it was in the past, and, therefore, let's forget it. This seems reasonable. Obviously, most of us today are not advocating the irrational beliefs and actions that characterized some of our predecessors. Consequently, only the most confused or disturbed personality would promote a witch-hunt. Slavery, too, is definitely out and few would suggest that adultery or doctrinal nonconformity be rewarded by death, as the Bible dictates. Certainly the argument for a flat earth (implied by Scripture) is almost nonexistent, although at one time people vehemently argued the point.

Such beliefs are ignored, rationalized, or thrown onto the junk pile of forgotten superstition. The biblical command to kill "witches" cannot be taken seriously because our society does not readily believe in witches. Unlike the religious zealots of the past, we cannot bring individuals to trial on the charge of witchcraft, much less execute them. So, biblical ideas that are out of sync with what has become morally or scientifically self-evident are quietly relegated to obscurity, as though they had never existed. Such conscious or unconscious denial is a natural defense mechanism, prompted by the pain and confusion that would result from admitting that some portions of Scripture are nothing more than reflections of a less knowledgeable age.

Be that as it may, looking back we can see, for example, that anti-Jewish sentiments are partly Christian and biblical in origin. But no one in the mainstream can condone what Christians or Hitler did to the Jews, using the Bible as justification. Therefore, if we can all agree now that anti-Semitism has no place in our morality (even as slavery and sexism don't), can we not recognize from past experience the fallacy and danger in presuming biblical teaching to be uncontestable? Evidently not: Christianity today is merely a carbon copy of the past; biblical authority remains sacrosanct.

Yet if we persist in clinging to the motivating principles which turned a blind eye toward the Inquisition and genocide, are we not still susceptible to the abuses and horrors of the past? If our clergy and the vast majority of Christians continue, however well-meaningly, to believe in and defend the Bible as ultimate truth, will it not drive them—in one way or another—to turn the thumbscrews on yet another generation?

Anyone who has never become indignant
about Christianity has never
really known it.

—Joachim Kahl
German scholar and theologian

Chapter III
Ongoing Bibliolatry

The malignancies of human behavior among past Christians were merely symptoms of an underlying problem—their total faith in the Scriptures as the irrefutable word of God. The fact that most Christians no longer display the misguided behavior of the Christian past does not mean they are rid of the problem that caused that behavior. In other words, although believers are no longer allowed to exercise the violent and destructive behaviors of the past (a legally forced restraint), and though they are less likely to follow or acknowledge those Bible verses that are colored by ancient bias and ignorance, their view of the Bible as God-given authority remains unchanged.

Although we cannot say that religious violence has been eliminated, it is no longer the norm. Aside from skinheads and other fanatical fringe groups that promote violence based on the indiscriminate interpretation of Scripture, Christians in general do not condone such behavior. Having said this, however, one is still dismayed at some of the statements made, and actions taken, by mainstream Christians against those who are different or have opposing opinions. Based on their ultimate allegiance to the Bible some Christians, not unlike their medieval counterparts, follow the letter of the Book. Thus, bibliolatry continues today, creating new and perplexing problems for us all.

Deadly Confrontations Over Abortion

We have seen where religious presumption of "rightness," based on the belief that one possesses ultimate truth, can lead. Today, one of the consequences of reliving the misguided passions of past Christians is evidenced by the hateful and murderous actions taken by religiously motivated antiabortionists. In 1993, while serving abortion clinics in Pensacola, Florida, Dr. David Gunn was murdered by antiabortionist Michael Griffin.

Presbyterian minister Paul Hill, who appeared on "Donahue," "Nightline" and CNN, defended Gunn's murder as "a fulfillment of the commandment of Christ."* Not surprisingly, in 1994 Hill shotgunned to death 69-year-old Dr. John Bayard Britton (Dr. Gunn's replacement). In the same point-blank encounter he also killed an unarmed escort, James Barrett.

According to an August 1994 *Time* magazine, other antiabortionists, such as Roman Catholic priest David Trosch, look upon such murderous acts as justifiable homicide and display public eagerness for the death of abortion doctors as well as their staffs and officials. Another activist, Michael Bray, editor of *Capitol Arena Christian News*, has written that abortion providers should be stoned to death. "With each blow . . . by the grace of God, he may confess his sins and be saved before expiring."[1] Although most Christians would not condone such behavior, there is an increasing undercurrent of approval since efforts to quell abortions have led to disappointment and frustration.

The Gay Issue

An equally volatile issue centers on homosexuality. But rather than focus on the highly publicized beatings and murders of gays, we need to candidly explore the general hostility directed against homosexuals in our society. Much of this homophobia (fear, dislike, or hatred of homosexuals), as might be expected, is partially a byproduct of Bible worship. The Bible is quite explicit in denouncing homosexuality and it would be very difficult for Christians to overlook this fact, especially if all biblical teaching is considered to be a God-given directive. Note the following verses:

> You shall not lie with a male as with a woman; it is an abomination (Lev. 18:22).

> If a man lies with a male as with a woman, both of them have committed an abomination; they shall be put to death, their blood is upon them (Lev. 20:13).

---

* *While it is true that Jesus accorded great importance to children (Matthew 18, for example), the concept of abortion being paramount to murder is not considered a conclusive argument by most Christians, certainly not as a justification for murdering doctors.*

As we have noted, we no longer condone the once-legal violent actions of past devotees. Even so, numerous gays have lost their lives to the murderous actions of the self-righteous. Furthermore, forms of torture other than the physical persist today. Discrimination and intolerance have many faces. Some of them would be laughable if they were not so dangerous and pathetic. For instance, during the Vatican International Conference in 1989, Rocco Buttiglione of Liechlinstein's International Academy of Philosophy went so far as to suggest that the AIDS scourge could be a "divine punishment."[2] This absurd notion has previously been raised by numerous Christian leaders from some of the largest Protestant groups, including televangelists Jerry Falwell, Pat Robertson, and James Kennedy (who said AIDS was from the hand of God). Such statements are sheer perversion, although they are grounded in biblical verse, such as:

> . . . and the men likewise gave up natural relations with women and were consumed with passion for one another, men committing shameless acts with men . . . Though they know God's decree that those who do such things deserve to die . . . (Rom. 1:27, 32.)

It is neither my desire nor the purpose of this writing to engage the reader in the pros and cons surrounding the gay debate. Nor do I presume to know the answers. That is not the issue—the issue is the overbearing influence of biblical thought on this matter. The presumption of possessing "truth" has once again served as a stumbling block against rational analysis and discussion. Flexible thought has all but vanished because Christians have been conditioned to believe that no other viewpoint can possibly have precedence over biblical views. Christian opinion becomes dogmatic by virtue of its unquestionable source.

Consider, for example, the verses we have already noted. What does the Bible actually convey about homosexuality? First, it categorizes homosexual behavior as an act that arouses strong disgust or loathing ("an abomination"). Second, it passes the death sentence on those who would commit to such a relationship ("they shall be put to death"). Third, the Bible goes on to tell us how God feels about gays—He decrees that such persons are deserving of death ("those who do such things deserve to die").

Are we to accept one, two, three, or none of these declarations? Is there room for discussion or must all three statements bear equal weight since they're biblical? Is there no room for a line item veto or perhaps a total veto? Can we not entertain other non-biblical assessments and alternative solutions, or must we forever go by the Book?

In this instance, no one is denying that Paul's actual intent is ". . . that those who do such things deserve to die . . ." He wrote what he believed God wanted—exactly what the verse explicitly states. But is this what God wants us to believe? Can this be true? It certainly is if you believe that biblical authors were led by God in such a way as to render them incapable of error or moral misjudgment. That is precisely what most Christians hold. They deny the biased, superstitious, and cultural limitations of biblical writers on the grounds that such misjudgments are not possible in a God-given document. It reflects the same narrow thinking of past Christians, which led them to absolutely all the wrong conclusions. It is extremely naive to proclaim: "The Bible said it! I believe it! That settles it!"

This is not to say that biblical teaching should be discounted. Such a suggestion would be ludicrous. Also, this should not imply that many Bible verses do not have a laser-like intensity for pinpointing truth. And in most cases, a rational holistic approach to the Bible can be of immense value. But we continue to trip over ourselves by pulling out bits and pieces of Scripture to support not only our religious notions, but also to justify any feelings, prejudices, theories, and actions peculiar to our own mental and social environment. It is no secret that the Bible can be used to uphold almost any cultural or personal opinion. But using the Bible as a reference to prove a point does not necessarily validate the point, although Bible-quoters like to think it does.

Sadly, gay bashing (be it verbal or physical) is not the only current problem prompted or exacerbated by misguided faith. The confusion generated about evolution and the Genesis account of Creation is a new high in absurdity. Owing to the New Religious Right (NRR)* influence, creationists managed to pass state laws requiring "equal time" for creationist views in the classroom. In doing so, they not only brought into question the well-grounded

---

* *"New Religious Right" or "Religious Right" is a collective term for fundamentalist, pentecostal, evangelical, and charismatic Christians who believe in a rigid, literal interpretation of the Bible. Further clarification of the Religious Right will be found in Chapter IV and Appendix IV.*

scientific theory of biological evolution, but nearly all of modern science, from astronomy to geophysics. The following information is drawn from several sources, summarizing the serious problems inherent in "scientific" creationism.[3]*

The Creation Issue

The twenty-first century is upon us, and the theory of evolution—that human beings and other life forms evolved from simple organisms over millions of years—is being undermined by the misnomered "creation science" theory of a six-day creation and a universe no older than 10,000 years (a concept considered ludicrous by the scientific community). According to the most recent Gallup Poll, a whopping 47 percent of Americans are creationists. So, more than half a century following the famous Scopes ("monkey") trial,† the same basic issues are still debated. This conflict is foolish not because the theory of evolution is flawless (it isn't) but because the central opinions of creationists are at odds with scientific data—data that is irrefutable. Creationist beliefs have no standing among scientists or biblical scholars (except, of course, in NRR circles).

Creation science is based not so much on science as on the literal interpretation of Scripture. And through the careful and selective manipulation of scientific data, it masquerades itself as a legitimate science.

In contrast, the theory of evolution is the graphic enlightenment of biology and is among the most elegant and fruitful structures of human thought. Most Bible scholars and scientists are perplexed and concerned about the vast amount of ignorance and misinformation surrounding the creation issue, especially since creationists

---

The information presented is a compilation of material obtained from articles addressing this issue in U.S. News & World Report *(January 18, 1982);* Science *(December 1981);* Newsweek *(March 29, 1982);* The Christian Work *(June 10, 1922); the Lubbock* Avalanche Journal *(January 15, 1984), and* Bioscience *(November 1994).*

† John T. Scopes, a high school biology teacher in Tennessee, was tried in 1925 and found guilty of violating a state law forbidding the teaching of any theory which denied the story of creation of man as taught in the Bible. In 1927 the state appellate court reversed the verdict.

continually seek to legislate their religious notions into secular education.

One cannot help but be reminded of the Rev. Harry Emerson Fosdick* who addressed a similar issue in 1922 while preaching his sermon entitled, "Shall the Fundamentalists Win?" More than seventy years ago, he said of the fundamentalists: "They have actually endeavored to put on the statute books of a whole state binding laws against teaching modern biology." Failing to do this, today the NRR has taken a different tact by seeking to inject into secular education a conflicting (and unscientific) theory of creation.

It is obvious this confrontation between scientists and creationists arose (again) because people of the Book failed to move beyond the most elementary understanding of biblical interpretation—a topic for later discussion. But there are other reasons for this needless conflict.

This clash is made worse by the ambiguity of terminology. Take for example the word "theory" which gives the impression that the concept of evolution is based on an "educated guess," since that's what "theory" means in casual speech. But scientists use the word to mean much more. The theory of evolution is based on well-grounded evidence, such as in the case of Einstein's theory of relativity. In fact, there is no disagreement in biology about the credibility of evolution, and no other credible explanation exists. On the contrary, all other scientific disciplines continue to support and verify the concept of evolution; astronomy and astrophysics,† for example, calculate the age of the universe to be billions of years old.

The theory of evolution, like the theory of relativity, is no longer a "theory" in the popular sense, but a scientific principle based on considerable, indisputable evidence. Of course, scientists

---

Harry Emerson Fosdick (1878-1969) was a progressive thinker who became one of the best-known preachers in the U.S. The conflict between science and religion troubled him. He preached the right of science to its place in the world and opposed the fundamentalists. He devoted his career as a preacher, professor, author, and radio preacher to this problem. He was Professor of Homiletics (preaching) at the highly acclaimed Union Theological Seminary (N.Y.) 1915-1946.

† Astrophysics is the branch of astronomy that deals with the physical characteristics of heavenly bodies.

disagree on specific details of evolution (such as the time rate of certain evolutionary changes) and the details are constantly being refined. Accordingly, a new modification of Charles Darwin's theory of evolution* is highly regarded among some scientists. This theory, developed by Stephen Jay Gould† and Niles Eldredge,‡ states that rather than changing gradually as one generation shades into the next, evolution proceeds in distinct leaps; therefore, there are no transitional forms between species, and, thus, no missing links.§ Right or wrong, such theory variations must not be construed by the public or creationists as evidence that the theory of evolution is in doubt.

The problem of ambiguous terminology also extends to the term "creation science" which fosters the impression—albeit untrue—that it is scientifically sound. This false impression derives not only from the clever manipulation and selectivity of scientific data, but also because some proponents of creation science possess doctoral degrees. Therefore, when creationists claim to follow scientific principles and sport doctoral degrees as garnish, the public is swayed to believe that creation science is a bona fide scientific discipline. Obviously a Ph.D. in physics is legitimately impressive, but it would not make one an authority in biological science, although it is understandable that some people would not catch the difference.

The real issue, however, does not center upon creationists' educational credentials (some are quite impressive) but on how

---

* *Charles Darwin (1809-1892), English naturalist, developed the theory of evolution: the theory that all living things developed from a few simple forms of life through a series of physical changes.*

† Stephen Jay Gould (1941-), Ph.D. Columbia University, 1967, is Professor of Geology, Harvard University.

‡ Niles E. Eldredge (1943-), Ph.D. Columbia University, 1969, is a paleobiologist and geologist. He was Adjunct Professor of Biology, City University, NY, 1972-1980, and is Adjunct Professor of Geology, Columbia University.

§ Since there is still insufficient evidence to verify the "punctuated equilibrium theory," the term "theory" used in this instance involves more speculation (i.e., an unproven theory) than a formulated probable principle. Unfortunately, scientists' double-meaning usage of the word "theory" will lead to confusion. Recently, researchers have preferred "model" to "theory."

their approach to evolution and earth science differs from that of biologists, anthropologists, and geologists. As one example of this differing approach, consider the creationist claim that if the earth and moon were 4.5 billion years old (as scientists believe), then there should be a layer of dust 50 to 100 feet thick covering their surfaces since the influx of meteoric dust from space to earth is about 14 million tons per year. But this estimate of dust influx is simply outdated. Space probes have shown that the level of dust influx from space is about 400 times less than previously thought. Creationists ignore these scientific findings because such data does not support their creationist views. In contrast, scientists rely on these findings to accurately predict probable outcomes. In the words of Tim M. Berra,*"Do these people [creationists] believe that the astronauts would have been allowed to land on the moon if NASA thought they would sink into 100 feet of dust?"[4]

In one's approach to any subject, there is a great difference between properly using the scientific method and manipulating evidence to support preconceived personal beliefs. Such maneuvering can be markedly seductive. So to argue that creationism is true because the Bible supports it,† despite most of the evidence, yields pitiful ideas that do not even rise to the level of half-truths. As U.S. District Court Judge William Overton concluded when he ruled against the Arkansas creation law:

> The creationists' methods do not take data, weigh it against the opposing scientific data and thereafter reach . . .

Dr. Tim Berra is Professor of Zoology at Ohio State University at Mansfield and a two-time Fulbright fellow to Australia. He is the former editor of The Ohio Journal of Science *and is the author of three books and more than 40 scientific papers. He received his Ph.D. in biology from Tulane University in 1969. His recent book* Evolution and the Myth of Creationism *demolishes most creationists' claims and arguments. Also, the National Center for Science Education (NCSE) offers free information on the evolution debate (1-800-290-6006).*

† *The Bible does not actually substantiate creation science. The creation story in Genesis was never intended as a literal description of how creation took place. This poetic parable simply proclaims the faith that God is the Creator.*

conclusions. Instead, they take the literal wording of the Book of Genesis and attempt to find scientific support for it.

Lacking rational examination of evidence and intellectual honesty enforced by the skeptical scrutiny of scientific peers, there exists not science but wishful thinking and self-deception.

Despite some setbacks, the NRR continues to battle for creationism. Their persistent influence has led the public to believe that a scientific controversy exists, as though we were at some pivotal point in history when half of the country's learned scientists believe the earth is flat and the other half believe it is round. But on the topic of evolution no such dispute exists in the scientific community, nor has it since the end of the nineteenth century. The scientific community as a whole does not accept creationism as a sensible discipline. Creationists do not present papers or publish in scientific journals; they are not part of the scientific community. The public must understand that creationism is not in fact a science. It is religion.

Another reason for the continuance of this clash between the scientific community and creationist Christians is directly linked to the mass, broadly-based financial support of the NRR and its phenomenal growth over the past decade. There are several creationist lobbying groups in the United States, the most effective of which is the Institute of Creation Research in San Diego. Its goal, says critic Wayne Moyer, Executive Director of the National Association of Biology Teachers, is the adjustment of all scientific knowledge to fit Scripture. The institute has published numerous textbooks and pamphlets for educators and librarians who want to present creationism.

There is no doubt that this creationist flurry has caused turmoil in science education. Several major textbook publishers have now omitted references to evolutionist Charles Darwin or toned down the importance of his theories. In some cases, whole chapters have been deleted. A Charles Merrill text, for example, has 82 percent fewer references to evolution than a previous edition. It is difficult to see where this debilitating hatchet job will end. In Texas, the Board of Education ratified a measure proclaiming that state textbooks do not have to mention Charles Darwin and his theory of evolution. This is akin to deleting Christopher Columbus from our history books. (Texas is the largest purchaser of public school textbooks in the nation.)

It is ironic that at a time when phenomenal advances in biological evolution are surfacing, schoolchildren are being deprived knowledge of this subject or confused by another version which willfully ignores the systematic procedure of the scientific method. This turmoil is unnecessary because the ideas of evolution do not contradict the Genesis statement of faith that God created, unless one insists on a literal Genesis account of creation. Such a literal interpretation is unwarranted since biblical scholars strongly affirm the account as a poetical parable.

Furthermore, it appears that major portions of the OT—such as the Creation account and the Flood story—have been borrowed from earlier alien cultural and traditional myths. Archaeology has unearthed Sumerian, Babylonian, and Assyrian writings that predate the OT; these literary forerunners disprove the idea that the OT is an unprecedented expression of God's word. As one example, the biblical narratives of Creation and the Flood appear to be almost exact copies of the Assyrian accounts (called the Epic of Gilgamesh, composed about 2500 B.C.) which predate the Bible by at least fifteen centuries.*

Whatever the case, the process of how creation took place must rest with the scientist. And if science presents evolution—or any other theory—as the most probable means of creation, this need not be construed as an attempt to exclude God. Indeed, the findings of science neither negate nor prove the existence of God. That remains a matter of faith. Science and religion serve different functions. Science deals with how things happen—how, for example, the world was formed. Religion deals with the *why* or *who* of creation, not the *how,* and so claims the existence of an ultimate intelligence to explain what happened.

Further Reflection

We have given considerable space to the NRR influence (as in the case of creationism) since it represents one of the most

---

* *For further reading on this issue, an excellent source is Manfred Barthel's 1982 publication,* What the Bible Really Says. *An extensive survey is made regarding how the OT writers borrowed and incorporated other people's ancient songs and myths into their own narratives. Manfred Barthel has a doctorate in philosophy from the Free University of Berlin.*

visible personifications of bibliolatry. It must be remembered, however, that allegiance to biblical verse is an *almost universal characteristic of the Christian community*—Catholic or Protestant, liberal or conservative, albeit in differing degrees.

We've touched on some consequences of indiscriminate Bible readings—homophobia, creationism, sexism, anti-Semitism, acceptance of slavery. There are many others, some of which were dominant long before recent times, and some of which are current developments—the presumption of rightness, religious intolerance, racism, demands for school prayer, mind control (cult mentality), the financial exploitation of people under the guise of evangelism, the "name it and claim it" theology of TV evangelists, wife abuse, child abuse, and non-human animal abuse.

Some types of militia groups pose yet another grave problem to our society, as they obviously misuse Scripture to justify acting out their own misguided actions. Through the ludicrous manipulation of Scripture—held by them to be God's instruction, of course—they erroneously draw conclusions that reflect ignorance and paranoia and act on those conclusions with violence and destruction. This is not to suggest that all militia groups pose such a threat; but there are those who, incredible as it may be to rational people, justify actions such as the 1995 bombing of the Oklahoma City Federal Building. It would be misleading, however, to focus on events as exceptional as bombings, for such a focus would lead to the mistaken notion that religious dogmatism and unawareness are characteristic only of extremists rather than the overall population. It is toward this misconception that we must turn our attention.

One of the most aggravating aberrations caused by the assumption of biblical certainty is a rather recent phenomenon, and is responsible for many of the abuses we have mentioned. A little more than 300 years ago Christianity came to a fork in the road and took the wrong turn. The mistake cost us dearly. Misguided religious conviction, as we shall see, once again pushed us in the wrong direction. On the basis of blind-faith devotion to the Bible, the opportunity for objective religious study during the last three centuries has been sabotaged (at least for the majority). Even now, in spite of living in the Information Age, most Christians have exempted themselves—and other unsuspecting Christians—from in-depth *critical* Bible study by embracing the false premise that biblical authority is sacred and, therefore, not to be questioned. Such an assumption has led to the dominance of faulty thinking and obsolete perceptions about Bible, Jesus, and Church doctrines. I am now, of course, referring to the *astrolabe mind.*

If a thousand old beliefs were ruined in our march to truth we must still march on.

—Stopford A. Brooke (1831-1916)
Anglo-Irish Unitarian clergyman and essayist

Chapter IV
The Astrolabe Mind

The symbol of the antiquated astrolabe conveys the general meaning of the astrolabe mind: one who perceives the present with a mind-set of the past. A classic true-life example of arrested perception is that of Lt. Hiroo Onoda, a Japanese soldier during World War II who, after hiding for some twenty-nine years on the remote island of Lubang in the Philippines, decided to come out and "surrender" in 1974. Talk about "cultural shock"! Onoda had to adjust his thinking on almost every aspect of what he had been conditioned to believe prior to the war's end in 1945. His concepts of morality, patriotism, religion, science, and social behavior—as well as his attitudes on women, Americans, and life in general—had to be radically reconstructed. In his isolation from the events, changes, and advances in knowledge taking place in the "real" world, Onoda's thinking had become antiquated. His overall mental development had been virtually arrested. For him, time had stood still while the rest of the world moved forward.

Thus far, the astrolabe mind has been defined as one which views the world from an outdated level of knowledge. Now let us further sharpen this definition. The astrolabe mind is more accurately described as a mind that comprehends all aspects of contemporary thought except in one area: *a specific blind spot in intellectual judgment*. In other words, the degree of mental obsolescence is restricted to only one specific area of perception, not overall perception. As an example, suppose Mr. and Mrs. Brown assume responsibility to educate their twelve-year-old daughter Tina. They provide her with the latest textbooks on history, English, geography, and so forth. But for natural science they provide information solely from the seventeenth century, which is far out of step with today's knowledge. Nevertheless, Tina learns all the material in her textbooks, including the outdated information on natural science. Tina will unknowingly possess an *educational blind spot*. She will have contemporary understanding in every field of thought except one; on the subject of natural science, her level of comprehension will be equal to that of the seventeenth century—more than 300 years behind the times. Her knowledge of natural science will be as outdated and useless as the astrolabe is for modern navigation.

If every child in the United States (or the world) were educated in like manner, the result would be devastating, as it would leave an entire generation with thwarted mentality in natural science. The repercussions of such a scenario would be grave and far-reaching, affecting the quality of life on many levels.

Admittedly, our example of Tina's scientific blind spot is unrealistic. And the chance of finding such a person, much less an entire society, appears unlikely. After all, we constantly derive new knowledge from watching television, reading newspapers and magazines, and accessing other numerous informational sources. But despite all the odds against it, a similar, seemingly impossible situation is a sad and tragic reality. In our earlier illustration, Tina personifies the precise nature of our mental condition, *the difference being that our lack of contemporary knowledge is not in science, but religion!* The vast majority of Christians—and for that matter non-Christians—are victims of a knowledge gap which places them at a level of religious understanding much more appropriate to the seventeenth century; ergo, the astrolabe mind.

No other field of thought has suffered such a prolonged, arrested condition in the general population. While the signs and dangers of antiquated knowledge might easily be detected in other fields such as medicine or physics, astrolabe mentality is not readily recognized because universal ignorance about this religious stagnation promotes the illusion that everything is perfectly normal! Sadly, people everywhere are caught in a mindless procession of unchanging beliefs, unaware of current information that would release them from primitive religious notions. The obsolete concepts I refer to are the entrenched doctrines and traditional theological assumptions of an earlier age, conceived in response to social and cultural influences that no longer exist.

To understand how the astrolabe mind developed, a few preliminary facts are warranted. We must recognize two events that occurred during the 1500s that radically altered the course of history: the Protestant Reformation and the Scientific Revolution.

The Protestant Reformation

By the fourth century, most of Christianity was united under the Roman Catholic Church, whose leader is the Pope. The first split within the Roman Catholic Church came in 1054 when a segment of the Church located in the eastern part of the Roman Empire withdrew from the main body after failing to resolve various disputes with its western counterpart. This departing group came to be known as the Eastern Church, which now dominates in eastern Europe, western Asia, and northern Africa. The remaining Roman Catholic Church (or Catholic Church, Catholicism) retained its name and continued to be the more formidable of the two.

A second division within the Catholic Church occurred in 1517. It was led by Martin Luther, a priest, and came to be known as the Protestant Reformation. Those who left Catholicism to join the movement were called Protestants, signifying "those who protest." Simply stated, a Protestant is a Christian not of the Eastern or Catholic Church, and one who denies allegiance to the Pope. The end result is that Christianity is basically divided into three groups: Roman Catholic, Eastern, and Protestant. Of course, most of us are either Catholic or Protestant since these two became the most dominant Christian bodies. It should be noted that after the Reformation the remaining members of the Catholic Church were able to maintain their unity—a positive side effect from allegiance to the Pope—while Protestants splintered into numerous alliances we call denominations, such as Baptist, Methodist, Presbyterian, and so forth. According to the *World Christian Encyclopedia*, Protestants proliferated into 20,800 denominations (some of them obviously quite small). To the best of my knowledge, most major splits have been prompted over disagreements on not only what the Bible *says*, but what it *is*.

The Scientific Revolution

The period between the sixteenth and eighteenth centuries was a highly significant time of discovery and invention that witnessed the challenging of long-dominant scientific, religious, social, and political authorities—an age in which opposing forces collided with irrepressible determination.

Prior to this period, most people blindly accepted traditional knowledge in every field, despite some noteworthy inaccuracies.

Almost everyone believed the sun rotated around the earth and that the earth was the center of the universe. Similarly, diseases were thought to be caused by supernatural forces or the positions of heavenly bodies. Cures for these diseases were thought to be effected by charms and animals. In short, popular beliefs were riddled with superstition, largely born of ignorance. All of this changed as interest in the *scientific method* underwent vigorous revival in Europe early in the sixteenth century.*

The Scientific Revolution of the sixteenth century was spearheaded by Nicolaus Copernicus with his 1543 publication *The Revolution of the Heavenly Orbs,* which established that the sun was the center of what we now call the solar system. In the seventeenth and eighteenth centuries (known as the Age of Reason and the Enlightenment)† further interest in natural law and human reason was generated by the scientific and intellectual achievements of Galileo Galilei, René Descartes, John Lock, Isaac Newton, and others.

The scientific method incorporates logical principles and procedures for systematically organizing information to develop knowledge. The first step is to gather data by observing phenomena. An hypothesis or premise is drawn from analyzing this data and then testing against the findings of further observation and experimentation. If the hypothesis is verified by the total findings, it is regarded as a scientific theory or law. If conflicting findings arise thereafter, this law or theory may be modified to accommodate the new findings or it may be supplemented by a new law or theory. The scientific method, then, is an objective research-based procedure which strives for knowledge through controlled experiments.

Before its revival in Europe, the scientific method had a long-standing history. The Greeks used it to make tremendous advances in systematizing knowledge between 600 B.C. and A.D. 200. Indeed, the renewed interest in science in late medieval Europe was stimulated by the recovery of some of these early Greek findings, especially those of Aristotle. Other notable Greeks who employed this method were Hippocrates, Pythagoras, Socrates, Plato, Euclid, Archimedes, Appollonius, Hipparchus, and Ptolemy.

† The Age of Reason was the period in Europe from the 1600s to the late 1700s in which philosophers emphasized the use of reason as the best method of learning truth. Within this time frame also, the Enlightenment was a philosophical movement in France and other European countries during the 1700s that emphasized rationalism and intellectual freedom.

In spite of these achievements, progress was slow as the majority of people continued to rely on ancient authorities and scriptural teachings as interpreted by the Church. Those who thought otherwise faced considerable risk, if not death. The Inquisition was not abolished until the 1800s, and freethinkers were still subject to persecution. Consider, for example, Giordano Bruno, the previously mentioned 52-year-old Italian philosopher who was executed as a heretic for arguing that many women being condemned as witches were simply senile or disordered old people. There were other reasons for his murder. Bruno was an astute and articulate person, a visionary, particularly in science. But his views on astronomy were considered too liberal, and he constantly opposed the Inquisition. For these and other reasons he was burned at the stake through the enthusiastic endeavors of Cardinal Bellarmine, the leading Catholic theologian of the day.

One cannot presume to know what Bruno thought as he was marched off to be brutally murdered by so-called servants of God, adorned as they were in dignified clerical robes—ironically and appropriately described in the NT as wolves in sheep's clothing. One can only hope that somehow Bruno took comfort in his own visionary spirit to see beyond his time, beyond the tyranny that sought to smother the truth he valued above all else. If nothing more, we can surmise that he was not surprised by his predicament; he would have known that the road to truth has led from cross to cross, from scaffold to scaffold, and from stake to stake—a never-ending sacrifice.

The classic example of this conflict is the struggle between Galileo and the Catholic Church. While Church leaders held that faith should rule, Galileo believed that *truth* should constitute the final authority. Thus, when Galileo, with the aid of a telescope (which he constructed), proved Copernicus' theory that the earth revolved around the sun, and not the sun around the earth, Cardinal Bellarmine (the same theologian who saw to Bruno's death) reacted sharply. In 1616 he told Galileo that he must not hold or defend the Copernican World System. After all, the Bible taught that the sun was in motion and the Earth motionless. Did not the Book of Psalms (104:5) tell us that God had ". . . set the earth on its foundations, so that it should not be shaken." And obviously, the Book of Ecclesiastes (1:5) states that "The sun rises and the sun goes down, and hastens to the place where it rises." Too, in the battle against the Amorites (Josh. 10:12) did not Joshua command the sun to stand still? This to the faithful conveyed that the sun rotated around the earth.

Galileo responded by seeking to demonstrate the truth of his findings. Soon it became the ambition and passion of his life. He was convinced that truth would persuade. The telling moment came in 1632 when Galileo published his work, *Dialogue on the Great World Systems.* Pope Urban VIII was outraged. To claim the view of Copernicus as true was to make the sacred Scripture false.

The following year the Inquisition, on orders from the Pope, charged Galileo with heresy and brought him to trial. At the meeting of the Congregation of the Holy Office, at which the Pope himself presided, the inevitable guilty verdict was passed. Galileo was sentenced to be tortured until he confessed and retracted his theories in favor of those of the Bible (and Church).

Elderly Galileo knew he could not survive the torture chamber. He sadly, but wisely, elected to renounce his scientific findings. The following is a partial account of his coerced confession:

> I, Galileo Galilei . . . age seventy years, arraigned personally before this tribunal, and kneeling before you, most Eminent and Reverend Lord Cardinals, Inquisitors General against heretical depravity throughout the whole Christian republic, having before my eyes and touching with my hands, the holy Gospels—swear that I have always believed, do now believe, and by God's help will for the future believe, all that is held, preached, and taught by the Holy Catholic and Apostolic Church . . . I must altogether abandon the false opinion that the sun is the center of the world and immovable, and that the earth is not the center of the world and moves, and that I must not hold, defend, or teach in any way whatsoever, verbally or in writing, the said doctrine . . . I abjure, curse and detest the aforesaid errors and heresies, and generally every other error and sect whatsoever contrary to the said Holy Church; and I swear that in the future I will never again say or assert, verbally or in writing, anything that might furnish occasion for a similar suspicion of heresy . . .[1]

Galileo retired to his house at Arcetri outside of Florence, where he was held prisoner until his death in 1642. Ironically, on Christmas day of the year Galileo died, Isaac Newton was born.

The Church had won the battle, but it soon lost the war. The opposition to unquestionable authority began to grow until it evolved into the Era of Enlightenment in eighteenth-century Europe. This era of mass awakening was characterized by the growing use of rational and scientific approaches to religious, social, political and economic issues. It emphasized intellectual freedom— freedom from prejudice and superstition. The continuing erosion of ancient religious and scientific dogma rapidly gained momentum. The Enlightenment produced formidable thinkers such as Francois Voltaire, Anne-Robert-Jacques Turgot, Jean Jacques Rousseau, David Hume, Adam Smith, Immanuel Kant, Thomas Paine, and Benjamin Franklin.

Clearly, the Scientific Revolution and subsequent Enlightenment ushered in an era of unprecedented discovery and, with it, a shattering collision of differing viewpoints. The movement crashed head-on into the superstitious concepts of the past. Traditional teachings were questioned and found sorely lacking. Established and intolerant authorities were challenged and many were forced into full retreat. Through the application of the scientific method, sacred beliefs that long held sway were tumbled from their centuries-old shrines, swept away like sand castles in the wake of the rushing tide. People were freed from the stifling dogma and imprisoning concepts recycled from ancient times. The continued application of the scientific method brought welcome relief to a stalemated world gone mad, long shackled by the chains of ignorance.

Modern science has prevailed for several hundred years now, and the quality of life for many humans has thereby profoundly improved. While some knowledge destroyed life or the environment, as in military weaponry or ecological pollution, it has nevertheless provided overwhelming benefits.

The practical value of the scientific method is that it can be applied to any subject under inquiry, from the existence of atoms or the mating habits of the mange mite to the age of biblical documents or the doctrinal claims of the Church. This is a debatable point for some Christians who do not believe the scientific method is appropriate for investigating religious claims. They believe that the nature of the object to be studied (the supernatural) is of another dimension than the tangible world, and therefore not subject to the methods of scientific inquiry. Such a position is only partially tenable. Although some segments of belief are not subject to tangible scrutiny, many claims by various religious groups can be investigated analytically. This point will be confirmed in coming chapters, and the rightful place of scientific analysis in religion will become evident.

In all fields of thought, new information eliminates falsehood and sharpens old knowledge. To illustrate this revisionary process, consider how the Apollo space program changed some of our beliefs about the moon. According to Dr. Gerald Wasserburg, Laboratory Director at the California Institute of Technology, the discoveries made by the Apollo mission refuted many highly-regarded beliefs about the moon. ". . . the facts changed everything," he said. "Pre-Apollo thinking is absolutely gone. The old moon is dead."[2]

Continued research forces society—sometimes slowly, sometimes rapidly—to make necessary adjustments in its beliefs. Normally, the insights from systematic inquiry first accrue to investigators, creating a temporary knowledge gap between them and us. In most disciplines, this gap eventually closes when the findings gathered by the few become the common knowledge of the many. *Religion continues to be the exception.*

The Birth and Perpetuation of the Astrolabe Mind

Protestant scholars pioneered analytical studies. Richard Simon (1638-1712) was the forerunner of NT criticism. His *Historie Critique du Text du N.T.* (1689) marks a date in critical interpretation of NT writing. As in other fields scrutinized by the scientific method, religion was found to contain discrepancies regarding long-held beliefs. Scholars discovered, for instance, through a reasoning process known as *biblical criticism*, that Moses was not the sole author of the first five books of the OT (a startling declaration in its day).

In this work, I will be using the term "biblical criticism" as a catchall expression to include the numerous analytical processes of biblical scholarship. Before proceeding further, it will be necessary to briefly clarify the nature of biblical criticism. To many the terms "critic" and "criticism" seem negative or hostile, as though the Bible were going to be deliberately maligned. This impression is incorrect since the words "critic" and "criticism" stem from the Greek word *kritikos,* meaning "able to judge." It is not defined in the modern sense of the book or film critic who leans toward subjective opinions. Biblical criticism is the objective, investigative science dealing with the text, character, composition, and origin of biblical documents. As with any other true science, its method of operation is dictated by the stringent procedures of the scientific method (readers are encouraged to examine the methods and findings of biblical criticism found in Appendix I).

Let us return to the focal point of this chapter—the phenomenon of the astrolabe mind. As analytical studies continued, it became obvious to many scholars that the Bible was not flawless and certainly not perfect. Some portions of Scripture were inferior to others in style, historical accuracy, and spiritual insight, and some were misleading and counterproductive to its central message of love. Even more controversial and shocking were the findings that suggested the Bible contained mythology. What had always been taken for granted as historical realities—angels, the Virgin birth, deity and resurrection of Jesus—were now being brought into question.

Expectedly, Christians refused to allow a question mark on what they considered to be divine truth. If the Bible was the word of God and the Church was created by God's own son, Jesus, there could be no error in how the Church interpreted the Scriptures. To question or challenge these foundations would undermine the validity and authority of the Bible, the Church, and Jesus. Thus, unlike other maturing disciplines that discarded faulty thinking in their struggle to obtain truth, Christianity almost universally rejected the findings of scientific investigation that conflicted with traditional views about Scripture. The intrusion of new perspectives into the exclusive sphere of Bible and Church was viewed as sacrilegious and therefore unacceptable.

It was the beginning of the astrolabe mind—a mind entrenched against truth on the assumption that the Bible possessed ultimate knowledge; a mind which declared all biblical stories to be historical happenings; a mind which declared that what it considered sacred was specifically unalterable; a mind which made authority its truth rather than truth its authority!

The refusal to view new information as an ally against faulty religious assumptions arrested most of Christianity within the mental framework of the seventeenth century. At its inception, the astrolabe mind was only slightly out of step with the newly discovered findings of seventeenth-century biblical criticism. But as time progressed, Christians increasingly failed to keep pace with these findings. Thus, the astrolabe mind became more and more antiquated and isolated from evolving knowledge.

Nevertheless, by the late nineteenth century new discoveries from Protestant scholarship were gaining ground, even as many enlightened views were being embraced in other fields. Christian scholars were creating a more flexible approach toward long-held dogmatic theology. If this evolving process had been allowed to continue *openly,* as it had in other fields, the astrolabe mind would never have survived into the twentieth century. But, early on, the Church could not tolerate its own scholars, especially those who clearly contradicted cherished beliefs. The Church became increasingly hostile with each discrepancy exposed from scholars' scrutinous light. Research represented threat.

Fortunately for these men, a growing awareness of human rights engendered by the Scientific Revolution, the Era of Enlightenment, and the abolishment of the Inquisition early in the 1800s helped establish a climate of forced restraint. Church leaders could no longer send heretics to the stake, but this did not discourage them from using other means to strike back at those who were theologically out of step. In 1862, the entire bench of Anglican bishops in England condemned the authors of *Essays and Reviews* for advancing biblical criticism. Similarly, in 1881 the General Assembly of the Free Church of Scotland dismissed its most noted historical critical scholar, W. Robertson Smith, for the same offense. The condemnation of these scholars for their historical and literary diligence simply reflects another dishonorable episode in the history of the Church.[3]

But in all fairness, when we look back on this stormy period it is not difficult to understand why the Church reacted so negatively. Although it was an unprecedented educational, scientific, and generally open-minded era of European history, serious problems nevertheless emerged—especially for religion.

When a revolution occurs, the pendulum inevitably swings too far in its new direction, and thus it did. Learned men became intoxicated with their newfound freedom, and philosophers and theologians were led into a mumbo-jumbo hodgepodge of ideas. From this environment sprang simple-minded idealism and theories of progress. Reason became a panacea, the freshly crowned god of a utopian age. As for sin, it didn't really exist and man could be perfected through reason. Miracles were said to be impossible since science had shown that the universe was governed by natural, inflexible laws. Also, Deism—the belief that God exists entirely apart from our world and does not influence the lives of human beings—became increasingly popular.

Church leaders were sorely irritated by these cavalier ideas and the extremist views of leading philosophers such as Voltaire,*

---

* *Voltaire (1694-1778) was a French author and philosopher.*

who looked upon the Apostles as forgers,[4] and Thomas Paine,* who concluded that reason alone was the avenue for discovering God.[5] Such thinking served only to cast suspicion upon science, reason, and analytical studies. It is understandable that Christians were unable to sort out the mess. Add to this confusion our leading culprit, the overriding devotion to biblical authority, and we have the makings of a serious derailment. It was a pivotal point in history, and most Christians were sidetracked because of conditioned belief, fear, and ignorance.

Although Protestant scholars pioneered in analytical studies, most Protestant clergy and lay people (not unlike their Catholic counterparts) were unable to assimilate any new information that challenged their inherited misunderstandings about biblical interpretation. Accordingly, it was expected that Christians would rise up and defend the sacred. The scholars were regarded as the villains trying to undermine the faith, while the traditionalists were seen as the good guys striving to preserve the infallible Christian heritage. The latter's uncritical devotion to tradition and biblical authority made them mentally inflexible. Indeed, their close-minded resistance to change was their virtual trademark.

It was not surprising, therefore, that from 1883 to 1897 members of various Protestant denominations gathered at what was called the Niagara Bible Conferences. In 1890, the Conference adopted a fourteen-point creed which included the verbal infallibility of Scripture, the universal depravity of humankind, salvation by faith in the blood of Christ, and the personal and premillennial return of the Lord to Earth. The intent was to preserve and maintain traditional interpretation of the Bible and what conference members believed to be the "fundamentals" of Christian faith.

Their organized protest against progressive scholarship caught fire in the early 1900s. The Moody Bible Institute in Chicago—a school founded by Dwight L. Moody and a stronghold of fundamentalist belief—published ten small volumes called *The Fundamentals*, which endeavored to return Christianity to its

---

* *Thomas Paine (1737-1809) was a famous writer on politics and religion who wrote* The Age of Reason. *Born in England, he eventually made his way to America. His writings greatly influenced the political thinking of the leaders of the American Revolutionary War. His writings also spoke in favor of the French Revolution.*

seventeenth-century, pre-biblical-criticism status. "Through the help of wealthy California businessmen, these volumes were distributed to millions of pastors and church members throughout the country, and they were influential in helping to shape fundamentalist bias among church members of most Protestant denominations.[6] Among the denominations most affected were the Baptists.

What emerged from this movement was a split in Protestantism. Thus, the early 1900s witnessed the emergence of a unique form of Christianity which was the product of, and exclusive to, twentieth-century Protestantism. This particular brand of Christianity came to be known as *fundamentalism*. Today, many fundamentalists are called *evangelicals*. More recently this movement has been referred to as the *New Religious Right.**

During much of the first half of the twentieth century, Protestant fundamentalism and Roman Catholicism were not far apart in their attitudes about biblical inerrancy and their rejections of modern scholarship. However, modernism represented less of a threat to Catholicism than it did to the new emerging Protestant fundamentalism whose authority was based solely upon an infallible Bible. Catholics could draw upon the equally sacred authority of Church and Pope to cautiously maneuver or reinterpret any conflicts arising from literary or scientific studies. Too, the official Catholic position regarding biblical criticism and biblical inerrancy was partially modified in comparison to the fundamentalist view.

Fundamentalism, more than any other group, rescued the astrolabe mind from its natural and rightful demise by rejecting the controversial findings of biblical criticism and by imparting new strength to traditional beliefs through vigorous support of the doctrine of inerrancy. This would be of little consequence today except for one thing: the majority of Christians have accepted this evangelical line.

The growth of fundamentalism, especially since the late 1940s, has been phenomenal. In fact, fundamentalism, with its astrolabe

---

Owing to the complexity if not impossibility of precise definitions, the terms conservatives, fundamentalists, and evangelicals will be used interchangeably in this discussion. I have no doubt that there will be objections to my using them in this manner since such an approach tends to create the impression that these conservative groups are identical—which, of course, they are not. For further definition and historical development of the fundamentalist movement, see Appendix VI.

character, is today the popular image of Protestantism. Although there are many non-fundamentalist Christians, this narrowly focused movement has engulfed the majority of Protestants in our society and continues to expand. A 1993 Gallup Poll asked: "Would you describe yourself as a 'born again,' or evangelical Christian?" Forty-six percent of those interviewed answered yes. This figure represents a 35 percent increase over 1986 figures.

There is no question that the more rigidly defined and structured system of dogmatic Christianity is overwhelmingly popular today. "Give me that old-time religion!" chorus millions of searching souls. They want to be told what to believe, clearly and firmly, in black and white. The very nature of dogmatic religion captures and hypnotizes its followers. Like the Pied Piper of old, there is nothing so compelling, disarming, and alluring as the claims of religious certainty which allegedly lead all who follow to the road of salvation. Akin to the swirling mass of a giant vortex, fundamentalism creates an irresistible pull which dominates and controls.

Nowhere is the growing force of evangelicalism more evident than with those who form the vast national television and radio audiences of what some have called the "electric church." Numerous television and radio stations are devoted solely to religious programming, and the numbers continue to increase. This proliferation has become worldwide. Also, more than 5,000 evangelical bookstores are operating today, and the number is growing. Financially, the electric church and fundamentalism in general brings in a weekly cash flow of millions. Their fund-raising appeals along with their magazines, books, T-shirts, bumper stickers, records, and cassettes represent an annual multi-billion-dollar industry in the United States and Canada.

The popularity and demand for a religion that promotes simplistic blind faith by claiming to possess divinely revealed truth continues to gather momentum. Many have heralded this as a great religious revival. Emotional zeal abounds and, with it, financial prosperity for the movement. Because of this success, a deceptive, self-validating assumption has begun to emerge. Many evangelicals believe that this startling surge of prosperity proves unquestionably that God is behind it all and that their absolute trust and faith in the traditional fundamental interpretations of Bible and Church are correct.

I disagree. I do not believe that the popularity and prosperity of this movement indicates an endorsement from God. On the contrary, the all-accepting blind-faith surrender to authoritarian religion today is indicative of widespread astrolabe mentality. This so-called religious revival merely demonstrates the antiquated mind-set of religious thinking; it reflects a vast dimension of ignorance and misunderstanding regarding the Christian faith. In the long run, narrow-minded belief systems are neither positive nor harmless. They lead to mind control, to the quest for personal power, and to the tragic manipulation of the masses.

Time for a reality check. It is vital to remember that the problem of astrolabe mentality is not restricted to fundamentalists although they seem to be the most affected. Regardless of their religious persuasion, most Christians—therefore, most of society—are characterized by this condition. The degree to which one espouses astrolabe thinking will depend on one's education, upbringing, and numerous other variables.

In any case, the astrolabe mind is one of the most astonishing and repugnant restrictions of our time. Much of what we are taught and readily believe about religion is oversimplified and untrue, much as seventeenth-century scientific knowledge would be markedly inaccurate in comparison with today's science. This is one reason the astrolabe instrument symbolizes our present antiquated condition. It is the perfect image of the contemporary Christian mind. The astrolabe mind is an archaic thought machine that should not be operative in today's world. Just as the astrolabe navigational tool gave way to the sextant in 1731, certain pre-enlightenment religious concepts should have yielded to more cogent knowledge; but they haven't as yet, at least not in the general population. [Despite the continued lack of awareness of lay people, the procedures and findings of biblical criticism were, of course, eventually validated by secular and religious institutions of higher learning—the exception being evangelical institutions (see Appendix I).]

Although the astrolabe mind has been with us for more than 300 years (becoming more obsolete with each passing year), the idea of unquestionable biblical authority which spawned it can be traced back to early Christian thought. Specifically, the astrolabe mind was and is a symptom of bibliolatry. Such a condition represents nothing less than a cancerous threat to our overall sensibilities and spiritual development.

The most debilitating trademark of astrolabe thinkers today is their almost universal lack of understanding about theology, Church history, and biblical criticism. As a result, they quickly succumb to erroneous or superficial interpretations of Bible and Church.

They simply have not armed themselves with enough knowledge to analyze what they are being told—or sold. The old proverb rings true: "What can you reason but from what you know?" If Christians are spoon-fed to accept Scripture or the Pope's word as God's personal messages and if they have no knowledge on which to weigh the validity of these messages, then they will receive them without reservation or scrutiny. Thereafter, they will be inclined to reject anything that challenges these alleged truths. Yet, if Christians cannot accept evolving knowledge because it conflicts with what they consider holy, then the gap between truth and what they believe will continue to widen, and the astrolabe mind will become even more entrenched.

Exacerbating this knowledge gap is the secular media, since it strictly functions from an astrolabe frame of reference. It follows the lead of popular Christianity without realizing that most adherents are afflicted with this disease. Thus, the popular press accepts and reflects the status quo of religious obsolescence. A perfect example of this mirrored delusion can be readily seen in the cover story of the April 10, 1995, *Time* magazine, entitled "Can We Still Believe in Miracles?" This pre-Easter edition did little but to confirm the widening gap between religious scholarship and the general population. The article attempted to endorse traditional religious views while simultaneously subjecting modern scholarship to the most ludicrous criticisms. Afflicted themselves with astrolabe mentality, the three contributing reporters proceeded to malign, denigrate, and mispresent scholarship with a hodgepodge of erroneous arguments that exposed their own lack of knowledge on the matter. They portrayed scholars as modern skeptics "working furiously to disprove the miracles in the Bible." As most uninformed people do, they confused the questionable notions (which do exist) of some religious scholars with well-established hard-core religious scholarship. They referred to Bishop John Shelby Spong, the Episcopal Bishop of Newark, for example, as an "enfant terrible" (indiscreet, irresponsible, unconventional) of liberal Protestant theology. Far from deserving such a label, Bishop Spong has authored several books that have helped bridge the gap between scholars and laity.

This characterization is exactly what one would expect in an astrolabe society. It is imperative that this religious anachronism be understood since it represents one of the most formidable obstacles to maturity. At the risk of being redundant, therefore, I will reiterate the problem by using the *Time* article as a point of reference.

The article's characterization of Bishop Spong as the *enfant terrible* of so-called liberal theology is the equivalent of calling scientist Carl Sagan* the *enfant terrible* of modern astronomy— which would, of course, be ridiculous. Carl Sagan will not incur this stigma because the knowledge gap between scientists and lay people has been virtually closed. Sagan sounds credible since the general population has been sensitized to enough scientific data to be readily accepting of his ideas. Also, science is replete with the tangible results of ongoing development. One cannot argue, for example, against the principles of aerodynamics when such an argument would be obviously silly every time a plane flew overhead.

But if we could transport Mr. Sagan in a time machine back to the seventeenth century, his teaching would sound shocking and unacceptable. He would indeed be castigated as indiscreet, irresponsible, and unconventional; worse yet, in all likelihood he would be called a heretic and burned at the stake. What we must not forget, however, is that Carl Sagan would have been severely rebuked *not because he was wrong, but because the masses he addressed would have lacked even the most basic knowledge necessary to grasp the plausibility of his comments.* How can anyone teach algebra, for example, to students who have never been exposed to the elementary concepts of mathematics?

Unfortunately, this same informational gap and, subsequently, this same hostile reaction are indicative of today's believer in relation to Bishop Spong and other mainline scholars—not because these teachers have traveled back to the pre-Enlightenment era, but because the religious belief system of that era has erroneously remained the norm of the present. Unlike other disciplines that did not labor under the false assumption of possessing sacred knowledge, conventional Christianity would not allow itself to be influenced or modified by the explosion of ongoing discoveries made available by analytical studies over the past three hundred years.

---

* *Carl Sagan of Cornell University and author of the best-selling book* Cosmos, *briefed the Apollo crews before their missions to the moon in 1969 and received NASA's Apollo Achievement Award. He is president of the Pasadena-based Planetary Society, the largest space-interest group in the world.*

In short, Bishop Spong and other religious scholars of this century, espousing only what is being taught by the most prestigious universities and seminaries worldwide, would not be regarded as extremists were it not for the amazing fact that most people are saddled with a seventeenth-century religious mind-set. Bishop Spong is no more an extremist than Carl Sagan. Without passing judgment on whether all their ideas are correct, we must acknowledge that they both use and draw from the same pool of twentieth-century knowledge, from the same methods and procedures of stringent investigative analysis. Furthermore, they both reflect the widespread knowledge of their respective fields.

Until our society recognizes the validity of religious studies, endless generations of Christians will continue to be led like preprogrammed robotic androids to accept concepts which inevitably lead to conflict and confusion. If young people are taught, for example, to embrace the OT creation allegory as literal history and then later are confronted with substantial evidence to the contrary, they will suffer a serious clash between religious faith and hard-core knowledge. A robot cannot assimilate data that conflicts with original programming. Sparks fly, the word "tilt" appears, and the lights go out; that is, faith goes out. This tragic loss arises from the inability to sustain what one has been taught about the Scriptures when such teachings are matched against twentieth-century knowledge.

Moderate and liberal Christians will not escape this dilemma, even though they have chosen *not* to look upon the Genesis account as literal; other theological issues will gnaw at their intellectual sensitivity. This is evident when we consider the deity of Jesus, the Virgin Birth, the Resurrection, the Second Coming, the Trinity, and other biblical reflections—reflections we will examine in later chapters. If any or all of these cherished beliefs are incorrect as traditionally interpreted, should they elude modification on the presumption that the Bible and Church are uniquely authoritative? Can one not gain important insights from theological and biblical studies, along with the findings of psychology, geology, anthropology, archaeology, history, philosophy, astronomy, world religions, and other such disciplines? And can one not be objective in viewing these findings, or must one forever examine them through the squinted eyes of bias and preconceived notions of "rightness"? To most Christians, such considerations are intolerable because they challenge beliefs which are held to be sacred.

Over time, these unattended questions translate into annoying ambiguities. In a futile attempt to shore up faith, many Christians superficially quell their anxieties by trying to reinforce the fading validity of an ancient world view. Such people remain fixated in the infantile stages of religious understanding, which ultimately impedes their self-development and drives them further from the "real" world. In relinquishing their right to challenge the dogma of another age, most Christians are by default responsible for the perpetuation of the astrolabe mind.

Further Reflection

We must remember that no other field of thought has suffered such a prolonged, arrested condition in the general population; no other discipline has been so afflicted with an informational blind-spot, the astrolabe mind-set. The gap between religious scholarship and lay people has never been closed. Astrolabe mentality is not easily recognized because universal ignorance about this religious stagnation promotes the illusion that everything is perfectly normal.

In other disciplines, although scientists may be a few steps ahead of the rest of us during the "discovery" time, the public sharing of their findings eventually closes the gap. But this gap between religious scholars and society has, for several centuries, widened instead of closed as the information has remained unknown, ignored, or rejected. Edward Farley, who teaches Constructive Theology at the Divinity School of Vanderbilt University (Tennessee) wrote an article which addressed the problem of unenlightened believers; it appeared in Princeton University's prestigious journal, *Theology Today*. Farley states:

> Why is it that the vast majority of Christian believers remain largely unexposed to Christian learning—to historical-critical studies of the Bible . . . Why do bankers, lawyers, farmers, physicians, homemakers, scientists, salespeople, managers of all sorts, people who carry out all kinds of complicated tasks in their work and home, remain at a literalist, elementary-school level in their religious understanding? How is it that high-school-age church members move easily and quickly into the complex world of computers, foreign languages, DNA, and calculus, and cannot even make a beginning in historical-critical interpretation of a single text of Scripture? How is it possible one can attend or even teach a Sunday school

for decades and at the end of that time lack the interpretive skills of someone who has taken three or four weeks in an introductory course in Bible at a university or seminary?[7]

Yes, the gap grows wider as scholars continue to accrue information that seldom reaches the laity. According to the late theologian James D. Smart,* the findings and resources of biblical scholars have remained largely limited to seminary classrooms and libraries. Only a minute fraction of this learning has been shared with congregants, and most Christians to this day are unaware that it even exists.[8]

The withholding of information by ministers is the cardinal reason for the perpetuation of the astrolabe mind. And yet, their lack of diligence in this area is understandable. Over the years they have inherited an assumption which has permeated the clerical leadership of the Church: While theological and biblical uncertainties arising from biblical criticism are essential knowledge for a minister, it is inadvisable to confuse congregants with issues better reserved for seminary classrooms.

Such reasoning not only occurs because they think it will upset the faith of their parishioners, but also stems from the fear of reprisal. As we have seen, it has been the scholars, ministers, and institutions of higher learning that have always born the brunt of indignant believers. As a further example, in 1893 the general assembly of the Presbyterian Church in the U.S.A. tried and convicted professors Charles Augustus Briggs and Henry P. Smith of heresy. They were dismissed from Princeton's School of Theology for disputing that Moses wrote the entire Pentateuch[9] (first five books of the OT), a concept that is accepted today almost without question. While the issues have changed, the threat of heresy trials is still very much alive in the more conservative and authoritarian churches. In Catholicism, for example, many priests are even today persecuted by the Church hierarchy (see Appendix IV).

The price for daring to challenge or inform may be high—so high that many clergy lose the resolve to pursue the quest. Even ministers in progressive churches are hesitant to introduce issues

---

* *James D. Smart (1906-1982) was a noted author, scholar, and professor at Union Theological Seminary (N.Y.).*

to enlighten their lay people since previous efforts resulted in harassment and accusations of not keeping the faith. Many a disgruntled congregation has replaced their minister. In those cases where the minister couldn't be removed, the members joined more conservative churches that catered to their astrolabe views. In this way evangelical churches, which claim to preserve traditional beliefs, have grown larger and stronger while the more open-minded churches have grown smaller and weaker, losing their disenchanted members to other churches that are Siamese-connected to the "old-time religion."

What are ministers to do? Can they drag seventeenth-century-minded believers kicking and screaming into the Information Age? The difficulty of the situation is such that relatively few ministers can bridge the two worlds. Usually, the clergy rationalize conflicts and give in to saying what their congregants want to hear, or take the schizophrenic path of "let's pretend," swinging between saying what their people want them to believe and what they themselves truly believe. Sadly, most clergy are forced to maintain the status quo at the expense of truth and integrity.

Ministers today are finding they must pay for the general unwillingness of past clerics to risk closing the knowledge gap. Unfortunately, the clerics of tomorrow may have to pay equally for this same reluctance today. This situation is worsened, as we will see, by the fact that many preachers are themselves unaware or uneducated about biblical criticism.

If, from the very beginning, the findings of religious scholarship had been *fully* shared (more precisely, allowed to be shared) with the entire Church body, the astrolabe mind would never have flourished. Had this occurred, Creationism and the other anomalies to which we have alluded would be nonexistent.

Before continuing I must be clear on the following point. I am not suggesting that the findings of biblical criticism reveal the Bible as unreliable or that it lacks authority; it is reliable and authoritative. That is not the issue. The issue centers on the overstated aura of absolute, sacred, *unquestionable* biblical authority to the exclusion of all else. It is exasperating to converse with Christians who hold the Bible as their ultimate answer-book to all matters, especially when they emphatically state: "The Bible says . . ." as though the discussion should now end.

Biblical imperfection is not of consequence to all Christians, since some hold a broader interpretation of biblical inspiration. They allow for historical and transmissional error as part of the natural process and do not regard them as threatening the truth of biblical writ. Thus, they concede the historical improbability of certain portions of Scripture, but not their theological improbability; therefore, they would not assume to question the validity of such doctrinal concepts as the Trinity or the divinity of Jesus. The end result has been that "enlightened" Christians no longer accept the doctrine of inerrancy and prefer a modified view of divine revelation. This modified view holds that even though Scripture may be flawed or inaccurate at points, these imperfections do not detract from the doctrinal and religious truths drawn from Bible and Church.

While acknowledging this "enlightened" view to be an improvement over the doctrine of inerrancy, we must note that it lacks credibility. It is simply a convenient rationalization, as anxious Christians with astrolabe minds scramble to avoid the serious theological implications arising from more than three centuries of biblical and historical studies. To substantiate this charge, the next two chapters will reveal information that strikes at the very heart of *traditional* Christian thought.

*A truth that disheartens because it is
true is of far more value than the
most stimulating falsehoods.*

—Maurice Maeterlinck (1862-1949)
Belgian author

Chapter V
New Testament Mythology

With the rediscovery of the scientific method in sixteenth-century Europe and the subsequent evolvement of the Enlightenment during the eighteenth century, it was inevitable that a more rational analysis of Scripture would occur. In a world becoming scientifically oriented, descriptions of walking on water, of demons, angels, resurrection stories, and other phenomena grew increasingly unacceptable as historical realities.

In 1835-1836, *The Life of Jesus Critically Examined,* by D.F. Strauss,* referred to some NT narratives as "myth" and defined those unhistorical elements as expressing a series of religious ideas.[1] Today, analytical studies continue to support and confirm this assertion. The majority of scholars regard the following NT accounts and Church-developed† doctrines as myth.[2]

1. the Virgin Birth;
2. the Incarnation (God in human form; that is, God as Jesus);
3. the work of Atonement (plan of salvation);
4. the Resurrection;
5. the Ascension (Jesus' bodily ascent into heaven forty days after the Resurrection);
6. the Second Coming (the return of Jesus to raise the dead and to summon all to the Last Judgment; and
7. the Last Judgment (the judgment of all by God at Christ's Second Coming).

D.F. Strauss (1808-1874) studied at Tübingen University (Germany) and later taught and lectured at the University.

†*Certain religious doctrines such as the Trinity and Plan of Salvation are not full-blown biblical concepts. These doctrines were developed by the Church only after the Church had interpreted biblical themes and implications.*

In order for one to understand why scholars view these doctrines as mythical, one needs to be familiar with the syncretized nature of biblical writing—syncretism being a process in which the religious doctrines, rituals, and beliefs of one religion are adapted or adopted by another religion—and the ancient world views from which these writings emerged. New Testament mythology was borrowed and customized from other belief systems that coexisted with Christianity. To illustrate this point, we will briefly explore historical criticism, one of the analytical branches of biblical criticism.

Historical Criticism

Historical criticism seeks to interpret biblical writings in the context of their historical settings. In doing so, numerous questions about the given document can be answered. Careful study of written content will normally yield clues to its time period, authorship, authenticity, purpose, and so forth.

To clarify how historical criticism works, let us examine the following document. Although an oversimplified example, it provides some insights into the application of historical criticism. Our objective is to determine if the following is an authentic writing of Abraham Lincoln, allegedly taken from his personal diary.

> June 17, 1843
> I find the evening difficult yet exciting. Tomorrow, Mary Todd and I will exchange wedding vows. Although one can never be sure in matters of this nature, I feel our union will be blessed by the Almighty.
>
> There comes a time when one senses the urgency of decision, and I trust I have made the proper choice; I believe I have.
>
> Sleep will not come easily this evening. The coming of tomorrow harbors no fear, and yet this headache persists. Admittedly, I am not without anxiety over other matters. The Kansas-Nebraska Bill has been most distressing. Perhaps an aspirin will ease the tension. Why is it that we mortals are so vulnerable? At best, we are seldom rested or content.

To the casual reader, the above record may appear genuine. But to the student of history, there are several reasons to question the authenticity of this diary entry. First, it is dated June 17, 1843, and historical records show Lincoln and Todd were wed in 1842. Second, the Kansas-Nebraska Bill was not introduced until 1854. Third, aspirin was not synthesized until 1853 and not used as medicine until 1899. These discrepancies strongly suggest this entry was not written by Abraham Lincoln on the date stated, or, if it was, the original text was altered and additions were made.

Historical criticism was applied in the analysis of the "Hitler diaries," which caused such a sensation in 1983. After careful inspection, it was determined the diaries were fakes. Not only were the paper, cover, bindings, labels, and glue manufactured after Hitler's death in 1945, but the historical content also contained errors. General Franz Ritter Von Epp was portrayed congratulating Hitler in 1937 on his fiftieth anniversary of army service. But in 1937, Hitler was only forty-eight years old and it was really the Führer who praised Von Epp for his fifty years in the army.

These same rigorous evaluations are used to scrutinize the Bible. Through the attentive efforts of many scholars, biblical records can be categorized in terms of origin, date, authenticity, and authorship.

Another objective of historical criticism is to probe the author's purpose and meaning discussed or implied in the work. Again, the historical setting is of utmost importance. Once critics isolate the historical backdrop of a work, they are less likely to impose their own biased interpretation into the text. Too often we unthinkingly define biblical writing from a twentieth-century Western perspective, which is too many centuries and cultures removed from the original historical surroundings; we fail to perceive its meanings and nuances. The Bible can be truly understood only by understanding the times in which it was written, and such an understanding includes the moral, political, ideological, cultural, social, economic, philosophical, and theological forces that prevailed. For biblical scholars this requires a profound understanding of the Roman, Jewish, and Greek cultures.

Although historical criticism has helped unlock the real meaning of the Scriptures, it has also produced many findings which have been ignored or rejected, owing to their controversial nature. For instance, Gustav Adolf Deissmann,* while analyzing secular Greek

---

* *Gustav Adolf Deissman (1866-1937) was a Bible scholar who studied the history of language, literature, and religion of Greek Judaism and primitive Christianity.*

documents, discovered that many NT words were not unique. He found that the terms used to describe Christ ("Lord," "Savior," "Son of God") were terms already in vogue prior to Christianity; they were not unprecedented.[3] Similar studies found that the religious language and concepts employed in the NT were not the exclusive property of Christianity. When Christianity emerged, several Greek mystery religions already embraced mythical concepts such as the virgin birth, baptism, sacred meals, and the death and resurrection of a savior. Among these sects were the followers of Attis, the vegetarian god of Phrygian religion and a powerful celestial deity in the Roman religion. The followers of Attis commemorated his death on March 22 and, three days later, his coming to life on March 25.[4]

Another resurrection account is that of Osiris, the legendary god-ruler of predynastic Egypt and lord of the underworld who was murdered on the 17th of the Egyptian month of Athyr, then found and restored to life two nights later on the 19th of Athyr. Still another account is that of the Greek god Adonis. It is not known when he is said to have risen following his death, but one papyrus text reconstructed by scholars indicates it was three days later.[5] Finally, Tammuz, an ancient deity worshipped in Babylon—in the OT (Ezek. 8:14) his disappearance is mourned by the women of Jerusalem—was loved by the fertility goddess Ishtar, who, according to early accounts, murdered him and later restored him to life.

Also interesting is the parallel between Christianity and the mystery religion of Isis, a nature goddess who was first worshipped in ancient Egypt. The faith expanded to the Mediterranean world and became one of the chief religions of the Roman Empire. Statues of Isis holding the infant Harpocrates (Horus) and the exalted hymns praising the Egyptian Queen of Heaven have their obvious counterparts in the subsequent admiration of Mary.[6]

Of course, there are many important distinctions between the mystery religious themes and their parallels in Christianity. In all of the mystery religions the deity dies by compulsion and not by choice, sometimes in bitterness or despair, but never in self-giving love.[7] And, too, the characters in these mystery religions are fictitious, while the central figures in Christianity have been living persons. Even so, the fact that Christianity reflects some of these same concepts, albeit in more ingratiating form, enhances the probability that it borrowed or absorbed these myths from the mystery religions of the day. It appears that the language and early teachings of Christianity, as captured in the Greek editions of the NT, mirror the popular street language and mythical beliefs of the Greek and Roman world.

The findings of historical criticism are a mixed blessing for most Christians. On one hand, these findings illuminate the setting in which the NT was authored and thereby afford a far greater understanding of the Scriptures. On the other hand, some of these findings detract from Christianity's centuries-old claim of theological uniqueness. Recent studies of Jewish writings contemporaneous with Jesus continue to highlight this dilemma. In the 1991 publication *Jesus' Jewishness (Exploring the Place of Jesus within Early Judaism)*, editor James H. Charlesworth* confirms that many of the earliest Palestinian Christians (who, of course, were Jewish) were highly trained, brilliant, and ingenious individuals. He states:

> . . . Early Judaism by Jesus' time was incredibly sophisticated, cosmopolitan, and brilliantly developed. Many theological, symbolical, and linguistic terms and ideas associated with Paul, John, and Christianity, and thus once labeled "Pauline," "Johannine," and "Christian," are now seen to be pre-Christian and sometimes even Jewish.

He then proposes the questions and ramifications of this insight:

> Wherein, therefore, lies the genius of Jesus' earliest followers? Wherein lies the unique theological perspective of Jesus himself? The "uniqueness" of Jesus has become less clear in light of the discovery deep within Early Judaism of many creative ideas once perceived as uniquely his.[8]

Further questions regarding the uniqueness of Christian theology will arise from the public debut of the Dead Sea Scrolls.†

James H. Charlesworth (1940-) is an educator and Methodist minister; he holds a Ph.D. from Duke University.

† The Dead Sea Scrolls are a collection of ancient papyrus and leather scrolls discovered in several caves in the Qumran Valley near the Dead Sea. They contain the oldest known copies of most of the books of the OT. They were written in Hebrew and Aramaic about 2000 years ago and contain comments and explanations on biblical writing and the monastic rule of the Qumran Community. The scrolls were discovered in 1947 and following years.

On September 22, 1991, the Huntington Library in California disclosed that it possessed a complete set of photographs of all unpublished scroll material and was making them accessible to any scholar who wished to see them. This material had been unavailable to the majority of scholars since its discovery in 1947. The unbiased inspection of these oldest biblical and non-biblical documents may have a tremendous impact on Christianity; it may leave the "uniqueness" of Christian theology open to question. *The Dead Sea Scrolls Deception* presents the following conjecture:

> If, for example, the scrolls could be dated from well before the Christian era, they might threaten to compromise Jesus' originality and uniqueness—might show some of his words and concepts to have been not wholly his own, but to have derived from a current of thought, teaching, and tradition already established "in the air." If the scrolls dated from Jesus' lifetime, however, or from shortly thereafter, they might prove more embarrassing still. They might be used to argue that the "Teacher of Righteousness" who figures in them was Jesus himself, and that Jesus was not therefore perceived as divine by his contemporaries.[9]

As a consequence of these and other studies, new evaluations regarding the uniqueness of Christian doctrine, including Jesus himself, will emerge. Whatever transpires through further research, Christians should not attempt to dodge the bullet of reality by side-stepping the findings of historical criticism; such denial will not serve our quest for truth.

The Unacceptable Finding

Since D.F. Strauss presented his work in 1835, scholars have not convinced the majority of Christians that biblical writing contains mythical expressions of NT times, even though studies continue to support and confirm this assertion—a serious sticking point for most Christians. There are several reasons for this impasse.

First is the misunderstanding of the term "myth," which, in the popular sense, is akin to fairy tales and fables, fictitious stories devised solely to entertain. Myth is sometimes equated with legend, that is, folk history. But philosophically, some myths relate stories of deep expression—that is, the beliefs of a people pertaining to supernatural events or gods or natural phenomena. Also, myth, like a parable, usually expresses a moral lesson. A myth, then, is a colorful expression which freeze-frames a concept that cannot be pictured as vividly in any other way. It forces one to focus at the point of insight. The purpose of NT myth was originally best expressed in the work of Rudolph Bultmann (1884-1947), a German theologian who advocated *demythologizing* the New Testament. He described NT myth as scriptural stories about the supernatural world told in terms of this world. Such myths, he believed, explain the unexplainable in ways we understand and to which we can relate. Unfortunately, the various conceptions of myth have blurred its unique quality and purpose, and have given it a negative connotation which most people have yet to overcome.

A second reason that Christians reject the myth hypothesis is the widespread belief in the Bible as God-given, which by traditional definition presupposes historical, not figurative, events. The contention that certain biblical stories are flavored by mythology shocks most Christians because they have long interpreted the Bible—aside from parables, proverbs, and such—as literal history. Even those Christians who hold a modified view of Scripture (recognizing its human imperfections) cannot accept the idea that our most cherished doctrines might be spiritual signposts and not historical happenings.

The third reason Christians reject the idea of NT myth comes from the manner in which Strauss and subsequent scholars presented their findings. Originally, the rejection might not have been so sweeping had he and his successors simply described the nature of NT myth from a different perspective. If Christians were adequately informed about the belief systems of the time in which the NT was written, they might be more apt to accept the Bible's mythology as a natural expression of the age in which it originated. The discovery and interpretation of NT myth must go hand in hand with an explanation of the factors that brought myth into the writing.

The final reason Christians turn their backs on the idea of biblical myth is that they simply can't recognize it. New Testament myth is interwoven into the fabric of historical events so as to camouflage its presence. There is no visible separation between an historical event and its mythical aspects. While it is relatively easy to recognize NT parable, the mythical content is written as though it were literal truth since, in all probability, the authors assumed it was. If the Gospel writers were not eyewitnesses to the stories they received about Jesus (see Appendix I) it would have been difficult for them to distinguish between myth and history, as they did not have sufficient scientific and philosophical perspective. It is doubtful these writers made a conscious distinction between myth, superstition, and historical reality. And if by chance they suspected a difference, they chose not to make this evident in their writings. For this reason, both mythical and historical information was interpreted and written as literal fact. For the NT authors, Jesus' divinity was just as plausible as any other reports they received about him. Thus, history and myth were indistinguishable and were fused as historical narrative. Christians today cannot identify them as two distinct elements because they probably were not originally perceived or written as such.

Bible myths at their inception were simply the expressions of people with an ancient world view. The recognition of and differences between fact, myth, and superstition can be more easily seen from our modern perspective. What Strauss, Bultmann, and other scholars call myth can be determined as such only from historical hindsight. Portions of the NT were labeled myth only *after* advances in scientific and historical knowledge made it possible to distinguish between the old and new world views. The way they perceived reality was in sharp contrast to our perceptions today. In Matthew 17:14-18, for example, a father brings his epileptic son to Jesus, who reportedly cured the boy by exorcising the demon that possessed him. It is not difficult to perceive the superstitious aspect of this story in the assumption that the boy's epilepsy was caused by demons. But how else could the author of Matthew interpret this condition, since the common belief then was that demons were the cause of epilepsy. We wouldn't expect Matthew to explain epilepsy as a chronic malfunction disorder of the human nervous system characterized by partial or complete loss of consciousness caused by a deficiency of glutamic acid in the brain thereby producing bodily convulsions, and that Jesus somehow managed to affect the brain's corpus callosum thereby restoring the normal electrical rhythm of brain cells to alleviate the condition. Of course not! Such knowledge was not even known and confirmed until the twentieth century.

This distinctive perception is now obvious, but one which most Christians have yet to seriously apply to the Scriptures. The truth is that most of them have a myopic view of biblical writing. I say this because a strange thing happens when Christians confront scriptural stories such as this one. Some will accept the account of demons causing epilepsy as literal truth, but most will readily attribute such thinking to an ancient world view, realizing that early people were less knowledgeable. But those Christians who support this distinction are unable to invoke the same logic when doctrinal belief is challenged, such as the divinity of Jesus (Incarnation). This is due to the reasons already discussed and to the grave importance most Christians attribute to these doctrines—an importance they believe can be maintained only by viewing them as tangibly irrefutable rather than mythically symbolic. And yet, even as we know today that epilepsy is not caused by demons, so we should suspect that gods do not assume human form.

Mythology: Its Function

Certain types of myth are not only desirable, but necessary for human adjustment and growth. According to Joseph Campbell,* myth has four primary functions: (1) a mystical function, to awaken and sustain in us a sense of spiritualism about the universe and our relationship to it; (2) a scientific function, to offer an image of the universe in accord with present scientific knowledge; (3) a cultural function, to help validate, support, and imprint the norms of our society; and (4) a practical function, to help us adjust emotionally and relate usefully throughout our lives.[10] Myth, in these applications, is not restricted to a narrow religious forum, but encompasses a broader meaning that fulfills one's total well-being.

We can see that when the OT and NT were written, they fulfilled all the functions of myth because they were in harmony with ancient beliefs. But today that is only partially true. Whereas the scientific function of myth is severely diminished since the image of the universe which the Bible conveys is no longer in keeping with today's science, it still achieves the mystical function as myth remains one of the most effective ways in religion for helping us relate meaningfully to God.

Our recent discovery of religious teaching as partially mythic should not negate its value. Whether employed by Judaism, Christianity, or any other religion, mythology helps us to clarify

---

*Joseph Campbell (1904-1989) was a prolific American author, the recipient of the Distinguished Scholar Award, Hofstra University, 1973. He also received the Melcher Award for contribution to religion, 1976, for The Mythic Image.

and thereby give meaning to, the enigmas of life, death, and God. The myth's truth and value are in its message, even as a NT parable conveys a truth through its message. The parable does not require historical verification to register its message. Neither should the truth channeled through the myth-story depend on a literal interpretation. Baden Powell* pointed out that ". . . parable and myth often include more truth than history."[11] To reject myth as nonsense because it reflects an unhistorical event, or unscientific viewpoint, is to miss its intent and value. The words of Episcopal Bishop John Shelby Spong personify the spirit of this reality:

> I am not interested in preserving the doctrine of the incarnation. I am interested in understanding the truth to which the doctrine of the incarnation points.
> Similarly, I am not interested in preserving the doctrine of the Trinity. I do not believe that the ultimate truth of God has been captured in the trinitarian formula. I am eager to embrace . . . the truth to which this doctrine points. There is, however, nothing sacred or eternal for me about the words previous generations chose to be the bearers of their truth.[12]

Truth or Consequences

As we have noted, NT mythology and consequently church doctrine are received by the astrolabe mind as factual, literal, and historical. Although in many respects such teachings are historically grounded, its mythical strand is either ignored or unrecognized. Yet does it really matter if we continue to ignore or be unaware of mythical elements? At what point does the ignorance or denial of myth interfere with human welfare? Several problems come to mind.

The first problem is the possible rejection of faith. If people continue to deny or be unaware of NT myth, religious teachings will lose their guiding value when thinking persons can no longer verify with integrity a literal interpretation. In the past many

---

* *Baden Powell (1796-1860?), a theologian and a professor at Oxford University, was one of the contributors to Essays and Reviews. The passage quoted from Hick's work originated in Baden Powell's* The Order of Nature.

Christians have abandoned their faith after discovering that some doctrines they thought to be historically grounded were mythical, symbolic, or did not necessitate a literal interpretation. Most Christians are appalled and bewildered when confronted with myth and often reject their entire belief system as unsound. This rejection is common among university students from a variety of religious backgrounds. Their denominations (liberal or conservative) have not exposed these young people to even the most widely accepted findings of biblical criticism. In the environment of true academic freedom, students are thus overwhelmed by the vast number of *credible* sources (both secular and religious) contradicting their astrolabe beliefs.

A second problem with "invisible" myth or the denial of myth is the continuing conflict many Christians feel between themselves and their culture. If one believes certain teachings unique to one's own religious heritage and is programmed with attitudes not of the general environment, the result can be painful and destructive. Those who are raised in religious sects, such as Jehovah's Witnesses, often feel uncomfortable in the larger social setting. They may even resent or feel hostile toward the cultural forms that surround them and be able to live and function comfortably only within their religious sect.[13] This same discomfort can afflict mainline Christians who continue to interpret myth as history, thereby clinging to antiquated assumptions about their faith which are not supported by biblical criticism or scholarship in any other field. The clash between Creationism and science personifies this needless division.

This brings us to our final and perhaps most important point. A third problem facing Christians who, for whatever reason, interpret myth as history is the failure to deal with reality. If people are unwilling or unable to grapple with life as it is, they are not likely to progress beyond the most elementary levels of religious understanding. Perhaps the following illustration about Voodooism, a religion practiced in Haiti, will be a starting point to clarify how and why the inability or unwillingness to perceive reality can be detrimental.

We begin by examining the concept of "voodoo death." In this ritual, the voodoo priest points a "powerful" charm at a subject, who, according to accounts, begins to scream, writhe on the ground and foam at the mouth. These accounts also state that unless the priest's hex is undone or the medicine man can supply a powerful countercharm, the victim usually dies.

Early reports of voodoo death were regarded by most psychologists as little more than superstitious stories. But over the past fifty years, eyewitness accounts by reliable scientists, along with psychosomatic research, showed voodoo death to be authentic.* According to these findings, it is the victim's strong faith in the power of the priest that convinces him his fate has been "taken over" by forces beyond his control. When the hex is cast, the victim's strong emotional reaction causes his body to experience an equally extreme physiological reaction. This is believed to generate shock, or blood circulation failure, which severely damages the heart and brain and causes death.[14]

What is significant is that the power attributed to the voodoo priest is believed to be the cardinal cause of all that follows to produce death. Thus, voodoo death is viewed as an outcome of the priest's power, a perception reinforced by the reactions of those upon whom he places a curse, even though he has no power at all! The victim succumbs not to any real power of the priest, but to his own misconceptions. In short, it is the victim's failure to recognize superstitious cause-and-effect assumptions that has killed him. As for the bystanders, they become erroneously convinced that the priest truly possesses such power—since they believe the result of his power is self-evident—thereby promoting this illusion as reality and making themselves psychologically (and therefore physically) susceptible to his hex. Such misunderstandings of cause and effect often lead people to the wrong conclusions, especially when they lack sufficient knowledge. In keeping with this train of thought, let us consider the sudden healing of the sick or disabled, often attributed to divine intervention or supernatural forces. What follows *is not* offered as a dogmatic explanation for what happens, but only as a *plausible* alternative to traditional assumptions.

In the NT we see that the healing power of Jesus was considered strong evidence of his divinity or close association with God. But it is possible Jesus' ability to heal the sick and disabled did not derive from divine power but from the mental and physical capabilities of the human body. Until recently these capabilities were virtually unknown. Thus it was natural for Christians over the centuries to regard Jesus' healing power as indication of his divinity.

---

* *We should note that voodoo death is not representative of Voodoo religion as practiced today.*

Such healings have been linked more recently to physiological and/or psychological forces invoked by the patient, the healer, or both. This hypothesis is scientifically probable. Controlled research in medicine and psychology continues to expose the previously unknown healing powers and resources of body and mind. Just as the mind can generate a wide range of psychosomatic illnesses as well as conditions ranging from false pregnancies to self-imposed death, so it can cure illnesses caused by psychological and physiological factors. Obviously limitations do exist. But as science understands and substantiates these processes, some of our assumptions about the "cause" and "effects" of healing and God's direct intervention therein will require modification. Over time, such reevaluations have helped us replace the gods of our ignorance. The continued gathering of knowledge has helped us to push the rain and fertility gods out of our belief systems.

Since the majority of Christians interpret NT healing stories with the mind-set that God's sudden miraculous intrusion is the only viable explanation, they are reluctant to accept or explore alternative hypotheses* (as in the cures of psychosomatic illness). They will point to the healing results as proof of God's power, even as less informed Haitians point to the results of the hex used in the voodoo death ritual as proof of the priest's power. Such knee-jerk assumptions leave little room for honest inquiry.

While this explains how inflexible interpretations obscure the truth, it need not detract from belief in the God-healer hypothesis. Originally, the purpose of the myth/story was to explain the unexplainable by declaring that God's power was the instrument of healing. Yet this can be seen as true regardless of the way healing occurs. The human capability to heal self or others can

---

* *The doctrine of God's omnipotent (unlimited) power is debated by theologians in terms of whether this power can be exercised at will or whether use of this power is self-restricted by God's design so as not to interfere with, as one example, people's free choice. Whereas God has the power to stop war, He chooses not to exercise this power so as not to violate our freedom of choice.*

Another viewpoint, known as process theology, suggests that God may not even possess absolute power and, therefore, does not have ultimate control. Process theology is reflected in the publication When Bad Things Happen to Good People, *by Rabbi Kushner.*

be seen as a God-given characteristic of humans, and is thereby no less a manifestation of deity since it resides in God's creation.

But if we insist on taking the myth literally (divine intervention as opposed to God-given aptitude) we obscure the truth as known today: Healing is a biological possibility for the body and mind themselves. Awareness of this possibility enables us to be in harmony with evolving knowledge and gain better perspective of our world, our human potential, and the manner in which God operates. Although this new consideration might be partially flawed, it would nevertheless drive us closer to reality and, perhaps, increase our faith and integrity.

Regardless of how we view miracles, what was traditionally termed "divine intervention" is much more the exception than the rule, particularly if one considers probable alternative causes and effects. We should come to realize that in many instances, causes and effects are misunderstood since results often issue from hidden causes. No one should rely on traditional assumptions. As in the case of unexplainable healing, for example, no one should presume that it necessarily originates from some external, supernatural force.

One can agree that faith often produces positive results even when cause-and-effect factors are misunderstood. For instance, belief in the idea that God heals through direct intervention—even when this is not the case—may provide a mental climate of faith that activates a person's self-healing mechanism. As one can die from belief in the power of a hex, so, conceivably, one can be cured through belief in God's power to heal. There is no doubt that positive results can accrue from belief in NT myths, even when, as has been the case, they are viewed as historical. Certainly the doctrines of Christianity, such as the divinity of Jesus, resurrection, salvation, and redemption, have provided security and comfort for people over the centuries, even though their mythical aspect was not recognized. By declaring the positive messages that these myth-doctrines render, and through the rite of conversion, Christianity has long been a powerful motivation for people to turn toward a more positive direction.

But the fact that this continues to occur does not necessarily mean it is the best approach to our religion, principally if that approach encourages the adoption of certain assumptions that in the final analysis are misleading or patently untrue. We have long since dismissed the presuppositions of seventeenth-century knowledge, Christianity being the exception. If in Christianity we find an inner peace based on a distorted premise—such as biblical inerrancy and/or failing to distinguish between myth and history—then our feelings of peace will prove to be temporary. Our edifice of faith may appear strong, but it will remain susceptible to ruin if the foundation is laid in the shifting mire of misinterpreted cause and effect.

To illustrate this point, what if a miracle turns out not to be a miracle? What then? If we thank God for healing someone who two weeks later dies, we are trapped with an ugly dilemma. Either we are misplaced in our faith or God has changed his mind. Either of these alternatives is unacceptable and leads to embarrassment. Take, for example, the publicized case of the unfortunate major league pitcher who suffered cancer and other severe complications in his pitching arm. A born-again Christian, he was certain that God would heal him and, before long, the cancer disappeared and he was healed! He published a book about how God healed him through faith, and how God wanted him to play baseball. Not long afterward, his arm had to be amputated and his career was of course over. What does this poor soul have to say now? That his faith wasn't great enough? That God told him he was cured, but then changed his mind? That the book he wrote was all for naught? Is his faith crushed for all time or was it all just a simple misunderstanding?

Of course, even when cause-and-effect factors are misunderstood, if the outcome is positive, God receives the credit (evidence the remarks of most survivors of catastrophes). If, however, the end result is negative, consider the horrendous emotional and theological gymnastics that Christians undergo when they attempt to reconcile their faith with the unresolved intrusions of disease, violence, death, and other uncontrollable events.

Many Christians do a face-saving (and emotion-saving) retreat by falling back on Bible verses such as Romans 8:28: We know that, "All things work together for good for those who love God . . ." That may be, but this verse is conveniently used as a backup system to excuse whatever goes wrong in their picture of what God is doing (or what they think God should be doing). This "escape clause" diverts them from ever coming to grips with misunderstood cause-and-effect factors. In short, it provides Christians with a one-dimensional theology that never questions what appears to be either the random forces of nature or the acts of a fickle God.

Further Reflection

When the myth issue came to light, the immediate response was one of denial and, for reasons we have outlined, very little has changed. Christians today are almost universally adamant in their rejection of this element and most do not even recognize its presence. We cannot place the blame for this educational oversight entirely on the Church, but it should bear the lion's share. It appears that for more than 300 years the Church, at least at the local level, has avoided or downplayed the controversial findings of biblical criticism. Bridging the knowledge gap between the Church's educational institutions and the lay person should become one of the Church's primary goals.

The result of this knowledge disparity is that Christians are caught in a time lag with a religious perspective equivalent to tunnel vision, and they are becoming increasingly estranged from their own faith. Serious mental conflicts arise for many Christians who are taught to regard biblical stories (such as the Virgin Birth) as historical fact. At some point, these astrolabe thinkers must compromise or rationalize their common sense in order to sustain the mythical underpinnings of ancient beliefs (even if they don't know or concede that they are doing so). If the Christian leadership continues to present myth as bona fide history—as most ministers do in their sermons—it will worsen the conflict between current knowledge and traditional Christian teaching. Caught in the center of this conflict are those Christians who, because they are not aware of or do not accept the idea of NT myth, struggle unsuccessfully to reconcile their beliefs with reality. They will become increasingly anxious as they are encouraged to live within smothering modes of thought no longer in accord with what is known. Ignorance and confusion will continue, reinforced by strange theological notions, perversities of thought, sheer nonsense, and pre-scientific concepts that are no longer reasonable or defensible.

Many Christians have already identified some elements of NT writings (epilepsy caused by demons, for example) which are conspicuously inaccurate against today's knowledge. Scholars, of course, have moved far beyond this transparent stepping stone. They now have applied well-grounded investigative litmus tests which have brought to light the mythical aspects of Bible stories that have been used as a basis for Christian doctrine.

The central myth of Christianity centers around the deity of Jesus, which we will explore in the upcoming chapter. Although

I consider the following information to be the most probable, the conclusions herein should not be viewed as a dogmatic claim for truth.

For the sake of Christianity's own survival,
the Church hierarchy must begin to explore
with their people the value and importance
of the myth-message, rather than
constructing make-believe shrines
to historical improbabilities.

Chapter VI
Christology

The question of the "divine-human" nature of Jesus forms the very nucleus of Christian faith. While scholarship has not yet put together all the pieces to reconstruct the development of Christological belief, there is sufficient evidence to indicate that in the early years of Christianity Jesus was progressively reinterpreted in new patterns of thought until he was gradually elevated to the level of divinity. *But at the outset Jesus was not considered a supernatural being.* There was a chain of events that bore him to this height.

The Messiah

Prior to Christianity, the Jews embraced two Messianic concepts and expectations. The first was the expectation of the coming of an ideal mortal ruler, a descendant of David,* who would liberate and defend the Jews against any opposition. This concept, which originated in the pre-exilic time (before 538 B.C.), gained acceptance among the Jews during their hardship and suffering after military defeats by Assyria and Babylon.

The second Messianic concept was of the Kingdom of God. The Jews believed the day was coming when God would banish evil and usher in a new age of righteousness.[1] This concept held that God would intervene on their behalf or assign an angelic being from heaven as the agent of their redemption.[2]

The first of these two Messianic beliefs was the more widely accepted. In fact, according to Alan Richardson,† the word "Messiah"

David, who in circa 1000 B.C. killed the Philistine giant Goliath, became second king of Israel, whose prosperous reign lasted forty years. David became the prototype of the Messiah through whom God would bless (rescue) Israel.

† Alan Richardson (1905-1975) was a theologian and prolific writer. He was Professor of Christian Theology, Nottingham University.

was used only in reference to the human "son of David" whom God would rise up to be king of a restored Davidic Kingdom.[3] Nevertheless, during the last two centuries before Christ there emerged a whole body of Jewish literature called the *Apocrypha,** which emphasized the second Messianic belief, the coming of a supernatural being who would lead the Jews to victory against their enemies. Some scholars believe this increasing acceptance of a divine Messiah was the result of repeated defeats by foreign powers and the Jews' subjection to persecution by Rome.[4] In other words, desperate Jews called for desperate measures. They believed that their only chance for escaping their hopeless situation was through some direct miraculous intervention by God.

Greek Influence

The NT was conceived in a Hellenistic environment. Hellenism was an extension of the culture, philosophies, and lifestyles of ancient Greece, principally in Athens during the fifth century B.C. and in related cities during the age of Pericles (Athenian general and statesman, 495-429 B.C.). When Jesus was born, the stamp of Greek civilization was everywhere, due to the wide military conquests of Alexander the Great. Although he lived to be only 33, Alexander established the greatest empire that civilization had yet known, and he prepared the way for the penetration of Hellenistic culture into most parts of the known world. Even after Alexander's death in 323 B.C. and the subsequent demise of Greece as a political and military power, Hellenism's influence expanded.

In fact, the culture of Rome largely derived from Hellenism.[5] Every person touched by this cultural influence was a Hellenist, regardless of race or social position.[6]

The effects of Hellenism on Judaism, and subsequently on Christological development, are most revealing. These effects were mild among some Jewish peoples and very pronounced among others. The variance is easily explained. The Jews at this time were

---

* *The* Apocrypha *is a class of Jewish and Christian visionary literature, written between 200* B.C. *and* A.D. *200, describing the ultimate victory of God over evil.*

geographically separated into two groups: the 1.5 million who lived in Palestine and the 5-6 million who lived in Greek or Roman territories outside of Palestine. In Palestine (where Jesus was born) Hellenistic influence did not significantly affect the essence of Jewish beliefs. These cohesive Palestinian Jews were aided by both a homeland advantage and the Aramaic language, which served as a buffer against the invasion of Hellenistic philosophy. But the Jews in the lands outside of Palestine did not enjoy geographic unity, although they still possessed ethnic and religious unity. This unity, however, was undermined by Hellenism, which consisted of numerous conflicting faiths and philosophies. The temples of Zeus, Apollo, Athena, and of all the great national divinities were frequented by the multitudes.[7] Existing side by side were the Greek cults of Demeter and Dionysius, the Phrygian cult of Cybele, the Phoenician cults of the Syrian Goddess and of Adonis, the Egyptian cults of Isis and Serapis, and still others, both Hellenistic and Oriental.[8] Thus, this much larger group of Jews (non-Palestinian Jews) shared the same culture and language as Hellenism, and eventually came to accept some of its beliefs—if not intentionally, at least by osmosis.[9] By virtue of this *partial* blending we will refer to these Jews as Hellenistic Jews, not to be confused with their Palestinian counterparts.

In Hellenistic religions, the back and forth movement between heaven and earth of gods in human form appeared in other literature written during this time. Visitation of the gods in mortal form can be found in the ancient myths retold by Ovid* around A.D. 8 in his poetic collection, *Metamorphoses*. How seriously these mythical concepts were accepted by the people of this time is debatable, but it does appear that such myth was regarded as natural. This is indicated by the way Paul and Barnabas, while traveling in Asia Minor (Acts 14:11-12) are mistaken for the Greek gods Hermes and Zeus.[10]

This mythical influence encouraged large numbers of Jews to shift from their original view of the Messiah as an earthly descendant of David to the belief that the Messiah would be a divine being. As might be expected, this belief was mainly championed by Hellenistic Judaism since the *Apocrypha* (which emphasized this

---

* Ovid (Publius Ovidius Naso) (43 B.C.-A.D. 18) was a talented Latin poet who enjoyed early and widespread fame. In the mythical category, Metamorphoses is considered a masterpiece and perhaps his greatest work.

concept) was written not by Palestinian Jews but by Hellenistic Jews;[11] they were undoubtedly more accepting of the prevailing mythical beliefs since such concepts were normal and culturally symptomatic.

Whatever the case, this influence gave rise to the fusion and confusion of Messianic concepts. Some expected the Messiah to be a mortal man from Davidic ancestry, while others believed a divine being would descend from heaven. From this we see the Jews did not have a clearly defined concept of the Messiah, but a conglomeration of perspectives as to the form, role, and essence of the coming savior. But it must be remembered that the concept of the Messiah as a divine being was made popular by the Hellenistic Jews who outnumbered the Palestinian Jews almost six to one, and it is *their* version of a supernatural Messiah that became dominant.

Jewish Christianity

While the words "Jewish Christianity" may seem strange, we must keep in mind that the first "Christians" were Jewish, and at the beginning did not consider themselves converts to a new faith. [Actually, the term "Christian" is not applied to the followers of Jesus until Paul and Barnabas preach in Antioch (Acts 11:26)].

After the death and resurrection accounts of Jesus, how did these followers perceive him? If they regarded him as the Messiah, did they believe him to be mortal or a divine being? To answer these questions, we must remember that Christianity had its beginning among the Jews in Palestine and not among the Hellenistic Jews. It stands to reason that the Palestinian Jews, who were less influenced by Hellenism, would favor the traditional Jewish concept of the Messiah as a mortal ruler, a "son of David," instead of a divine being.[12] In this respect, Harry Emerson Fosdick and others have pointed out that the first Christian Jews believed Jesus was chosen by God for a supreme mission, but they did not characterize him as divine.[13]

We should not generalize from this that all Palestinian Christian Jews shared this view. Some were undoubtedly hoping for some miraculous act from God to deliver them from Roman domination. Others were probably influenced by the popular concept (which had already circulated for two centuries among Hellenistic Jews) that the Messiah would be a divine being from heaven. But even if some of these early Christian Jews considered Jesus to be more than human—a supernatural being—they would not have equated him *with* God, but *from* God. It is critical to understand that the Jews were/are strictly monotheistic. Whereas they might view Jesus as a God-given supernatural entity, it would be highly improbable that they would view him in terms of sharing godhead as later defined in the doctrine of the Trinity. This is one reason why many scholars believe that, at the inception of Christianity in Palestine, Christian Jews could not have fostered the viewpoint that Jesus was God incarnate.[14] Such an idea would have been considered blasphemy. Why and how, then, was Jesus elevated to the status of deity as the Christian movement evolved, especially as reflected in NT writing? What bore him to the heights of Godhead?

Gentile Christianity

From its inception, the Christian Palestinian church in Jerusalem numbered among its members a few Greek-speaking Jews who are mentioned in Acts 6. Those Jews who could speak Greek eventually became missionaries for Christianity in territories outside of Palestine, where they carried the teachings of Jesus to other Greek-speaking Jews and to Greek societies. While their efforts to convert Jews outside of Palestine were unfruitful, many Gentiles (non-Jews) responded enthusiastically to these teachings and the Christian movement rapidly gained momentum. This runaway trend can be seen in Barnabas' experience at Antioch (Acts 11:20-24) and his mission with Paul at Antioch of Pisidia (Acts 13:44-49) where great numbers of Gentiles were converted.

Thus, there developed alongside Jewish Christianity what we shall call "Gentile Christianity"—destined to outgrow its Jewish counterpart. In time, Gentile Christianity would no longer depend on the Palestinian church that spawned it and, in its new environment, would reach new understandings of itself and Jesus through the interpretation of the Hellenistic culture.[15]

New Interpretations

When Christianity spread from the Palestinian Jews to the Gentiles, the words *Messiah* and *Christ* lost their meaning. (The Hebrew word *Messiah* translated into Greek was *Christ;* the terms are synonymous.) The Gentiles could neither comprehend nor identify with the original Jewish notion of Messiahship. The title

Christ, representing a statement of faith in the saving mission of Jesus to restore the Kingdom of Israel, was of little interest to the Gentiles. They didn't care about the national cause of Judaism. In time, the statement of hope within the title Christ was lost. It became, instead, a proper name. *Jesus the Christ* became *Jesus Christ.*[16]

Since the word *Christ* did not have the meaning for Gentiles that it did for Jews, Paul sought a word that would be equally meaningful to the Gentiles among whom he was working. He knew the term *Lord* (as a reference to God) was familiar to both the Jewish and pagan worlds. Although the term *Lord* was applied to Jesus by some members of the early Christian community, the extent of its use is questionable as it would have been unacceptable to Jewish Christians trained in the strict monotheism of Judaism.[17] On the other hand, the word *Lord* (*Kurios* in Greek) was extensively used by the Gentiles, and certainly by devotees of the mystery religions. In the worship of Osiris and Dionysius, *Kurios* was the common designation for the savior-god.[18] It is not surprising, therefore, that when Paul used *Kurios (Lord)* in reference to Jesus, the Gentiles looked upon Jesus as a divine or supernatural being. In Gentile territory, it was a term that enjoyed a common ground of understanding.

Whether Paul viewed Jesus as deity is not clear. Certainly Paul boldly applied OT passages to Jesus in which the word *Lord* meant *God.* A prime example is Romans 10:9-13, where Paul quoted the promise of the prophet Joel that ". . . everyone that calls upon the name of the Lord [God] shall be saved." Here Paul used the word *Lord* in reference to Jesus.[19] In contrast, Paul consistently subordinated the Lord Jesus Christ to God the Father. In 1 Corinthians 11:3, he characterizes the authority of Christ as secondary to that of God. Some scholars believe there is no way to determine Paul's precise meaning when he called Jesus *Lord.*[20]

Whatever the case, the point remains that most Gentiles of this time interpreted *Lord* in accordance with the prevailing Hellenistic view. If Jesus was Lord, then Jesus was *divine.* Note that the Gentiles comprised the fastest growing and most populous sector of Christianity; their views had great impact on Christological development.

Another significant factor in the augmentation of Christology might have been early Christianity's common use of the title "Son of God," which in the OT referred to any specific close or faithful servant of God. This title (Son of God) was bound to be misunderstood by Gentile converts to the point of accepting it as a literal statement regarding Jesus' nature.[21] While some scholars, such as Alan Richardson, disagree that this led to the portrayal of Jesus as divine being,[22] strong evidence exists to the contrary. To the Jews, "Son of God" referred to one who demonstrated obedience and devotion to God, but the Hellenists looked upon the title as a condition of divine nature. John Charlot* recognizes a great turning point here in Christian theology as the interpretations given to such titles and expressions by Gentile Christians became radically different from those intended by early Jewish Christians.[23]

There is little doubt that the Christian movement was significantly influenced by Gentile Christians with their Hellenistic god/man mythology (the mobility of gods in human form between heaven and earth). This is clearly reflected in NT writings which depict Jesus as a Redeemer who, via a miraculous birth, descends to earth from a higher sphere, fulfills his assigned mission and then ascends to be with God (Phil. 2:6-11; Col. 1:15-20; 1 Pet. 3:18-19, 22; 1 Tim. 3:16; Eph. 2:14-16; Heb. 1:3). The late Norman Perrin† believed that "The understanding of Jesus as a descending-ascending redeemer is one of Gentile Christianity's most significant contributions to Christological development."[24]

Projecting deity upon Jesus must have been an easy step for most Gentiles since belief in god/man mythology saturated Hellenistic culture, even outside of their religious formats. Take for example the non-religious myths attesting to the miraculous births of Plato,‡ Heraclides of Pontus,§ and Hermippus.+ Also, Greek philosophers Pythagoras (582-507 B.C.) and Empedocles (495-435 B.C.) were the subjects of myths of incarnation and

---

*John Charlot (1941-), graduating Magna Cum Laude, received his Th.D from the University of Munich (Germany) in 1968. He taught NT theology at St. John's University in Collegeville, Minn.

† Norman Perrin (1920-1976) was Associate Professor of New Testament, 1964-1976, University of Chicago Divinity School.

‡ Plato (427-347 B.C.) was one of the greatest philosophers of Western culture.

§ Heraclides of Pontus (388-315 B.C.) was a Greek astronomer and philosopher. He was a student of Plato and perhaps Aristotle.

+ Hermippus (450-400 B.C.) was an Athenian writer of the old comedy, which flourished during the Peloponnesian War.

deification. The prevalence of such myths is further confirmed by the most famous work of Greek biographer and essayist Plutarch (A.D. 46-120?), *Parallel Lives of Illustrious Greeks and Romans,* in which divine genealogies and stories of the supernatural are assigned to the founders of cities and leading rulers such as Alexander the Great and Romulus, in Roman legend the founder and first king of Rome (traditionally set at 753 B.C.). In fact, the ancient myth of Romulus was also recorded in the work of Livy* just prior to 25 B.C. It is similar to the Gospel accounts of Jesus, including conception by a god, virgin birth, and resurrection.[25]

With the abundance of mythical stories pervading the Greco-Roman world, it is natural to ask whether the divinity of Jesus was an honorific attribute issued from the need to make him equal with contemporary superstars, a sincere belief based on superstition, or an historical reality as Christians claim. One thing is certain: The framework of New Testament storytelling was not fashioned in a vacuum, but had its contemporary counterparts.

The deification of Jesus is completed in the Gospel of John, the last Gospel to be written and one of the last NT books to be written (A.D. 100-150). In the prologue, Jesus is identified as the *Logos;* few terms were more meaningful for Hellenistic people. In Hermetic† religious literature, *Logos* denoted, among other things, a divine power enabling one to know God. Among Greek-speaking Jews, *Logos* referred to the creative power of the word of God, through which God created the universe. In Hellenistic philosophy and religion as well as in the OT, Logos was a divine instrument whereby the knowledge of God is revealed. While many efforts have been made to explain *Logos* as used in the Gospel of John, it is probably historically correct to recognize a multiple influence.[26] The growing need to share the meaning of Jesus with the Hellenistic culture reached its pinnacle with the interpretation of Jesus as the Logos, the eternal Word of God: ". . . and the Word was with God, and the Word was God" (John 1:1.). It appears that the Gospel writer attempted to interpret the meaning of Jesus in terms that would have the greatest influence in the Greek world.[27]

---

* *Titus Livius (59 B.C.-A.D. 17) was a Roman historian.*

† *Hermetic derives from Hermes Trismegistus, the Greek name for the Egyptian god Thoth, reputed founder of alchemy and other occult sciences.*

Further Reflection

In the original Messianic portrayal of Jesus, he was generally esteemed as uniquely chosen, anointed by God to fulfill a supreme mission. But as the ranks of the Hellenistic Gentile converts grew, the terms applied to Jesus, such as "Lord" and "Son of God," were bound to be interpreted by Hellenists in terms of their mythical beliefs; namely, viewing Jesus as divine. This affected some NT authors who did not produce their works until the Christian movement was well under the influence of Gentile Hellenism. Before the NT writers finished depicting Jesus, he was elevated to the supernatural realm, a being sent to earth to achieve God's will. Using all the majestic terms of the ancient world, he was the "Messiah," "Lord," "Son of God," and "Logos."[28] The final result: Jesus was deified. Whether this gave rise to Christian beliefs far beyond those originally intended—and without basis in the facts of the life and ministry of Jesus—has long been debated. Let us review (and expand upon) the evidence for this hypothesis.

It is obvious that Christianity spread rapidly from the Aramaic-speaking Jews of Palestine to the Greek-speaking Hellenists. Within twenty years after Jesus' death, Christianity moved from Aramaic to Greek, and from Palestinian Jews to Hellenist Jews and Gentiles. Even then the majority of the NT had not yet been written. We must remember that with the exception of seven Pauline letters, the books are anonymous and pseudonymous (bearing a false name) and some were not written until fifty to seventy years after Jesus died. Certainly it cannot be assumed that the NT was chiefly authored by Palestinian Jews, especially when we realize that most of the NT was not written until after Christianity swept the Gentile world.[29]

Even if the NT had been authored primarily by Palestinian Jews, it is possible that these Jews themselves were influenced by Hellenism in spite of their cohesive language and geographical advantage. Martin Hengel, a member of the Faculty of Protestant Theology of the University of Tübingen and one of the world's most respected scholars on this issue, argues against traditional differentiation between Judaism on the one hand and Hellenism on the other.[30]

For the sake of argument, however, let us assume that Hellenistic influence on Palestinian Jews was inconsequential. They would still not be totally myth-free. The fact is, Jewish belief in divine visitors was not caused solely by Hellenism. One prominent work, *The Myth of God Incarnate*, shows that the mythical beliefs of the ancient world were not exclusive to pagan cultures, but also permeated Jewish traditions dating to the very beginnings of Judaism. According to Frances Young, a lecturer in NT studies at Birmingham University, England, "The descent of heavenly beings to intervene in earthly affairs, often to render assistance, is clearly a feature of both pagan and Jewish legend, and certainly pre-dates the New Testament . . ."[31] These supernatural beings were described descending to earth disguised as men. Popular Hellenistic myths included Zeus and Hermes (Greek gods) descending to visit unsuspecting Philemon and Baucis (husband and wife). In comparison, the Jews embraced accounts of Abraham entertaining divine visitors (Gen. 18). Similarly, two angels disguised as men approach Lot while he sat at the gateway to Sodom (Gen. 19). Another example is found in Judges 13:16, where Manoah (father of Sampson) spoke unknowingly with an angel incognito. Such OT myth is reaffirmed in the NT: "Do not neglect to show hospitality to strangers, for by doing that some have entertained angels without knowing it," declares the author of Hebrews (13:2). Also, the naturalness of this mythology is indicated by the way Paul and Barnabas are mistaken for the Greek gods Hermes and Zeus (Acts 14:11-12). The bottom line: We cannot assume a mythological black-and-white contrast between orthodox Jews and the pagan world.

Obviously, both pagan and Jewish mythology were common expressions prior to and during the time of Jesus. To what extent the mythical concept of the demigod (one who is partly divine and partly human) affected Christological development is open for discussion.

One final note. The Church wrestled for centuries with its effort to clarify its official position on the nature of Jesus. Was he divine? Was he human? Was he both human and divine? Was he God, man, or something in-between? In short, how does one define the Trinity? Argumentative and diverse opinions continued until A.D. 451 when, at the Council of Chalcedon, the Church finally came to agreement on the present Trinitarian formula. This Trinitarian concept was originally formulated at the Council of Nicea (Nicene Creed, A.D. 323).

The grandest of all laws is the law of progressive development.

—Christian Nestell Bovee (1820-1904)
American author and editor

Chapter VII
Progressive Revelation

Until we learn to view the Bible as something other than divine revelation—God's ultimate authority—we will remain in the infantile stages of religious understanding. Not all Christians support the doctrine of inerrancy, but most would balk at the idea of challenging what is considered to bear God's imprint. In light of biblical criticism (and other disciplines) both positions prove too narrow. The findings of biblical criticism showcase the Bible as an unfolding process of spiritual understanding—not in terms of perfection, but in terms of imperfection. It is apparent that traditional viewpoints about the Bible no longer represent the most plausible reality; therefore, a more authentic alternative needs to be considered.

One can note that *biblical revelation* is used synonymously with *divine* (or *direct*) *revelation*. These terms are familiar to most of us and are used interchangeably. With *divinely* revealed religions, the underlying assumption is that God intervenes *directly* into the natural order: God directly affects nature and impacts human affairs. This impact is emphatic and, in most cases, is considered "miraculous." This type of religion contains a central nucleus of doctrine that is used to separate "true" from "false" and has taken form in a sacred canon (such as the Bible or Koran). In this mold, *divine revelation* becomes unalterable, absolute, and indisputable!

In contrast are the *non-divinely revealed* religions, a term which needs elaboration. It is not meant to imply that, in all cases, such a religion is not God-influenced; the term is *not* meant to be construed as meaning religion without God. Rather, with non-divinely revealed religions the underlying assumption, at least from a Western perspective, is that God works *through* the natural order. God's influence is not explicit but subtle. God pulls, pushes, or nudges people through the human faculties of reason, intuition, conscience, and courage. The written documents of non-divinely revealed religions, although highly regarded, are not usually considered sacrosanct or exclusive. The revelation that is the basis of non-divinely religion can be termed *progressive revelation.*

Although progressive revelation is indicative of non-divinely revealed religions, we must acknowledge that this assertion is a generalization; it is not intended as a dogmatic portrayal of any specific religion. In other words, when contemplating divine revelation as opposed to progressive revelation, we should not view these differing concepts as a black-and-white division; they are not always mutually exclusive. In some cases—in fact, in Christianity—it is probably correct to assume an intermix. Nevertheless, owing to its positive characteristics, it is imperative to emphasize progressive revelation rather than divine revelation.

The Case For Progressive Revelation

Unlike divine revelation, which primarily relies on some spectacular manifestation, progressive revelation pursues the "natural course" of discovery characteristic of other disciplines. It is based on the belief that religious knowledge and spiritual understanding emerge through the same channels as *all* knowledge—through a process of human insight, trial and error, and continued refinement. The word *progressive,* in this usage, denotes forward movement or progress. Progressive revelation is even better described by the word *evolving,* defined as unfolding, opening out, or, in this application, reaching a highly developed state by gradual growth and change; in short, open-ended. Again, this does not exclude God from the process. I offer the following reasons for the belief that biblical revelation is progressive and as such is the most plausible explanation for the way God generally touches the human spirit.

The first reason is based on simple deduction. *Every field of knowledge has developed slowly.* Be it physics, astronomy, psychology, anthropology, religion, or any other field, there is a pattern of growth evolving from a simple beginning to ever more complex and challenging discoveries. The journey from Wilbur and Orville Wright's first flight to our present space program was not accomplished in one giant step. No school of thought emerges fully developed and mature. On the contrary, each one begins in raw, embryonic form and proceeds through the painstaking stages of trial and error.

We can say, therefore, that both science and religion have been developing (progressing) for thousands of years, even though at times their respective developments have been interrupted. Their concepts were tried, accepted or rejected, and continually refined.

They were never pure, whole, or infallible at any point in the journey. The process of refinement is continuous. Over the centuries, the result of both quests has been an increase in knowledge, yielding a greater understanding of ourselves, the nature of the universe, and the more meaningful aspects of life.

It's obvious that science moved from outmoded theories to advanced principles, expanding continually, sometimes slowly and sometimes quite rapidly. While religion may seem innately different and not subject to this same trial and error procedure, history tells us quite the opposite. *The origin and progression of religious thinking has been similar to that of every other field of study.*

This process of maturation is clearly reflected in biblical writing. As Fosdick observes:

> Beginning with a tribal war god, leading his devotees to bloody triumph over their foes, it ends with people discovering that "God is love; and he that abideth in love abideth in God, and God abideth in him" (1 John 4:16);

> Beginning with a territorial deity who loves his clanspeople and hates all others, it ends with a great multitude of "every tribe and tongue and people and nation" (Rev. 5:9), worshipping one universal being;

> Beginning with a god who walks in a garden in the cool of the day and shows his back to Moses as a special favor, it ends with the God whom "no one has seen" (John 1:18) and in whom "we live, and move, and have our being" (Acts 17:28);

> Beginning with a god who commands the slaughter of infants and sucklings without mercy, it ends with the God whose will is that not "one of these little ones should perish" (Matt. 18:14).[1]

We see religion's progressive movement from polytheism to monotheism, from belief in a nationalistic God to faith in a universal God, from belief in an anthropomorphic deity to an omnipresent spirit, and from the portrayal of a God of wrath to that of a loving, compassionate God.

The second reason for accepting progressive revelation comes from observing the personality traits that arise in most people who accept the alternative: divine revelation. There is no doubt that the personal belief in the supremacy of Scripture creates within the majority of believers what might be called an "attitude of presumption." This attitude, which is not exclusive to evangelicals, is characterized by one or more of the following: (1) feeling that those who have different beliefs are "wrong" and out of step with God; (2) needing to convince others to accept the Bible and Jesus as ultimate truth or suffer God's condemnation; (3) feeling superior and self-righteous; (4) feeling intolerant, sparking critical, negative views about oneself and others; (5) a sense of impending certainty about the Second Coming, Armageddon, and so forth; and (6) hostility toward the findings of biblical criticism and other knowledge that conflicts with or challenges traditional beliefs.

This attitude of presumption was responsible for the murder and oppression that characterized centuries of Christian thought and, more recently, for molding and perpetuating the astrolabe mind. Although Christians who are obsessed with the supremacy of biblical writing no longer express their devotion through physical persecution of others (with some exceptions), mental and emotional persecution still prevail against those who do not accept their reasoning. This aura of presumption slowly divides people, even parents and their children, husbands and wives, brothers and sisters and long-time friends. Few people have escaped its destructive effects. To maintain peace and avoid hurting loved ones, those Christians and non-Christians who do not share this attitude must either pretend to accept it, ignore it, remain uncomfortably silent, or avoid contact with those who take this obstinate posture. It is ironic that Christians, whose guiding principles spur them to be amiable, loving, and selfless, can simultaneously evoke oppressive attitudes of exclusivity, arrogance, and intolerance.

The third reason for preferring progressive revelation comes from analyzing divinely revealed religions alongside non-divinely revealed religions. Examples of divinely revealed religions are: Judaism, in which God revealed the Ten Commandments to Moses; Christianity, in which Christ, the Son of God, revealed the Word of the Father; and Islam, in which the angel Gabriel revealed Allah's will to the prophet Mohammed. In contrast are the non-divinely revealed religions: Buddhism (in which Buddha is revered not as a god, but as an enlightened leader); Jainism; and Taoism, all of which regard the individual as evolving within the natural order of human knowledge and insight.

A significant and amazing difference becomes apparent when

the histories of divinely revealed religions are compared to the non-divinely revealed religions. Acts of intolerance, bloodshed, conquest, death, and destruction occurred exclusively among those religions claiming to have been *directly inspired by a Supreme Being*. At the beginning of the Jewish nation, its bloody conquest of Canaan was regarded as the holy will of God and was the first of many wars sanctioned by Jewish prophets who claimed to speak in God's name. Christianity was no exception, with its military expeditions (the Crusades) to recover the Holy Land from the Moslems and its other numerous atrocities already examined. The Islamic faith also has a history of extensive violence, including the mass slaughter of groups who refused to accept Islamic beliefs after being conquered by the armies of Islam.

In the 1980s, the eight-year border conflict between Iraq and Iran was one of the world's bloodiest religious wars. This was far from a secular war—it was a war of faith. The Iranian war cry was "God is great!" Iran's Shiite Moslems cherish the idea of dying in battle since martyrdom guarantees entrance to heaven. Similarly, Lebanon's tough Druse militiamen, inspired by religious convictions, are fearless in the face of death, and India's Sikh terrorists equate religious fervor with warlike spirit. Religious conflicts continue to erupt in the 1990s, as is the case in Bosnia-Hercegovina, along with the clash between the Hindus and Moslems of India.

While these religions claiming to be directly led by God have been (and continue to be) serious offenders of human rights, the non-divinely revealed religions have had few such incidents throughout their histories. Their development has been peaceful and positive.

Clearly, the followers of those religions claiming to possess divine truth maintain their faith to be the true one! They vigorously declare to have the better way or the *only* way! This attitude leads almost inevitably to arrogance and abuse (be it physical or psychological) and thwarts the positive aspects of religious influence and development. I do not mean to imply that I reject Christianity in favor of non-divinely revealed religions; I simply point out this inherently destructive feature of our faith which needs to be replaced with attitudes more in tune with progressive revelation.

The fourth reason for accepting progressive revelation as the most credible interpretation of God's imprint derives from faith in the God-given human ability to pursue and unveil reality. One is born to think and to trust one's own judgment, provided that one's judgment is not based on frivolous thinking or formed in the absence of collective knowledge. But the argument for progressive revelation is not based on vacuous reasoning, but on the well-grounded findings of critical studies. These findings provide virtually no evidence that the Bible is (or ever was) a direct, unblemished message from God. On the contrary, they strongly confirm that the biblical message is fluid, not static, reflecting the same process as all other fields of knowledge: God allows progressive discovery over time through the evolution of human experience.

It serves no constructive purpose to reject the findings of qualified scholars because they contradict or undermine long-held and obviously faulty assumptions about the Bible and the origins and idiosyncrasies of early Christianity. The willingness to consider and benefit from these scholarly findings clearly leads us to understand the Bible realistically. Those who reject these findings to protect what they believe to be the divine truth may be denying themselves access to the greater learning and understanding it offers. By clinging to a fail-safe concept of divine revelation, they emasculate their powers of judgment.

This coincides with the thinking of past great teachers and spiritual leaders who urged their followers to place personal judgment, discovery, and learning above the sacred status quo. Buddha, for example, encouraged independence of thought among his followers, saying:

> Believe nothing because a so-called wise man said it. Believe nothing because a belief is generally held. Believe nothing because it is written in ancient books. Believe nothing because it is said to be of divine origin. Believe nothing because someone else believes it. Believe only what you yourself judge to be true.[2]

Inherent in Buddha's last sentence is an explicit trust in one's own judgment. Again, this assumes that one's judgment has not been fashioned in a vacuum or from one school of thought, but has been enriched by *various* sources of knowledge.

Similarly, Jesus did not view his religious heritage as incontestable authority; he consistently challenged the authoritative teachings of his faith. Although the Gospel of Matthew portrays Jesus as saying, "Think not that I have come to abolish the law and the prophets; I have come not to abolish them but to fulfill them" (Matt. 5:17), these words cannot imply that Jesus remained within the framework of Jewish law. Quite the opposite.

The written law was based on the first five books of the OT, which included the Ten Commandments. The oral law was a series of complex regulations pertaining to religious societal behavior and was based on the written law. These oral laws are referred to in the Gospels as "the tradition of the elders."* Both the oral and written laws were considered sacred and vital, and were accorded great respect. Yet Jesus did not find them infallible. He personified humanity's changing, progressive spiritual quest.

The Written Law

As James Dunn[†] has noted, Jesus clearly valued his insights above those of the OT. In the Sermon on the Mount, he did not merely reinterpret the law of the Jews; in some cases, he advocated it be altered or abolished.[3] In Matthew 5:38, Jesus cited and revoked the OT edict that was also the oldest known law: "An eye for an eye, and a tooth for a tooth." According to William Barclay,[‡]

> That law is known as the *Lex Talionis,* and it may be described as the law of tit for tat. It appears in the earliest known code of laws, the Code of Hammurabi, who reigned in Babylon from 2285 to 2242 B.C.[4]

This law became part of the OT ethic and is repeated in Exodus 21:23-25, Leviticus 24:19-20, and Deuteronomy 19:21.

Another instance in which Jesus challenged the Jew's written law was with his sweeping denunciation of the OT dietary law. Leviticus 11 contains a long list of animals that Jewish law decreed unclean and forbidden to be consumed. These laws were stringently obeyed, even under the threat of death. Such was the case in

---

These oral laws were eventually written down long after the time of Jesus (about 200 A.D.); they became known as the Mishnah.

† James D. Dunn (1939-) received his M.A. and B.D. from the University of Glasgow and his Ph.D. from Cambridge University, 1968.

‡ William Barclay (1907-1978), Scottish biblical scholar, educator, and author of books on religion, was a professor at Glasgow University. His Dailey Study Bible *commentaries sold more than five million copies.*

Palestine when the Jews were under the rule of Syrian King Antiochus Epiphanes (175-163 B.C.). He had demanded that the Jews eat pork. The king was trying to undermine their faith, but the Jews died by the hundreds rather than violate their religious law.[5] Nevertheless, Jesus declared such dietary laws irrelevant: "Do you not see that whatever goes into a man from the outside cannot defile him . . ." Mark concludes: "Thus he [Jesus] declared all foods clean" (Mark 7:18). This declaration was simultaneously an indictment against the oral law; at the beginning of Mark 7, the Pharisees complain to Jesus that his disciples are breaking the tradition of the elders (the oral law) by eating with unwashed (unclean) hands.

The Oral Law

Jesus reacted sharply against the oral laws of his people, particularly those governing the Sabbath and ritual purity. He regarded these oral traditions as irksome and alien to a spirit motivated by love of God and neighbor, and continually rejected them.[6] In the third chapter of Mark, for instance, Jesus violates the oral law by healing a man with a withered hand on the Sabbath. The Jewish law was quite explicit. Any kind of work (healing was considered work) was strictly forbidden on the Sabbath. Medical attention could be administered only in a life-and-death situation. To his accusers Jesus declared: "Is it lawful on the Sabbath to do good or harm, to save life or to kill?" (Mark 3:4) In an earlier incident, Jesus and his disciples were charged with breaking the law of the Sabbath after they plucked ears of grain (they were hungry) on the holy day. When the Pharisees questioned their motives for breaking the Sabbath, Jesus proclaimed: "The Sabbath was made for man, not man for the Sabbath" (Mark 2:27).

The manner in which Jesus dealt with his religious heritage holds a valuable lesson for us all. He selected from Judaism those teachings he regarded as practical and meaningful, discarding the rest. This "selective attention," as Fosdick called it, is one of the most creative processes in human thinking. It can alter the nature of religious or philosophical thought by reconstituting human thinking so ". . . as to achieve without the contribution of a single brand-new element, a startling new result."[7]

The point is, Jesus never looked upon "sacred" teaching in a manner that forbade altering or rejecting such instruction should it no longer promote, or should it stand in the way of, human well-being. Yet how do Christians today react to one who similarly challenges Christian tenets? It is ironic that most people insist on a concrete, rigidly defined system of belief, when, in fact, Jesus did not. His actions indicate he regarded religious teaching as something which had to change or be changed, clearly reflecting an attitude supporting revelation as progressive (evolving) and not absolute (perfect).

Buddha directly encourages this insight for progressive change. He tells his disciples that his ". . . teaching is like a raft which they are using to cross a river: Once they have reached the other side of the river, it would be foolish to lift up the raft and carry it away on their shoulders out of gratitude for its aid in crossing. Rather, they should leave it there on the riverbank and walk away unburdened."[8]

Unlike the founders of the world's great religions, their followers seem to be spellbound by authority and tradition. They continue to impute unreasonable (sometimes blind) allegiance to their holy books, institutions, and leaders. This is not to suggest that they should ignore or reject these sources of authority, but rather that they should realize, as Jesus did, that authority is not unerring.

The last argument for favoring progressive revelation, as opposed to divine/direct revelation, is linked to Albert Einstein's theory of relativity. Perhaps no one concept (with the possible exception of Darwinism) has affected twentieth-century thought more profoundly than that of relativity. This theory, as applied to physics, emphasizes the relative rather than the absolute with regard to motion, velocity, and the interdependence of matter, time, and space.

The principle of relativity can be applied even more profoundly to social, moral, historical, and religious knowledge. In these applications, "relativism" means that our basis of judgment differs from others' according to the ways we have been conditioned to perceive events, institutions, ideologies, issues, and all of life in general. Simply stated, relativity means that what you see and what I see are different, relative to numerous factors that affect our perception. Thus, we cannot know exactly what the real world is like; we can only relate to what we see, and we each see the world uniquely. Our perceptions are shaped by every influence we experience, right from birth, including parental and environmental influences, education, friendships, injuries, and genetic factors (to name a few). The unique combination of these factors over time causes us to perceive life differently from *any* other person. That is why at times we find ourselves at odds with others on political, religious, or social issues. But even if we are in agreement, our perceptions about life as a whole can never be identical, only similar. As a result, no one ever fully knows reality (truth) since our perceptions of it are colored by these factors. No two of us think exactly alike, nor can any one of us claim "absolute" knowledge as our knowledge derives from relative thinking and perception. We can only strive to come closer to accurate, objective knowledge by continuously comparing and refining our viewpoints. Thus human knowledge, whether scientific or religious, is decidedly in a constant state of progressive change or evolution.

Many Christians will contend that "relativism" cannot and does not apply to the Scriptures since they are God-given and therefore pure, supreme, incorruptible, and timeless. But this view is totally unsupported by biblical and historical scholarship, which show the authors of the NT and the early Church leaders (not to mention everyone who came after them) were divided by relativity of thought. Robert L. Wilkens,* in his book *The Myth of Christian Beginnings*, clearly demonstrates that at no time has the Church's thinking been whole, perfect, and pure, nor has it even possessed a consensus of opinion on the nature of Jesus.[9]

Granted, relativism does not afford us the warm security many Christians enjoy by believing they possess ultimate knowledge. But neither can we turn our backs on relativism simply because it lacks this comforting quality. As H. Richard Niebuhr† said, "If theology is developing into a relativistic field of thought, it is not to emulate the natural or behavioral sciences, but to achieve greater self-knowledge."[10]

Further Reflection

Early on, the NT was considered the ultimate source of truth, based on the belief that the Third Party of the Trinitarian Godhead (the Holy Spirit) inspired, preserved, and watched over the Holy Writ since its inception. Over the past three centuries, this rigid belief was abandoned by most biblical scholars to incorporate a more natural and realistic view of biblical writing. Measured against analytical studies, the doctrine of inerrancy no longer persuaded.

---

* *Robert Louise Wilkens (1936-) was associate professor (1972-1980), Department of Theology, University of Notre Dame.*

† *Helmut Richard Niebuhr (1894-1962) was Sterling Professor of Theology and Christian Ethics at Yale University Divinity School.*

On the other hand, progressive revelation recognizes the relative and evolutionary qualities of religious knowledge. It affords us a basis for flexible and evolving belief rather than limiting us to centuries-old concepts of absolutism. In this, progressive revelation joins with science in contending that absolute knowledge is something we strive for, not something we fully possess. As the late J. Bronowski noted: "Those who claim absolute knowledge, whether scientists or religionists, open the door to tragedy since all information is imperfect."[11] The continuing accumulation of knowledge may never give us the all-perfect answers to our numerous questions, but it will help clarify our perception by eliminating ignorance; it will drive us closer to the truth by exposing what is false. But this journey of discovery and growth will stall if we assume to own the "ultimate" truth.

Imagine the fate of science had its early practitioners, about 2,000 years ago, viewed its knowledge as early Christians did their own. All then-existing scientific data could have been assembled into one volume. The claim would have been made that this data was divinely communicated and no one thereafter could question, challenge, or alter it. Nor could anyone conceive, follow, or disseminate any scientific theories other than those in the works. Any challenge to this scientific canon would result in severe punishment for heresy. Had this repressive atmosphere existed, scientific progress would have stagnated and humans surely would never have landed on the moon, nor would any scientific discipline have progressed much beyond its embryonic state.

Yet this is precisely the position in which many Christians seek to arrest religious knowledge by freezing the theological and ethical teachings of the Bible at their inception stage. They insist the Bible is God's untouchable masterpiece, but it is increasingly apparent that religious knowledge must also traverse the bumpy road of trial and error.

Christians have found it difficult to accept this line of reasoning. The idea of "sacredness," always associated with revelation, has led them to believe that biblical revelation must somehow differ from scientific or any other form of unfolding knowledge. In part, they are correct in recognizing this difference, since all forms of knowledge vary. The problem arises, however, in the *degree* of difference we Christians ascribe to this revelation—a difference that has been misconstrued and exaggerated. Believers are encouraged to elevate religious knowledge above all other knowledge. This belief is based on the further assumption that there are basically two realms of existence: the natural and the supernatural. This superficial dichotomy (between the "natural" and the "divine") dictates the manner in which most Western people view revelation. All information believed to come from the supernatural realm, or God, is automatically elevated to a level of superiority over information derived from human effort (the natural realm). Whether these two domains are exclusive of one another or operate in a separate and restricted manner is highly debatable, but most people believe they are and do.

Whatever the case, we must not lose sight of the issue—the issue is about reality. This is not a question about God's power, as though God were unable to bring about miraculous direct revelation. The question is not "What *can* God do?" but rather "What *did* God do?" From historical evidence we see what God did and the manner in which it was accomplished; namely, progressive revelation.*

Some may object that progressive revelation reduces religious knowledge to the same level as secular knowledge by eliminating all possibility of miraculous disclosure of divine truth. Really? While progressive revelation may appear less spectacular and impressive, it is no less miraculous. It is a matter of perspective. Progressive revelation does not make religious knowledge secular, but it makes secular knowledge religious; that is, all knowledge, whether religious, scientific, philosophical, or any other is a gift from God. All truth, whether revealed through physics, Buddhism, psychology, sociology, or any other discipline, is part of the same whole. All systems of learning journey through an identical process of discovery, trial and error, failure and success, truth and false-hood. Viewed in this light, both "sacred" and "secular" learning travel the same winding road to enlightenment. Declaring one form of revelation divine (superior) and the other secular (inferior) becomes meaningless. *Truth is truth; no special declaration of authority is needed to make it so.*

Certainly, if we are to escape our astrolabe mentality, our understanding of what we have heretofore considered sacred must be modified. Perhaps it will serve our purpose to identify more

---

* *We are assuming cause and effect here; namely, that what we have identified as progressive revelation has actually been initiated by God, as opposed to random historical meanderings.*

clearly some of the obstacles to maturity. Aside from the domineering influence of bibliolatry, what drives believers to cling to faulty assumptions surrounding biblical revelation? What deters people from seriously questioning, reevaluating, or modifying their belief system?

The dangers of knowledge are
not to be compared with the
dangers of ignorance.

—Richard Whately (1787-1863)
Archbishop of Dublin

Chapter VIII
Obstacles to Maturity

On January 1, 1889, an eclipse of the sun was viewed with awe by a Paiute Indian named Wovoka (1858-1932) and other members of his tribe. As darkness spread across the midday sky, the expanding eclipse ignited his vivid imagination and emotions. Since he was unaware of the real nature and causes of the eclipse, Wovoka, and later his followers, interpreted this phenomenon as a divine message—a direct sign from God (another misinterpretation of cause and effect). This "miraculous" and unexplainable happening was quickly accepted as conveying the power of divine intervention (reminiscent of the OT rainbow incident*).

In the excitement of Wovoka's wishful vision, God's message became clear: The time would soon come when all white men would disappear from the earth and all Native Americans would be reunited and dwell in harmony, free from disease, misery, and death. To receive these benefits and to appease God, the ritual of the Ghost Dance was introduced. This ceremonial dance, involving shaking and hypnotic trances, was to be performed for five successive days and repeated every six weeks. One specific promise of this new religion was that the Native Americans would be shrouded with special "bulletproof" ghost shirts to protect them from the white man's bullets. The idea spread like wildfire through most of the Western tribes.

It is difficult to estimate how many Native Americans were killed because of their misplaced faith in this "divine" message they thought was received under supernatural circumstances. We do know the Sioux of Wounded Knee, followers of the Ghost Dance religion, were wearing their bulletproof ghost shirts the day U.S. Army Col. J.W. Forsyth ordered them disarmed. Record

---

* In Genesis 9:13-14 is a primitive notion of how and why the rainbow exists, i.e., a message from God.

has it that in response the medicine man, Yellow Bird, threw a handful of dust into the air. Another Sioux pulled a gun from his blanket and fired. Within minutes, nearly 200 Native American men, women, and children were massacred.

We may look back upon those Native Americans and wonder how they could have believed an eclipse of the sun was a divine message from God. How could they have been so deluded as to accept the promise of divine protection via bulletproof ghost shirts? Were they unintelligent? No. But they were, obviously, uninformed.

The Role of Ignorance

There is no question that many beliefs are based on sheer ignorance. Whether one defines ignorance as a lack of knowledge or a lack of education, the consequences of being uninformed can be very serious and even deadly. The person who surmised that "what you don't know won't hurt you" had an ostrich mentality; the truth is the precise opposite.

Today we would never interpret the natural phenomenon Wovoka observed as a sign from God. Our understanding of the solar system would not allow us to seriously entertain such a notion. But keep in mind that it is knowledge and reason that help us perceive and understand reality. Reality denotes the quality of being true to life: authentic, factual, genuine, one with nature. Truth and reality, then, are synonymous.

Yet, while we may be too aware to accept that an eclipse of the sun is a message from God, certain areas of our thinking continue to be just as uninformed and, therefore, vulnerable. Consider the catastrophic venture of America into Vietnam. Are we not easily led and misled when knowledge is lacking? Given enough wrong information from what appears to be an authoritative source, the human mind and body can be led into the innards of hell. In the words of American author Charlotte Gilman (1860-1935), "To swallow and follow, whether old doctrine or new propaganda, is a weakness still dominating the human mind."[1]

Sometimes we cannot help being in the dark because certain facts are not yet known (a cure for various diseases) or they are being concealed by special interest groups (corruption in politics or national security). Still other facts may be available, but are beyond our personal level of understanding (nuclear physics).

Unfortunately, however, much of our ignorance is self-imposed, not because the knowledge is yet unknown or unavailable, but because we fail to take advantage of it. And when we are uninformed, we become vulnerable to every wind of doctrine and to those in authority. We can be led, herded, manipulated, and even guided willingly to our destruction, as was the case in the mass murder/suicide of hundreds of ill-fated followers of the Rev. Jim Jones at Jonestown, Guyana.

Without adequate knowledge, we lack the basis to question, challenge, or reject what we are told or directed to do. We have no alternative but to follow like sheep and, in many sorry cases, follow like sheep to the slaughter. Of course, the Jim Jones incident is extreme and not likely to be our fate. Nevertheless, on everyday levels of experience, ignorance can affect us negatively and ruin our lives in a multitude of ways, be it collectively as a nation or personally as individuals.

Only the open-minded pursuit of knowledge can save us from this course, and, in fact, help us create a more positive course. Knowledge is power; it helps us develop insight, and insight generates right, rational action. Even as ignorance can be our self-imposed prison, the search for truth can be the key that helps us escape our mental dungeon—perhaps escape from astrolabe mentality. We were created to be knowledgeable, for the opportunities are all around us, awaiting our taking. In the words of J. Bronowski, "Knowledge is our destiny."[2]

Knowledge Versus Love

The Greeks made a major contribution to the advancement of human society by declaring knowledge to be the greatest good. Unlike NT writers, the Greeks regarded intellectualism as the supreme virtue. For NT writers, on the other hand, the greatest good was love (1 Cor. 13; 1 John 7-8). This difference of focus is further emphasized when Paul states that the faith he preached was regarded as foolishness by the Greeks who demanded "wisdom" (1 Cor. 1:22), which to the Greeks meant rational philosophy, not religious faith.[3]

New Testament authors did not err in making love the cornerstone of their faith, for this was in keeping with the proclamation attributed to Jesus and other religious leaders (that love is the greatest of all human virtues). But the unfortunate result of elevating love above all other qualities is the negation of some very important attributes. Among these are reason and knowledge, which have come to be regarded as secondary virtues, and many times erroneously considered to be in opposition to Christianity. Intentionally or otherwise, Paul fostered this negative attitude by downgrading human wisdom again and again, notably in the first chapter of 1 Corinthians.

Again, this is not to infer the Greeks were right in designating "knowledge the greatest good, but to point out the historical consequences of Paul's emphasis on love at the expense of knowledge and reason. It would be foolish to argue about which is the greater good, love or knowledge. Such an argument would be similar to arguing about which player position is the most indispensable to a football team. Even if we agree the quarterback is the key to the team's success and, therefore, the most indispensable, we also have to concur that every other player is vital to the team's successful performance. These players cannot function independently of one another, nor can any one player be looked upon as less important (though technically this may be the case). Should this occur, the interrelatedness of the players would break down, and the team would become dysfunctional. The same is true for love and knowledge. They are essential components within the human personality, and when either is absent or diminished, the game of life is not well played.

Christian faith has a tendency to nullify this even-handed approach. For most Christians, faith preempts reason. After all, God's truth (the Bible) is authoritative; therefore, conflicting knowledge must be downgraded. When irrepressible evidence indicates the Scriptures are amiss, many Christians are forced to rationalize the discrepancy or reason that it is only because the things of God are unknowable to man, and man's wisdom is but foolishness in His sight. Does not the Bible say God will destroy the wisdom of the wise? (Ps. 33:10; Isa. 29:14; 1 Cor. 1:19) It also states: "Has not God made foolish the wisdom of the world?" (1 Cor. 1:20b) and "For the foolishness of God is wiser than men, and the weakness of God is stronger than man" (1 Cor. 1:25).

In these last two statements denouncing human wisdom, Paul refers to those, such as the Greeks, who could not comprehend the concept of a Messiah or the suffering and death of God's son. To the Greeks, then, the Christian message was foolishness, and this is what Paul was alluding to in his anti-wisdom proclamations (an understandable criticism in his time). But unfortunately, many Christians today continue to cite these verses to defend against a multitude of questions raised by the swelling tide of knowledge.

Paul provided a perfect excuse for rejecting any information contradicting the Bible by declaring man's wisdom to be inferior to that of God. While Paul's assessment of the human condition is precise, this truism has been misconstrued and generalized beyond credibility. To the non-discriminating Christian, words such as *knowledge, reason, wisdom, logic, scholarship, intellect,* and *science* are interchangeable. Thus, the word *wisdom* in Paul's writing has become a red flag, a dirty word easily replaced by the word *science* or *intellect,* and so forth. Hence the verse, as one example, can be interpreted, "God has made foolish the *intellect* of the world." Such a misguided reading is disheartening and sheds light on the continuing conflicts between analytical studies and traditional religious beliefs.

Traditional blinders continue to be a major factor in maintaining the extensive, astrolabe-minded Christian perspective. But ignorance alone cannot explain the present dominance of astrolabe thinking because we know that many Christian ministers and some congregants are aware of the "new" findings of biblical criticism. Yet, among these persons prevails an attitude of complacency toward—or outright rejection of—scholastic findings. Why? One reason is that such knowledge often runs counter to conventional teaching which for the believer causes emotional trauma; denial of the evidence alleviates the pain. Also, the respect and awe accorded to the Bible may simply cause a mental knee-jerk reaction against whatever appears to undermine that which is considered sacrosanct. Therefore, while knowledge may help liberate the mind from false perceptions, it does not always succeed in getting past well-indoctrinated, solidified mind-sets. The mental watertight compartments separating contemporary knowledge from religious beliefs are strongly built; they withstand great pressure and amazingly function side by side without any meaningful interaction.

The Role of Conformity

Another obstacle to religious maturity is based on the "monkey see, monkey do" principle of conformity. The way we walk, talk, dress, eat, and even think and believe is mimicry. This inclination to mimic is found in all cultures and is even essential for the preservation of the community.

It is not difficult to see why so many people possess and readily embrace astrolabe thinking. They are born into traditionalist families and into a society regarding it as the norm. The late noted psychologist Erich Fromm* stated that people are herd animals, and concepts of right and wrong, good and bad, true and false, are determined by the herd, by the group in which they exist.[4]

What is accepted as the norm, then, is dictated by our cultural time and place, factors over which we have no control. We are shaped by the relative values and attitudes of our time.† We need only reflect on the teachings of past and present cultures to realize that most people, regardless of where they live, accept as truth that which the majority of *their kind* deem to be truth—*their kind* meaning family, peer groups, or, with a broader brush, the Church, community, or country. So, depending on one's culture, one might variously regard the best form of government to be fascism, socialism, capitalism, communism, or some other "ism." Similarly, one might be born a Jew, Christian, Hindu, Buddhist, Jain, Moslem, or even a Ghost Dance devotee and be genuinely convinced of one's good fortune. Of course, this good fortune is a partial delusion. As Fromm observed:

> The assertion that "my country" [or religion] is the most wonderful, the most cultured, the most powerful, the most peace-loving, etc., does not sound crazy at all; on the contrary, it sounds like the expression of patriotism, faith, and loyalty. It also appears to be a realistic and rational value judgment because it is shared by many members of the same group. This consensus succeeds in transforming the fantasy into reality, because for most people reality is constituted by general consensus and not based on reason or critical examination.[5]

Perhaps we can see, then, why many Christians continue to tenaciously cling to outmoded concepts and teachings they deem indispensable, believing that they posses the "truth," the "way." We can also begin to see why irrational, dangerous, or even plainly insane thought systems can so easily hold the minds of people.

Erich Fromm (1900-1980) was a German-born American psychoanalyst and prolific writer.

†*There are certain moral values and attitudes, however, which seem to be a part of every place and time. Incest, murder, injustice, and so on, are negative to all cultures and are sometimes referred to as universal laws.*

When we are confronted with differing views of life—even if they are sound—we may regard them as unsound, illogical, worthless, or just plain silly because they conflict with our own. And outsiders are equally baffled about our ways of thinking. So who's right? We are, of course! Carried to the extreme, the tendency to "swallow and follow" without reason can be detrimental to the human spirit, as was the case in Hitler's Germany.

The need to conform also stems from the fear of isolation, which is linked to the need to be loved and accepted. To be different is to risk alienation from the group, whether familial or social. We remain with the herd to avoid the emotional pain of humiliation, exclusion, condemnation, and rejection. But by cleaving to the group we create an interesting problem as none of us want to feel dependent and sheep-like, but self-sufficient and independent. This problem is neatly resolved through the numerous choices within the framework of conformity. Acceptable options help sustain our illusion of being independent while we remain part of the herd. Protestant Christians, for example, may choose between numerous denominations reflecting a variety of theological beliefs. But to avoid the pain of confrontation with their personal herd, they are less likely to become Catholic and certainly not Moslem.

More importantly, the tendency to conform may be the result of our physiological makeup. A quick look at non-human animals may help clarify this statement. As we all know, non-human animals respond rapidly and without instruction at birth to certain stimuli, resulting in life-sustaining behaviors. These are called "instinctive behaviors," actions that do not require experience prior to performance. According to Joseph Campbell,

> Both the readiness to respond to specific triggering stimuli and the ensuing patterns of appropriate action are in all such cases inherited with the physiology of the species. Known as "innate releasing mechanisms" (IRMs), they are constitutional to the [non-human animal's] nervous system. And there are such in the physical makeup of the species Homo Sapiens, as well.[6]

Although the human nervous system is also characterized by innate releasing mechanisms, they are somewhat different from other animals. The IRMs of a human being are not *fixed*, whereas the IRMs of other animals are almost completely functional at birth. In this sense, all animals (human or otherwise) can be seen as computers, with one major difference: non-human animals are born *programmed* by nature, while human nervous systems are *imprinted* during the first twelve or more years of life by the behavioral patterns and belief systems of their cultures. These patterns are engraved, largely by socially transmitted practices.[7] The words of Supreme Court Justice Oliver Wendell Holmes, Jr., come to mind: "We are all tattooed in our cradles with the beliefs of our tribe; the record may seem superficial, but it is indelible."*

We can see, then, the enormous power and influence a culture registers in determining the mind-set of its citizens. Unlike other animals, who from birth have predetermined behavior patterns, people, over time, are taught to respond "properly" according to the dictates and customs of the culture in which they are raised. Once the IRMs have been programmed and have become part of our nervous system, mental and emotional responses to certain signals within our environment become permanent. In short, our feelings and responses become biological and instinctive, even though they were not original to our nature. This is precisely what adds conviction to our feelings and beliefs even if they are irrational or opposite to the feelings and beliefs of others. Of course, this kind of cultural/biological imprinting is bound to create extreme differences in outlook, as would be the case between Blacks and Whites, Jews and Arabs, men and women.

Accordingly, as adults we tend to respond in predictable fashion because we are now firmly set in the hardened concrete of our rearing. This is why many people find it difficult, if not impossible, to alter their behavior. The same is true for intense feelings of faith and belief when individuals have been programmed to respond to certain signals (ideas and symbols) related to religious, political, philosophical, or social systems. Thus, we do not *think* as much as *react* to environmental stimuli. If, for example, gentiles have been conditioned from youth (either by family and/or society) to regard Jews as greedy, it is unlikely they will ever respond to Jews without some concern or suspicion. The reason for this pattern, according to Campbell, is that old messages are not always

---

* *Oliver Wendell Holmes, Jr. (1841-1935) was one of the most significant U.S. Supreme Court Justices (1902-1932). His dissent in* Abrams v United States *(1919) was a powerful defense of free speech. The passage quoted is taken from* Dictionary of Thoughts.

addressed to the brain—to be interpreted there by rational thought and then passed on—but are directly passed to the nerves, the glands, the blood, and the sympathetic nervous system which controls involuntary feeling and action.[8]

As Campbell notes, some of these messages must pass through (register with) the brain, and it is here the "educated" brain may intercept biased messages.[9] The intellect, exposed to enough factual information about or experience with Jews, might modify its thinking sufficiently to eliminate some of its prejudice. Even so, all the negative emotional feelings are not automatically eradicated, due to the deeply-felt influence of the programmed IRMS. In the words of Oliver Wendell Holmes, Jr.: "You cannot educate a man wholly out of the superstitious fears which were implanted in his [childhood] imagination, no matter how utterly his reason may reject them."[10]

One can recognize that the IRM theory is, at least in part, a mythological expression that helps us to deal with "reality" as we understand it today. This is to say that mythology will always be an evolving aspect of our belief systems, be they scientific or religious. We are never free of mythology; it is the canvas upon which our beliefs are painted. And any painting, bad or good, cannot be expressed without the canvas.

Sophistry

A major obstacle to the updating and maturing of the astrolabe mind is the prevalence of sophistry. *Sophistry* is defined as subtle reasoning that appears to be true but is false, unsound, or misleading. Through the clever filtering and manipulation of facts, many false ideas can be made to look as though they have substance. As English clergyman Caleb C. Colton (1780-1832) observed, "Falsehood is never so successful as when she baits her hook with truth, and no opinions so fatally mislead us as those that are not wholly wrong."[11] Even science has not escaped this negative influence. Ptolemy's incorrect theory of the heavens held sway for fourteen centuries until Copernicus established in 1543 that the sun was the center of the solar system. But science today is far less vulnerable to any long-term effect of sophistry. Continuing experimentation and analysis shows each hypothesis probable or improbable, the sole exception being those theories beyond the current capabilities of scientific measurement.

Tragically, traditional Christianity is saturated with sophistry, the result of its faulty presuppositions. Unlike science, religion usually begins by assuming it already possesses truth and then sets out to "logically" support this assumption. The upshot is a number of doctrinal, theological, and dogmatic declarations largely based on convoluted logic and ending in complex but misleading conclusions. No other major field of human endeavor is so permeated with sophistry as religion. There are several reasons for this debilitating peculiarity.

First is what I will term the "self-appointed expert" problem. This problem springs from the inescapable fact that religion is a mystical, personal *feeling* experience, and feeling is usually the measuring stick—aside from general consensus—by which we form our religious opinions.

One is reminded of the atheist who, while sightseeing about the countryside, accidentally fell into an open well. Although not seriously injured, he found himself utterly trapped. After two days of futile cries for help, he panicked at the prospect of his own demise. In desperation, he sought to strike an agreement with his Creator even though he had always denied His existence: "God, if you do exist and if you'll get me out of this mess, I promise to change my ways and help non-believers like myself find the road to salvation." A few minutes later he was "miraculously" rescued by a passerby. The now-reformed atheist was deeply moved by what appeared to be God's intervention and could hardly wait to get started on his side of the agreement. True to his prayer of desperation, the man changed his ways and served God by leading others to salvation. To this day, he can be seen roaming the countryside, pushing people into open wells!

Once we are convinced that God is the author of our experience, then the experience becomes the "way." We become self-appointed experts on the basis of our experience while emotional feeling serves to solidify our thinking. The credibility of this logic is seldom questioned. Our feelings tell us it is too real to be otherwise even though numerous differences of opinion arise between ourselves and others. This in itself should cause suspicion among reasoning followers. Unfortunately, the opposite occurs. People are polarized by their feelings and then proceed to select information that fits their particular religious convictions, leading in turn to the creation of self-appointed experts, most of them puppets and perpetuators of sophistry. This process becomes apparent in the ever-popular Christian bookstore, with numerous examples of sophistry in writings catering to virtually every intellectual and emotional level. This conglomeration of differing viewpoints collides persistently. It's like a thousand rock bands playing different songs simultaneously, each one increasing its volume in an effort to establish dominance.

More often than not, the primary purpose of these works is to describe the author's personal history and conversion experience, to encourage others to accept Christianity, and/or to claim validity for a specific theological viewpoint. There is nothing wrong in sharing one's personal religious experiences or beliefs. But the self-interpretation of these factors could be erroneous, especially if one has ignored or been unaware of advances in religious studies.

Even seasoned Christians fail to see that they are interpreting their experiences from a very limited perspective because they have neither the findings of biblical criticism nor the educational tools to critically analyze their beliefs. Their religious experiences require not only introspection, but evaluation against available knowledge to ensure that they are not adrift on the sea of sophistry. This is not to deny the mystical, subjective nature of religious experience which is not always subject to analytical clarification (of course). Nevertheless, the use of reason can and does eliminate irrational systems of thought or erroneous cause-and-effect assumptions, mainly when they are contrary to more plausible knowledge.

If we look to any other field of study, such as medicine, we find a different situation than in the field of religion. While there is diverse opinion among the medical profession, it remains within general consensus; its hypotheses are developed through scientific method by trained and qualified persons. To ensure competent medical practice and to protect the public from quacks, laws and professional standards permit only properly trained physicians to practice. Patients generally do not prescribe remedies for themselves or others, nor do they challenge their doctors' advice. They may seek other doctors' opinions, but most do not have the medical knowledge or clinical know-how to improve upon their physicians' prognoses.

Members of the clergy, religious scholars, and theologians are "doctors" in a spiritual sense. But, owing to the personal nature of religion, many followers regard themselves as experts. They find it difficult to know when to heed the clergy's professional judgments rather than their own opinions (on theological matters).

Strangely enough, the self-appointed expert problem is seriously compounded because many clergy also fit into this unenlightened category. Believe it or not, unlike doctors, lawyers, and other professionals, no legal requirements are necessary to practice ministry (a side effect from the separation of Church and state policy) though each religious group sets its own minimum standards. Some denominations, such as the United Methodist Church, require a four-year college degree plus a three-year postgraduate masters degree (a total of seven years of higher education). At the other end of the spectrum, some denominations require only that persons *feel* a call to ministry, even if they have little or no formal education. Many TV evangelists fall into this latter category, and, tragically, their influence is extensive—extensive only because their astrolabe preaching caters to the astrolabe mentality of the masses. In effect, the blind is leading the blind.

Isn't it odd that no one can practice medicine without a license, but anyone can claim ministry? In fact, many dethroned celebrities such as athletes, film stars, rock stars, and politicians often find their second spotlight by simply adding the title of Rev. to the front of their names. This is not to say that such persons are less dedicated or sincere than their educated counterparts, but only that they are usually unaware of secular and religious knowledge that would liberate them from their astrolabe views. Without this advantage they can only perpetuate arrested religious perceptions. This indeed is a sad predicament.

In addition to the self-appointed expert syndrome, a second powerful contributing factor to religious sophistry is what I call "intellectual ambiance": the atmosphere of authority, principally found in books authored by highly educated people, but with little or no theological education. Their works are quite persuasive owing to their intellectual tone. They express their religious views in a sophisticated style and language that seemingly imparts credibility. One such author is the late C.S. Lewis,* a prolific and influential writer (also noted for his fiction writing). Although many of Lewis's religious views had merit, his indoctrination into traditional Christianity, along with the absence of any formal religious education, might have caused him to fall into the whirlpool of sophistry. He simply refused to acknowledge the value and

---

* *Clive Staples Lewis (1898-1963) was a British author, literary scholar and Christian apologist. He taught medieval literature at Oxford University and Cambridge University.*

cogency of biblical criticism, which consequently never altered his religious presuppositions. In his work *Christian Reflections*,[12] Lewis condemned biblical criticism for too much guesswork and for reconstructing "imaginary" history. These criticisms grew out of his personal involvement with certain book critics of his day, who, Lewis stated, missed the mark when they analyzed the feelings and motivations behind his writings. How then, he reasoned, could Bible critics possibly understand the motivations of those who wrote the NT nearly 2,000 years earlier?

Lewis appears to either ignore or be unaware of the various shades of meaning as applied to the term "critic," but we must not be misled by this apparent oversight. *Critic,* as we have defined the term, is synonymous with an objective, investigative scholar. Lewis, on the other hand, has interpreted *critic* to mean one who makes subjective judgments of the merits and faults of books, music, motion pictures, theater, and so forth. But it is illogical to compare the arbitrary and subjective views of a book critic to the research-based findings of a biblical scholar. While art critics often draw conclusions from personal preference and matters of taste, the critic/scholar employs analytical tools of investigation. Efforts to reconstruct what happened are based on precise methods which, if not always perfect, produce reliable information that helps to establish a greater realism.

The bottom line is that C.S. Lewis rejected biblical criticism in his writings and embraced an astrolabe interpretation of divine revelation. He accepted the Bible as an unquestionable authority. On Christology, for example, he affirmed without reservation that Jesus was a divine being. In his book *Mere Christianity*, Lewis wrote:

> I am trying here to prevent anyone saying the really foolish thing that people often say about him [Jesus]: "I'm ready to accept Jesus as a great moral teacher, but I don't accept his claim to be God." That is the one thing we must not say. A man who was merely a man and said the sort of things Jesus said would not be a great moral teacher. He would either be a lunatic—on a level with the man who says he is a poached egg—or else he would be the Devil of Hell. You must make your choice. Either this man was, and is, the Son of God: or else a madman or something worse.[13]

These views are a perfect illustration of sophistry and astrolabe mentality. Lewis would have us believe that we have no choice but to equate Jesus with God as a divine being because the Gospels depict Jesus as claiming divinity. (Implied in Lewis's statement is the infallibility of Scripture.) Lewis then reasons that if Jesus isn't God, then he lied about his divinity which would indicate he was either insane or the devil himself. As such, Jesus could not even be considered a moral teacher. William Barclay, the well-known NT expositor, also falls into this ill-founded assumption when he states: "Clearly one of two things must be true—either Jesus was mad, or he was unique; either he was a megalomaniac or else he was the son of God."[14]

This argument appears logical, but it is not! It is erroneously based on the unstated assumption that the Gospels are infallible accounts of what Jesus said. It also implies that the term *Messiah* (before and after Jesus' life) had a singular definition making it synonymous with God; but it had at least two variant meanings—both of which were far removed from being synonymous with God, as equated in the doctrine of the Trinity. Lewis either ignores this information or is oblivious to it. He accepts and interprets the Gospel accounts in traditional fashion, leading him to declare that we have but two choices: we must either regard Jesus as wicked or insane, or accept his claim to be God. But we know from biblical criticism that the Bible can no longer be viewed from such a stringent perspective, especially in reference to Jesus' so-called claims of divinity. How could Lewis or anyone interpret the Bible without considering the historical influences we now know helped shape biblical thought?

It is obvious that most Christians have sugar-coated their understanding of biblical revelation. Such an approach is immoral since it not only creates self-deception, but retards the very progress of the human family. If we are to learn greater degrees of truth about Jesus, the Scriptures, God, and ourselves, we must openly consider the findings of scholarly investigation and seriously apply them to the foundations of Christian beliefs. We must be realistic! Honest, objective inquiry *cannot* begin with the assumption that Jesus is God simply on the face-value interpretation of Scripture; it must begin with the question: "Did Jesus truly claim to be God?" It also must ask: "When the Bible states that Jesus claimed divinity, is the Bible trustworthy on this issue or the manner in which it is reported?" Further: "Were the original accounts about the life of Jesus altered, either by the early Church or the Gospel writers?" [See Appendix I (section on Form Criticism) and Appendix II (section on Resurrection Conflicts.)] And: "Has the term *Messiah* been overstated or misstated?" Finally: "How did Hellenism influence the biblical development of Christology?" Only when these and similar questions are answered to the best of our knowledge can we begin to understand the meaning of Jesus for his contemporaries and for us.

Sophistry, generated through intellectual ambiance, is also commonly found in books authored by ministers who received their education primarily from fundamentalist colleges and seminaries. These evangelical writers employ (albeit not intentionally) the most elaborate forms of sophistry to persuade the less informed to their views.

One of the most successful examples of this type of literature is *The Late Great Planet Earth* by Hal Lindsey* and his follow-up book, *The 1980's: Countdown to Armageddon*. Both works are equally absurd—absurd because, like many misguided clergy before him, Lindsey predicted that the world's last war (the Battle of Armageddon as described in the biblical Book of Revelation) would occur in the 1980s. He believed this would usher in the second coming of Christ and end human history as we know it. Such predictions have been with us since the apostle Paul first believed the return of Christ was imminent. In Lindsey's work, the main culprit was the now-defunct Soviet Union.

Of course, no one is denying the ever-present danger of a nuclear holocaust, although such threats have abated in recent years. But even if we unleash our doomsday weapons, the unfolding drama of human history will not follow the pattern of so-called biblical prophecy, except possibly the promise of mass destruction and God's final resolution (whatever that may be). But interpreting the mythical/allegorical Battle of Armageddon, the anti-Christ, the seven-year Tribulation, the Rapture, the 1000-year utopia, and so forth, as literal future events is as far off target as viewing the Genesis story of Creation as a literal account. Lindsey seems to interpret biblical writing with a total disregard for the well-established findings of biblical criticism, resulting in works characterized by literal interpretation of myth and allegory blended with fact and fancy. The level of sophistry is alarming. As a result, these

---

* *Hal Lindsey is a Southern Baptist minister, a graduate of Dallas Theological Seminary.*

works lack credibility and realism. Professor James Barr of Oxford University termed *The Late Great Planet Earth* a type of science fiction with shadings of astrology and the occult.[15]

I am not bothered that Hal Lindsey presents a position contrary to the findings of biblical scholarship. What alarms me is the mass acceptance of such works. In 1980, the *New York Times* reported that this work had become the best selling nonfiction book of the 1970s; it sold more than 18 million copies! This is incredibly sad. It is a startling indictment of the level of Christian maturity. It exposes the raw nerve of religious ignorance today—the prevalence of world-wide astrolabe mentality. In contrast, scholarly works on the subject (Book of Revelation) remain cloistered in the libraries of major universities and seminaries—their sales limited to academic circles. (Some larger, well-stocked, local libraries do carry many scholarly works, but they remain generally ignored since the terminology is not usually geared for the general public.)

As we have noted, the astrolabe mind is characteristic of most Christians regardless of their theological leanings. This vast segment of Christianity spreads its traditional teaching through the majority of Christian churches, as well as by television, radio, bookstore, film, community program, class, and seminar. In contrast, there does exist a small number—small in comparison to astrolabe thinkers—of scholars, professors, ministers, and lay persons who acknowledge, study, and teach the findings of biblical criticism. Not surprisingly, this minority group spearheads religious studies in academic circles but remains virtually unknown, ignored, or severely criticized by the multitudes of Christians who function outside of the educational system.

Many Christians generally consider the institutional bastions of education as arch enemies, in regard to religious studies and perhaps some segments of science. They are at odds not only with the cutting edge of religious knowledge, but with the entire array of religious scholarship gathered since the seventeenth century.

While much of the Church continues to appease the astrolabe mind by failing to engender awareness and acceptance of biblical criticism, most institutions of higher learning do quite the opposite. A Christian high school graduate who goes on to higher education and takes an introductory course to the NT may be in for a rude awakening, primarily if she or he is from a conservative background. There is no conspiracy; nor is the university anti-Christian. But it is directed chiefly to making knowledge available to its students, regardless of the subject matter. The fact that much of this information conflicts with traditional viewpoints of the Church is not the fault of the university, but of the Church.

A final note on sophistry. We all possess and project a certain degree of bias through our own sophistry. There is *no* purity of thought. It is presumptuous for any of us to believe we are wholly objective and free from prejudice. Therefore, the continued search for knowledge is critical if we are to detect our self-imposed sophistry and to keep from being influenced by the sophistry of others who would alter our judgments. Through an erroneous but well-worded argument, an uninformed person is easily persuaded to accept that which appears to be a logical premise but which, under close scrutiny and compared with enough alternative information, would be rejected. In matters of faith, knowledge must be an integral part of the belief foundation because the opportunity for sophistry, along with its potential for persuasiveness and deception, is enormous.

Further Reflection

Considering the premise of this writing and the information discussed thus far, we come to a highly important question: What should we believe? This is a difficult and sometimes perplexing question since no school of thought corners the market on truth, and virtually every religion and ideology has sufficient merit to attract. All have unique, often opposing viewpoints that in combination overwhelm us. How, for example, can we distinguish the truth between biblical criticism and the conflicting arguments of astrolabe thinkers? An answer must be sought not by claiming truth, but by illustrating the process that leads to truth. What should be the basis of our belief?

We begin by admitting that our search for truth is hampered from birth. Our popularly supposed truths are first imprinted upon our minds and spirits by the dogmatic consensus of the herd, and subsequently reinforced by our fear of isolation and our need to be loved and accepted. And if we show signs of becoming mavericks, of seeking out truth for ourselves, we are quickly shoved back into the corral by the weighty influence of majority opinion. Subdued by ignorance and led by the nose of conformity, we are herded through twisting tunnels of sophistry whose only signposts are scripted with the conflicting messages of self-appointed experts. Suddenly we find the path turning not toward truth and enlightenment, but circling back to the cradle, harkening us to come back to the culturally imprinted, old-time religion, the faith of our fathers that feels so good because it's been there so long.

Such obstacles to maturity can be hurdled if leaders can move away from dogmatic teaching practices. Religion has been preoccupied with telling people what to think instead of teaching them how to think. If we accept ideas without challenge or critical examination and merely accept them because they issue from some authoritative source, they will forever enslave our minds. It is extremely vital to realize that in order to know *what* to think, we first must know *how* to think. Clearly, the ability to discern between truth and falsehood is a serious and necessary undertaking.

Seize upon truth, wherever it is found,
amongst your friends, amongst your foes,
on Christian or on heathen ground; the
flower's divine where'er it grows.

—Isaac Watts (1674-1748)
English hymn writer

Chapter IX
What Is Truth?

Mortimer J. Adler,* in his excellent book *Six Great Ideas*, gives us several valuable insights into the question "What is truth?" He states that ". . . the truth of thought consists in the agreement or correspondence between what one thinks, believes, or opines and what actually exists or does not exist in reality that is independent of our minds . . ."[1] If the moon, for example, revolves around the earth in an elliptical orbit, not circular, as scientists have shown, then what I believe about its movement will either correspond with reality (making my belief correct) or it will not correspond with reality (making my belief incorrect).

Our goal should always be to sharpen our beliefs until they coincide with reality. Since reality is not always knowable (depending on when we live, the knowledge accessible, and the nature of the subject) we can nevertheless say we are closer to the truth when our viewpoints most closely resemble reality. If I say the moon's orbit around the earth is circular, I would not be entirely correct (since it is elliptical), but I would be closer to the truth than someone who says the earth orbits the moon.

Still, the fact that one is closer to the truth does not mean one possesses the truth, at least not the absolute truth. The understanding of what we call truth will therefore be modified as more information becomes available. This does not mean truth is relative. On the contrary, truth does not change; only our opinions and perceptions of it vary. "We do not make statements true or false by affirming or denying them. They have truth or falsity regardless of what

* *Mortimer J. Adler (1902-) is the chairperson of the Board of Editors of Encyclopedia Britannica, director of the Institute for Philosophical Research in Chicago, and a senior associate of the Aspen Institute for Humanistic Studies. He holds a Ph.D. from Columbia University (1928).*

we think .. "[2] Reality is not changed by what we believe or don't believe. What is true is true for all of us; it has universal application. (We are speaking here of objective truth, not matters of taste, flux, or subjectivism.)* In keeping with this, it is incorrect to say something might have been true, but is no longer true. Centuries ago people believed the earth was flat. That false opinion was replaced with an accurate explanation based on greater knowledge. But as Adler states:

> This should not be interpreted to mean that the objective truth has changed—that what once was true is no longer true. If it is now objectively true that this planet is spherical, it never was true that it is flat. What has changed is not the truth of the matter but the prevalence of an opinion that has ceased to be popular.[3]

When we are in accord with reality, we have truth. But as Adler rightly points out, this definition of truth may tell us what truth is, but not what is true. It does not answer the question "Is it true?" How do we know which of a number of conflicting beliefs, ideas, or statements is true? How do we know when our thinking is in accord with reality, especially in areas that are more subjective than objective (such as religion compared to physics)?

In determining the truth of any idea or, at least, what is closest to the truth, the question is how can we distinguish scientific explanations from non-scientific ones, the rational from the irrational, truth from falsehood? Why should or shouldn't we believe Jesus is divine, Einstein's theory of relativity is correct, the moon is made of cheese, or biblical criticism is credible?

A process of verification is needed to accept or reject such hypotheses. We verify a statement or hypothesis by direct and/or indirect evidence. I can verify directly that I have ten fingers simply by counting them. But suppose you told me that the University of Southern California just beat Notre Dame in football. If I had not attended the game, I could not directly verify your statement. I would have to rely on indirect (secondary) evidence,

---

* *In his book,* Six Great Ideas, *Adler addresses the differences between varying matters of taste and truth; the subjective from the objective, and so forth.*

such as information from a sports editor of the local newspaper, game scores from the radio and television, or information from a phone call to friends who are sports fans. But hearsay evidence is not always reliable (usually inadmissible in a court of law). Suppose the newspaper sports editor accidentally gave me the wrong information and the radio announcer and my friends made similar mistakes. The fact that these indirect sources supported your claim still would not make that claim true. While these types of errors may be unlikely, it is important to gather as much verifying data as possible to minimize the likelihood of error. When direct evidence is not available or possible, indirect evidence becomes the basis for belief, and the more indirect evidence we have to support a statement or theory, the more believable it becomes. Of course, any point of view will be compromised if the integrity of the sources are questionable. Thus, distinguishing between what is possible or probable depends squarely on the kind and amount of direct or indirect evidence we gather.

This is the difference between scientific and speculative views. Whether the premise being tested is biblical inerrancy or Einstein's theory of relativity, such belief must rest upon substantial verifiable evidence, direct and/or indirect. But evidence can be found to support almost any hypothesis, even one that is false. Evidence once indicated that the world was flat, this evidence chiefly being that it looked flat (apparently direct evidence). Again, it is important that more than a minimal amount of evidence be examined when testing any proposition.

The Model of Probability

To understand the validity of the arguments surrounding any hypothesis, theory, or law, there is a process of reasoning we should employ. This reasoning is not a black-and-white, yes-or-no, true-or-false method of judging reality. Rather, it says this statement *appears* to be true, and there are also other alternative answers that may be almost certainly true, very probably true, possibly true, probably not true, almost certainly not true, and so forth. This is the kind of logic used in the model of probability. It is the only sound, logical way to draw conclusions when viewing evidence that cannot be classified in terms of true-or-false certainties.

To visualize this model, it is important to understand the difference between *possibility* and *probability*. According to Webster, *possible* means "may or may not happen"; *probable* means "likely to occur or to be so; can reasonably be expected or believed on the basis of available evidence, though not proven or certain." For example, anyone jumping without a parachute from an airplane at 15,000 feet might *possibly* survive, but *probably* would not.

Most of our beliefs, including those relating to science and religion, are based upon possibility and probability. And that includes the beliefs in our daily lives. When you board a 747 airliner, the possibility of a crash may enter your mind, but if you believed for a moment the crash were probable, you'd no doubt head for the exit. The importance of and common use of probability logic cannot be denied. Every day we make decisions and reach conclusions based on evidence at our disposal. Whether such day-to-day conclusions are relatively unimportant (deciding to carry an umbrella on a cloudy day) or serious (authorizing a surgeon to perform surgery), they usually can be reached only by using probability logic.

If most of our beliefs are based on possibility and probability, then what about certainty? Science confirms that there is no such thing as certainty or absolute proof. This concept is supported by the quantum theory, which establishes that even the laws of nature are not absolutely predictable. (In physics, this concept is sometimes referred to as the *theory of indeterminacy*.) The very electrons, protons, and neutrons that comprise our existence do not always behave as expected. Once in a while, they seem to go berserk! (Although what is "berserk" today will probably be understood by tomorrow's science.) Thus, modern physics says: "You cannot say what an electron will do; you can only say what it will probably do." It follows then that you cannot predict with certainty what anything in our physical realm will do. You cannot even prove that a rock, when dropped, will always fall downward—though you can predict with the highest probability it will. Even so, science acknowledges the rare possibility that a stone, when dropped, might move upward, or that a pot of water placed over a flame might freeze instead of boil.

We know that exceptional happenings such as these have such a high degree of improbability that they do not threaten the certainty of expected occurrences. While we recognize the possibility of such events, we choose to believe what will probably happen, not what might possibly happen. The laws of nature may not be absolute, but they are highly predictable and dependable.

Obviously, the probability of any subject, theory, law, or belief system will vary according to its unique characteristics. An outcome may be 99 percent probable, 80 percent probable, 63 percent probable, and so forth. At 49 percent, the probability factor has passed from the positive to the negative. So, probability logic can indicate for or against, depending on which direction you approach the percentages. If, for example, you acknowledge a 70 percent probability for rain, then it is equally true there is a 30 percent probability it won't rain.

Probability logic is easy to employ when investigating the laws of nature since they tend to be highly predictable. But what about philosophy, religion, psychic phenomena, or other abstract subjects? It is precisely within such categories that the model of probability can be of particular value. We must use this model to arrive at valid, intelligent conclusions about the belief systems that summon to us. Although nothing can be absolutely proven, when enough evidence supports the probability of what we are investigating, we can then believe it (or vice versa).

Of course, the search for truth can require extensive effort. Even within the same subject, we will find that verification factors vary greatly. If we try to answer the questions "Does God exist?" and "Is the Bible fallible or infallible?" we will discover that probability factors will be more convincing for the second question than the first. Whether God exists or not is much more difficult to ascertain since the question lends itself more to subjective rather than objective interpretation of the evidence. While many sound arguments have been made for the existence of God, they have been based primarily on religious and philosophical interpretations of the evidence that could easily be interpreted differently by those who oppose the God hypothesis. This centuries-old question continues to be mainly a matter of faith, buoyed by intellectual arguments for the existence of God, such as those by Aquinas in his *Suma Theologica*.*

On the other hand, the question "Is the Bible fallible or infallible?" lends itself more readily to scientific probe. As it turns out, there is sufficient evidence showing a high degree of reliability for many portions of Scripture, but the concept of biblical inerrancy can be easily refuted. In fact, the evidence drives us to the opposite conclusion.

---

* *The* Suma Theologica, *written 1267-1273, is an incomplete but systematic exposition of theology on philosophical principles and the rigid application of reason.*

Every question, every issue, every hypothesis has unique characteristics that must be critically analyzed to test its validity. Responsibly used with the scientific method, the model of probability is a very effective tool in determining the truth of the matter.

It must be noted that when a given proposition has not been proven (proven by the preponderance of data) or disproved, we cannot conclude it is either true or false. Many otherwise enlightened people are prone to this fallacy. An example is the late noted author and philosopher Ayn Rand, who said during an interview on the nationally televised "Phil Donahue Show" (May 15, 1979) that she did not believe in the existence of God since it could not be proven. But if we say something is false because it has not been proven true, or true because it has not been proven false, then we commit the fallacy in logic known as *argumentum ad ignorantiam* (argument from ignorance).[4]

My limited approach to the issue of truth should be displayed on a much broader canvas, but space does not permit. I must, however, include Adler's explanation of the term *knowledge*, which is often made synonymous with *truth*. Even when we speak of the sciences as branches of organized knowledge, this knowledge should not be regarded as unalterable. These disciplines are subject to change because of:

> ... new discoveries, improved observations, the development of sounder hypotheses, the substitution of more comprehensive theories for less comprehensive ones, more elaborate and more precise analysis or interpretations of the data at hand, and rectified or more rigorous reasoning. Less adequate formulations are replaced by better ones—better because they are thought more likely to be true, or nearer to the truth being sought, and, therefore, better approximations of it.[5]

This line of thinking is in keeping with what we have already discussed about progressive revelation. I mention it here to ensure that people are not misled into believing that branches of authoritative knowledge—be they scientific or religious—are beyond question. On the other hand, verifiable knowledge (though in the process of refinement) possesses weighty credibility since it is based on rational grounds, not emotional grounds (as is the case with most opinions).

Further Reflection

This book is of course more than a compilation of information. It reflects my evolving religious awareness. But readers must make their own interpretations. We are continually putting the puzzle together, but the total picture will never be seen. And sometimes it becomes even more remote when we explore some aspects of reality that cannot be defined in tangible form or visible shape. The enigma of Jesus, the Bible, or the existence of God defy complete analysis even when we call upon probability factors. But, clearly, what one believes about Jesus and God should ultimately be based on *informed* faith, not *blind* faith. It cannot be overstated. Ignorance is our greatest enemy. If Christianity is to survive as a credible force for human development and spiritual expression, then today's faithful must come to grips with the findings and implications of twentieth-century knowledge and, particularly, biblical criticism.

Still, many Christians will insist that the evidence gathered through biblical criticism is misinterpreted or we have misunderstood the mysterious way in which God works. Then how are we to perceive reality? Obviously, whenever possible we must rely on the same procedures of logic and investigation that we apply to other fields. How can we validate, accept, and live by the findings of the scientific method as applied to every human endeavor, and then reject these procedures and findings in religion on the ridiculous assumption that they no longer apply?

As we have noted, scientific measurement has its limitations. It cannot validate certain questions regarding faith and divine spirit. Nevertheless, faith should not be a substitute for reason, nor should it become a catalyst that marshals opposition to advancing religious and secular knowledge. The problem is not that Christians have too much religious faith, but that they have too little faith in human capability.

I do not suggest we need to understand all things before we invoke faith. We must, however, recognize that mature faith resides at the end of qualitative and quantitative knowledge, not biased and limited information. Our faith will grow and modify as our knowledge and understanding grow and modify; it is a progressive, lifetime journey. But is such a journey of discovery possible for those who refuse to venture beyond the centuries-old concept of divine revelation? And will those who enter the Christian faith even be aware of the choice of religious attitudes, or will they be forced out of ignorance to accept traditional Christian beliefs? These two cardinal questions may determine the fate of Christianity.

*Accurate knowledge is the basis of
correct opinions; the want of it
makes the opinions of most
people of little value.*

—Charles Simmons (1798-1856)
American clergyman

Chapter X
Possible Solutions

We have seen that the astrolabe mind is merely the by-product of bibliolatry. The belief that divine revelation is absolute is an aberration that is woven into the fabric of our faith and, for that matter, all belief systems that claim special knowledge. This crippling presumption prohibits personal growth by denying the validity of any new knowledge which conflicts with the sacred scrolls. On this basis, we have misdirected the Christian family—and everyone else—for almost 2,000 years. We can understand why discernment of this disabling viewpoint was not possible for most people prior to the seventeenth century. But following the Age of Reason and the Enlightenment and, consequently, the development of biblical criticism, what should have changed, didn't change. Instead we got the astrolabe mind, which in turn led to creationism, homophobia, and other present-day anomalies. The question is: How can we eliminate this perennial Christian practice of going by the Book? How do we eliminate bibliolatry?

First, we must modify our definition of *sacred knowledge* to incorporate the natural process of evolving truth. The Bible must not be viewed as a closed system of thought, nor as the ultimate and final expression of what constitutes reality. The Bible must be recognized as only *one* reflection of many parts of a greater whole. To assume it is the whole is a grave mistake. To make it the best and final message for all time is to ignore the evolving spirit of truth and deny humankind further theological development. Although the Bible represents a masterpiece in spiritual, ethical, and moral values, it must not be considered the final chapter in our religious evolution since it is neither perfect nor without serious problems. As we have seen, some aspects of Scripture are inferior to others in style, accuracy, and insight, and some are counter-productive to its central message of love and justice (see Appendix II). Had the Christian faithful realized these inequities early on, the tragedies of the past and those that persist today might have been avoided. But here we are moving into the twenty-first century with most Christians still denying the prejudice, ignorance, and cultural limitations of biblical writers on the grounds that such misjudgments couldn't exist in a "God-given" document.

In some respects, we need to *decanonize* the Bible. We must redefine (not remove) its mystique and downgrade its aura of authority which distorts our perception of reality and blocks further growth. All forms of knowledge, regardless of their station, are in flux—not static. Until the Bible is viewed in this proper perspective, we will not make significant strides in combatting Bible worship. Such steps will not eliminate the Bible's importance in our lives, but will pave the way for new highs in personal development as we consider new information that sheds light on our religious journey. As yet, some of our greatest truths, insights, revelations, and discoveries lie unexposed.

Second, to eradicate biblical absolutism we must also come to realize that biblical truth does not depend on biblical perfection. It is not necessary to contend that the "Holy" Bible is an all-authoritative message from God in order to lend credibility to its teachings. The Bible must, and can, stand on its own—on the merits and enduring value of its message for humankind. Its imperfection does not eliminate God as the moving force behind its development, but merely reshapes our understanding of how human influence is also registered.

Some persons will argue: "If the entire Bible isn't true, then how do you know which parts of the Bible are true and which parts aren't?" This thinking clearly lacks perception. If you took a course in American History and were assigned to read a specific history textbook, you would not expect its every statement to be without error. You couldn't always perceive which areas of the book were accurate and which were not, but you would assume the majority of the text was correct, based on the reputation/credentials of the author and of your professor, the History Department, and the University. Thus, you would accept the textbook to be historically reliable even though you acknowledged its natural imperfection. If segments of the book were incorrect, continued research by the author, together with any new findings, could result in a new edition with greater authenticity. Or your research into suspected portions might produce information pointing to the author's bias or lack of knowledge. Such data could come from your independent study of other history works, as well as late data from sources to which the author did not have access. But you would not invalidate the entire work because it was flawed.

This analogy is not watertight since the process of development for the Bible, as compared to a textbook, is significantly different. But the point is twofold. They are both subject to analytical review for the discernment of truth; and the fact that they are flawed does not invalidate them.

If biblical integrity is to survive, biblical content must be dealt with realistically; namely, in terms of the imperfections relating to the religious and cultural influences that shaped it, and the human limitations of its creators. It also must be understood as part of a long process which did not begin or end with it. Similarly, if we speak of the Bible as special, it should not mean inerrant nor should it be considered unquestionable authority. Instead, we should regard the Bible as having been accomplished through the extraordinary elevation and stimulation of the natural powers of people who yielded themselves devoutly to God's will and who sought, with great success, to create and convey truth useful to all humankind. To assume anything more is to invite the disastrous consequences we explored earlier and to encourage people to worship at the shrine of bibliolatry.

Third, to further erase Bible worship we must come to grips with the findings of biblical criticism, especially in terms of myth. In doing so, we must educate our people away from the restrictive notion that God's truth is inseparable from the literal interpretation of the Bible story. The Resurrection account, for example, viewed as myth can equally proclaim the teachings of the Church: good is more powerful than evil, love can achieve more than hatred, and life endures after death. Acceptance of these teachings is based on faith, even as belief in the literal Resurrection of Jesus (which declares these same teachings) is based on faith.

Faith, as the Bible succinctly defines it, ". . . is the substance of things hoped for, the evidence of things not seen" (Heb. 11:1). Simply stated, faith is believing without proof. Obviously, if something could be "proven" it would no longer rest within the realm of faith; this is what gives faith its character. Although a certain amount of faith must be exercised at almost every point in our lives, the real meaning of faith is usually reserved for matters which have little or no supportive evidence; e.g., the difference is clear between faith in tomorrow's sunrise and faith in life after death.

In our approach to biblical stories, the key element is faith—but faith in what? Can we have faith in the truth of the message as conveyed by the biblical story without the story-event itself being historical? After all, having faith in the truth of the message as conveyed by the story is not the same as having faith in the story as historical reality. We have here two separate and distinct concerns; namely, belief in the truth of the message and belief in the narrative as historical. As an example let us return to the Resurrection account.

Traditionally, Christians have been taught that biblical stories—aside from parables and such—must be historical to make the story-message valid. Herein seems to be the stumbling block for most Christians. Even Paul reflects this limited perspective when he states: "And if Christ has not risen, then our preaching is in vain, and your faith is in vain" (1 Cor. 15:14).

Apparently, Paul entwines (as most people do) our two separate and distinct concerns (history and message) into the unacceptable proposition that you can't have one without the other; that is, if Jesus didn't literally rise from the dead, then there is no salvation or life after death. But to argue that the message is invalid unless it is undergirded by an actual historical event is not necessarily true, especially in this case since one cannot verify historical substance (resurrection) any more than one can verify the truth of the message (life after death). These are matters of faith, not proof.

In other words, one should not claim the assurance of life after death based on the resurrection of Jesus since belief in the resurrection itself is based on faith. As logic dictates, you cannot prove one statement of faith with another. You cannot prove one unverifiable idea with another idea that itself is unverifiable. Although this type of co-dependent argument creates the illusion of verification, the attempt is simply cosmetic. In the final analysis, belief in a literal resurrection (which is based on faith) does not prove the belief in life after death (which is also based on faith).

Of course, many Christians argue that their "proof" is based on the authority of the Bible which they feel should be taken at face value. But this again is not proof since allegiance to biblical authority is also based on faith—faith that the Bible as traditionally esteemed and interpreted is correct. This may even be obstinate or blind faith which flies in the face of biblical criticism—but it is, nevertheless, faith.

It is obvious that faith is the common denominator for whatever and however we believe. It is equally clear that faith does not have a universal starting point. That is, one person's faith may *begin* with the belief that God's message has come through an inerrant Bible which depicts unquestionable historical events. Another person's faith may *begin* with the belief that God's message, as reflected in the Bible, has been expressed through the human and cultural limitations of an ancient time. In either case, both beliefs require faith—faith that is not, however, focused at the same point. Thus, it is not faith that has changed; only the starting point of faith has changed. In a manner of speaking, Christians who do not interpret the Resurrection literally have simply leapfrogged their traditional counterparts on the continuum of faith. For these Christians, such repositioning is essential in preserving personal integrity against the onslaught of what has become intellectually self-evident (the presence of mythology). Whatever the case, we must conclude that no matter how one approaches the Resurrection story (literally or mythically), the approach proceeds on the basis of faith and faith alone, and the final message is equally embraced.

In preceding chapters, we explored the idea that some matters of faith are subject to rational scrutiny through the scientific method and the model of probability. As a result, biblical criticism has produced strong evidence which indicates that myth is one of the structures underpinning the NT message. This does not mean that the historicity of biblical characters is in doubt, but to illustrate the prominent role of ancient myth in biblical narrative. Increasingly, biblical criticism requires a reevaluation of where one's faith should reside so as to avoid denial of, or conflict with, reality. Therefore, it is not unreasonable for informed Christians to place the emphasis of their faith at nontraditional points. In so doing, their faith becomes centered on the affirmation of the message (where it should be) regardless of whether its underpinnings are historical or mythical. And, if these underpinnings should prove to be mythical (as biblical criticism continues to indicate), the value of the message will not be lost.

Even if the erosion of historical substance continues, the concept of the Resurrection will not lose its guiding value unless we impose restrictions by insisting on literal interpretations of the Bible and, therefore, on how God communicates. And if we should discover that Adam and Eve are symbolic figures, or that a big fish didn't swallow Jonah, or that Noah's Ark never sailed, are we to conclude that the messages these allegories proclaim are no longer valid? Would we not, as the old cliché tells us, be throwing the baby out with the bath water?

The need for most Christians to regard biblical myth as history reflects mental self-limitation created by centuries of indoctrination. Contrary to what such persons think, faith does not require belief in all biblical stories as historical happenings. Rather, faith grows out of our honest endeavor to understand them for what they are—expressions of early Christianity, some of which are couched in mythical imagery—and then draw their meaning and message. As in a parable, the absence of history does not invalidate the message; the truth of the message is not dependent upon the vehicle in which it arrives.

The question arises: "Won't Christianity lose its uniqueness if most of its fundamental doctrines are reduced to mythological constructs?" The answer is a qualified yes. If, for instance, the Incarnation is accepted as mythical, it will lessen Christianity's uniqueness, but only in its doctrinal assertions. Maurice Wiles* explains, ". . . the most likely change would be towards a less exclusive insistence on Jesus as the way for all peoples and cultures . . ." and he believes such a change would be a gain for the faith.[1] I agree. It would remove presumptuous attitudes which spring from the claim that Jesus is God's exclusive savior of the world, to whom every knee shall bend, and that he is the only one through whom the Father can be reached.

But this will not weaken Christianity's message since its validity and authority do not depend on the claim that Jesus is divine. The teachings of Jesus that emerge from the pages of the NT will be valued and preserved because they are compelling, or they will become secondary to a more lucid message. This is true of all instruction. Truth has its own authority; what is true will survive, and what is not true will eventually pass. If God delivered a message of love and hope through the Jesus event, why must Jesus be divine or the Bible sacred to make the message valid? Envision truth as a cork at the bottom of the ocean. By its nature it cannot remain submerged and will eventually break the surface. The course of knowledge is similar, and no special claims of divinity or sacredness are necessary to make it so.

Accepting the Incarnation as myth also eliminates the demand for uniform belief within Christianity. While the life, role, and nature

* Maurice Wiles is regius professor of Divinity and Canon of Christ Church, Oxford, England, and chairman of the Church of England's Doctrine Commission.

of Jesus have long been interpreted differently by various churches within the faith, any deviation from the fundamental belief in Christology has been viewed as unfaith, or heresy, giving rise to condemnation and persecution. If what holds Christians together could be seen as varying interpretations of the same Jesus event rather than as one dogmatic, doctrinal belief, far greater harmony and understanding would prevail among all who embrace these perspectives. The result would be new unity.

This brings us to our fourth means for eliminating bibliolatry—the clergy. We have already touched upon the hesitancy of ministers to share with their congregants any information that would create ripples in the holy water. History is replete with examples of disastrous consequences for those who would make the attempt. Even so, the clergy have a moral obligation to help bridge the gap between the "knows" and the "know nots." The shirking of this responsibility is immoral as it perpetuates ignorance and deception.

Members of the clergy have a tremendous responsibility to help their lay people clarify the nature, purpose, and meaning of biblical revelation and help them resolve the overwhelming contradictions within traditional Christian concepts and doctrines as they relate to religious and secular knowledge today. The fact that congregants may have to be dragged kicking and screaming into the present should not inhibit ministers from performing their duty, nor should the possibility of reprisal intimidate.

A fifth possible solution to this problem could rest with secular education, although such a prospect is not very promising. Academic institutions do offer religious studies, but their impact is minimal since such courses are usually offered as electives. Also, most students, unless specifically interested in religion, will not sample this knowledge menu. Those who do show interest rarely have enough spare academic time to pursue more than one semester of study unless they plan to continue postgraduate studies at seminary. Frankly, most college graduates have little or no understanding of religion and biblical development.

If possible, a similar curriculum would be of tremendous value at the high school level. Unfortunately, many adults will interpret religious education to mean a program that indoctrinates or proselytizes students, like a Sunday school. But the curriculum I advocate for secondary schools is not instruction *in* religion, but *about* religion; that is, the study of the historical and developmental characteristics of religions in general—a simpler version of what is being taught at the university level. Handled objectively, such instruction would not violate the principle of Separation of Church and State, but it would help drive out aspects of astrolabe thinking and also keep young minds from succumbing to religious cults and harmful winds of doctrine.

The acceptance of religious education in the secondary schools, of course, is highly unlikely. Three major barriers stand in the way: a lack of qualified instructors, public misunderstanding of the nature of and need for such a program, and lack of funding. For the present, religious education will probably be confined to institutions of higher learning and perhaps a few churches on the cutting edge of reality.

A sixth means for eradicating biblical dogmatism must rest with scholars and other educators. One suspects that our present predicament might have been avoided had scholars written their works in readable fashion. Instead, they wrote and continue to write to each other, or so it seems, using incomprehensible language. Consider the following words from a prominent religious publication: "The hermeneutical principles laid down in the last chapter dealt with antiquarian historiography and the interconnection between historico-exegesis and historico-critical dogmatic theology." Is it any wonder that people have not kept pace with religious scholarship? Granted, intellectual gymnastics can be enjoyable and sometimes absorbing, but not for most believers. They have neither the background nor the inclination nor the time to laboriously hammer through alien language. We desperately need to make scholarly writing—to borrow a computer phrase— "user friendly."

Further Reflection

Some may interpret these recommendations as a compromise and adaption of Christian teachings to the modern mind, making it more palatable to the masses. This is not the case. The motive is not to compromise the faith, but to bring it to reality—and that reality begins with the acknowledgment that we need not base our beliefs on centuries-old cosmology. Christianity today must clarify the nature, purpose, and meaning of biblical revelation, and be prepared to shed long-held assumptions that threaten its credibility and, therefore, its survival. This process will depend on the willingness of clergy and lay people to resolve the contradictions within traditional Christian thought as they relate to religious and secular knowledge today. The concept of divine revelation and doctrinal statements of faith are no longer convincing in the traditional sense and sorely require reinterpretations that speak to the minds and hearts of twenty-first-century believers. Unless we recognize the enormous fallacies and self-deceptive inconsistencies with which we approach religious faith, we will discard it altogether or remain at a level of understanding that will alienate more enlightened persons, reduce our numbers, and doom us to live in conflict with the ever-swelling tide of knowledge. This will be a tragedy and great loss since Christianity holds great value for us all.

Unfortunately, confusion and misinformation are so prevalent in this area that it may take another century or more to rectify the problem. Even as biblical criticism strives to free the Christian majority from centuries of erroneous assumptions, the popular Christian movements and media of our day actively work to strengthen their hold.

All that is known now is that astrolabe devotees are continually well-programmed to resist new theological perspectives. Therefore, the very fate of Christianity may rest on whether individualistic thinking and self-determination can take precedence over the programming of the masses. Then and only then can the legacy of Christianity survive.

Those who so become accustomed to walk
in darkness weaken their eyesight so
much that afterwards they cannot
bear the light of day.

—René Descartes (1596-1650)
French philosopher.

Epilogue

Two roads diverged in a yellow wood,
And sorry I could not travel both
And be one traveler, long I stood
And looked down as far as I could
To where it bent in the undergrowth;

Then took the other, as just as fair,
And having perhaps the better claim,
Because it was grassy and wanted wear . . .

—Robert Frost (1874-1963)
American poet

The fork in the road described so eloquently by Robert Frost in his poem "The Road Not Taken" clearly illustrates the dilemma of decision-making. As life unfolds, such fork-in-the-road decisions must be made, and no matter what path we follow, we leave behind still another path—"the road not taken."

When such a decision is made, and if the angle of the fork is not too great, companions who chose the other road may be kept in sight for some time until the ever-widening distance obscures them. But whether the roads move apart quickly or slowly, the result is the same; the experiences of the one become isolated from the experiences of the other.

At times, while moving forward on our chosen path, we may glance back with a curiosity about the road not taken and wonder, "What if?" But we made our decision and there is no turning back. We are committed to following the road we chose, and our experiences thereon will determine whether we made the right choice—or at least a good choice.

Theologically, I know many will choose a road different than mine. Some because they are less informed, others because they are more informed. And their road to them is as real as mine is to me. It would be foolish and presumptuous of me to believe that this work has laid out the one true path that everyone should follow, or that anyone should follow. But even though I realize no individual or school of thought can corner the market on truth, I cannot help but believe that my path is appropriate, at least for me, since its direction was determined by both the collective knowledge of humankind and by my own sensitivities.

Be that as it may, there is no argument that the findings of scholarship have raised perplexing questions—questions that have not been fully answered. These unresolved questions, with their serious overtones, will not bring aid and comfort. But as I stipulated early on, this work seeks only to create a framework of knowledge, a starting point for discussion. One must continue to wrestle with these mysteries and perhaps, along with many others, help lend perspective to these troublesome insights. Of course, some answers rest far into the future. For the present, we must avoid relying on simplistic answers or, as has happened, try to put new wine into old wineskins. All too often, our fear of the stark truth has led us to denial. Even some Christian scholars, in an attempt to salvage traditional beliefs, have tried to force square pegs into round holes—an attempt to preserve the foundation of a religious system badly shaken by the continuous jackhammer impact of evolving knowledge.

Lovers of truth must find their own way through the maze of knowledge and spirit. You and God must touch in your own way. Any outside authority such as the state, the Church, the Bible, our peers, or parental influence may point us in the right or wrong direction. But, ultimately, we are responsible for the direction we take. In the quest for truth, there can be no substitute for personal perseverance. If, after examining the evidence, we adopt beliefs that conflict with "the powers that be," we must summon the strength to keep faith with our growing awareness. From an historical perspective, we will be in good company. Some may accuse us of arrogance, especially if we choose to adopt beliefs that modify those of our parents, the Church, or the Bible. But we must stay true to the course, our chosen road.

The success of this quest will depend upon the maturity, honesty, courage, and resolve of the seeker. Such human traits are essential for this journey. While it may be fulfilling, it will also be difficult and painful.

Pain is likely whenever we are forced to reexamine and, perhaps, change our belief systems. When one is separated from one's security blanket, emotional pain results. I suppose it wouldn't be so difficult if the pain were swift and brief, but this is not the case. The personal struggle for growth involves long-term doubt, anguish, and turmoil and requires courage to retreat from the familiar and comfortable answers of the herd. But there can be no other way, for change is essential to a vibrant existence. Without change there is stagnation and, ultimately, decay and death. A contemporary poem entitled "Change" expresses this concept powerfully:

> *if you stare at one*
> *corner of the world*
> *for too long your eyes*
> *may get stuck*
> *glued to that land of*
> *repetition, seeing no*
> *new colors and*
> *hearing no new songs*
> *your mind dancing*
> *to the echoes of dullness*
> *and crying as it*
> *reaches its lonely hands out*
> *for change[1]*

The key to renewal and growth, according to Professor John S. Dunne,* is the "seeking and finding" we experience at each new stage of life: infancy, childhood, adolescence, adulthood, and maturity. This is true, Dunne says, if we perceive our lives as a journey for discovery, and if we expect each new plateau not merely to repeat what we know, but to give us new insights and new perceptions.[2] Similarly, noted psychologist Dr. Carl R. Rogers† states:

John S. Dunne (1929-), ordained to Catholic priesthood in 1954, is professor of theology at Notre Dame (1969-); he was Riggs Professor of Theology, Yale University, 1972-1973.

† Carl R. Rogers (1902-1987) was a psychologist and author. He received his Ph.D. from Columbia University and attended Union Theological Seminary, New York.

> Life at its best, is a flowing, changing process in which
> nothing is fixed . . . When I am thus able to be in process,
> it is clear that there can be no closed system of beliefs, no
> unchanging set of principles which I hold. Life is guided
> by a changing understanding of and interpretation of my
> experience. It is always in process of becoming.[3]

When serious moments of doubt ensue, we must search deep within ourselves to discover the great reservoirs of faith. Indeed, in order to continue our journey successfully we will need a stronger faith than previously held because all of the props and security of traditional Christianity will be gone. Forever lost will be the absolute assurance of a "divine" Jesus or an all-authoritative Bible. Instead, we will have to struggle to discover how God has worked through the human dimension of Jesus, Bible, and Church, as well as through the other unfolding disciplines of the world. And there will be times when we long for the warm shelter of the "old-time religion" in which simple, unquestionable answers soothed the troubled soul. But we cannot return to that system any more than we can abandon the road we have chosen to take; one cannot return to that other easier-seeming path.

Our chosen byway may also lead to feelings of isolation as we discover that the most cherished and accepted religious doctrines are no longer attuned to our evolving level of awareness. We also will find that our ability to relate to the system and the people that nurtured us will substantially diminish, not only because we are different, but because they cannot accept or control our "difference." The seeker's fate is well presented by the words of Kahlil Gibran*:

> Said the Eye one day, "I see beyond these valleys a
> mountain veiled with blue mist. Is it not beautiful?"
> The Ear listened, and after listening intently awhile,
> said, "But where is any mountain? I do not hear it."
> Then the Hand spoke and said, "I am trying in vain
> to feel it or touch it, and I can find no mountain."

Kahlil Gibran (1883-1931) was a Lebanese poet, philosopher, and artist. He is best known for his classic masterpiece The Prophet, published in 1923.

And the Nose said, "There is no mountain, I cannot smell it."

Then the Eye turned the other way, and they all began to talk together about the Eye's strange delusion. And they said, "Something must be the matter with the Eye."

Still, we will find the rewards of our journey are commensurate with the trials endured. We will feel alive as never before. As we become the *eye* of our spiritual quest, we will also perceive a reality beyond the superficial one surrounding us. No longer will we be fettered by religious dogma and mind conformity. Instead, like a bird on the wing, we will soar into open skies, above the mediocrity of human invention, toward ever brighter and more meaningful insights of faith. This will be possible only if we allow the continuing light of truth to illuminate our minds, and if we take seriously the implications and responsibilities of love.

For myself, I am grateful for the journey thus far. It has not been easy, but that is what has made it special and valuable to me. I am also indebted to my Christian heritage, without which I could not have made this pilgrimage. Nor do I know what lies ahead, except to feel deeply confident, as echoed in these concluding words from "The Road Not Taken":

> *I shall be telling this with a sigh*
> *Somewhere ages and ages hence:*
> *Two roads diverged in a wood, and I—*
> *I took the one less traveled by,*
> *And that has made all the difference.*

Appendix 1

Biblical Criticism

Before we explore the findings of biblical criticism, a few disclaimers are warranted in order to prevent false impressions.

First, biblical scholars do not unanimously agree on all the issues. On the contrary, great differences of opinion prevail, notably between fundamentalist and nonfundamentalist scholars. But this writing will not project fundamentalist/evangelical teachings since they are not considered a cogent, objective, educational discipline by mainstream—both secular and religious—academic institutions. In fact, except for fundamentalist colleges and seminaries, no major institutions of higher learning rely on fundamentalist scholarship as a basis for religious studies. More than any other group, they are perceived as lacking commitment to the essential principles of analytic investigation. Too often, "truth" is determined by whether or not it conforms to the Holy Writ. In fairness, it must be noted that no scholar in any field of study is free of bias. But this bias becomes insurmountable when it becomes the driving force in the investigator's procedure. By virtue of this fact, the material presented herein will reflect the knowledge issued and accepted by the widest spectrum of educators associated with higher education.

Second, there are many reputable scholars, both Christian and non-Christian, who, insofar as is humanly possible, objectively pursue the quest for truth. Unfortunately, many of these scholars have been unfairly perceived as anti-Christian solely because their findings have not always harmonized with traditional beliefs. Regardless of what Christians may think, however, it is the objective pursuit of truth that makes the findings of these literary critics uniquely valuable. Such would be the case in any field of study. This is not to imply that the findings of biblical criticism are flawless. As with any investigative discipline mistakes are inevitable, and the process of refinement, ongoing.

Finally, due to the numerous findings and subdivisions of

biblical criticism, it is not possible in this short space to be inclusive of all aspects. Therefore, my efforts will be limited to the basic methods of this discipline and those findings that I believe will be of most interest to the reader.

Biblical criticism consists of several scholarly and scientific analytical processes which include: (1) source criticism, (2) textual criticism, (3) historical criticism (already discussed in Chapter V and therefore not addressed in detail here), (4) form criticism, and (5) redaction criticism. Some of the methods and findings of these investigative disciplines will be examined (primarily with regard to NT writing).

Another important and emerging fator in understanding the NT is the method of midrash—the Jewish tradition dictating that everything to be venerated in the present must somehow be connected with a sacred moment in the past. For example, the power of God working through Moses, seen in the parting of the waters (the Red Sea) when the Hebrews escaped from Egypt, is reapplied to ongoing events in Jewish history. It later appears in the saga of Joshua when the waters of the Jordan River are parted. Elijah was also said to have parted the waters of the Jordan River. The midrash tradition continues into the NT, when Jesus enters the Jordan River to be baptized, although it is not the waters that are parted, but the heavens themselves. The implications of midrash on our understanding of the Bible are enormous. This subject is well-covered by the 1994 publication *Resurrection: Myth or Reality?* by Bishop John Shelby Spong.

Source Criticism

Source criticism is concerned with the written sources used by the Gospel writers to develop their works. The following are the most important and most widely-accepted conclusions from source critics.

The Gospel Authors. The majority of scholars agree it is unlikely that any of the Gospels (Matthew, Mark, Luke, and John) were written by Jesus' disciples or eyewitnesses to his ministry. The names of the original authors are unknown and may never be determined. It is believed, for example, that the Gospel of Mark (like the other Gospels) originally circulated anonymously. In the second century it became important to give authority to the Gospels, and so this Gospel was attributed to John Mark, a companion of Paul (mentioned in Acts 12:12, 25; 15:37, 39).

The Synoptic Gospels. It is popular to speak of the four Gospels as Matthew, Mark, Luke, and John. But, since the 1780s, three of these books—Matthew, Mark, and Luke—have been called the "synoptic" Gospels (from the Greek *synoptikos*, "seeing the whole together") as they relate very similar accounts of Jesus' ministry.[1] From this it is obvious that Matthew, Mark, and Luke shared the same sources. The Book of John, on the other hand, is strikingly different. It refers to few of the events recorded in the other Gospels. The writing style and language in John also contrast markedly with those in the other three books. For biblical scholars studying and reconstructing the life and ministry of Jesus, the books of Matthew, Mark, and Luke are the major focal points.

The Priority of Mark. Source studies indicate Mark was the first of the Gospels written and became the basis for the writings of Matthew and Luke. That is, the authors of Matthew and Luke used the Gospel of Mark as a primary source for writing their Gospels. This is evident from a careful cross-analysis of these three books. Of the 661 verses in Mark, 637 reappear in Matthew and Luke (51 percent in Matthew, 53 percent in Luke).[2] The remaining content of Matthew and Luke comes from another source.

The Q Source. Other segments of Matthew and Luke not in Mark are so similar they appear to have been drawn from another common source. This unknown source is commonly called *Q*, from the German *quelle*, "a source." These findings are the basis of the classic "Two-Source Hypothesis," which maintains that two sources, Mark and Q, were the primary sources used in composing Matthew and Luke. While other theories have been advanced, this one remains the most popular among source scholars. Other possibilities could be considered, but would be of interest to only a select few.

It is further believed that the Gospels were composed between A.D. 70 and A.D. 100.

Textual Criticism

Many people assume that our modern English-language Bibles are simply translations of the original NT books. This cannot be true as we do not possess, nor have we ever possessed, any of these books since the time of the early Christians. They were lost or destroyed early on. What we do possess are copies of these books, most of them incomplete and several times removed from the originals. Over the centuries, early editions were translated, copied, and recopied by different people throughout the known world.

Textual criticism tries to uncover, with the highest attainable degree of certainty, what the authors of the original NT wrote. Yet, how can this be achieved without the original writings?

The task is made even more difficult because our partial and complete Greek-language translations of the NT manuscripts total nearly 5,500 and *none* of these agree with each other.[3] Consequently, if we examined twenty Greek translations of Matthew, we would probably not find two of them identical throughout even a single chapter.[4] Not one of them contains a complete text identical to any other document. We then have to ask, which of the nearly 5,500 translations and which of the scriptural passages within these manuscripts most authentically reproduce the original NT writings?

To answer these and similar questions, a complex process of study is needed. Each manuscript must be carefully analyzed and compared with the others to determine which are the most accurate renderings, truest to the original documents. Hopefully, the result will be the most authentic reproduction of what the NT authors intended. This is the painstaking task of textual criticism.

Textual criticism may begin with the scientific physical examination of the manuscripts, apart from their contents. The material on which the manuscripts are written, the arrangement of pages and columns, the styles of handwriting, the scholia (or marginal notes), and even the ink, can help researchers determine the date and sometimes even the places of origin.[5]

Even more revealing is the meticulous inspection of the manuscript's content. By painstaking cross analysis, scholars seek to discover which of many and divergent early readings most closely resemble the writings of the original NT, and which of these works have added to or subtracted from the original text. Even though we do not possess any of the original writings for comparison, a third-century manuscript would carry more credibility as reflecting what the original stated than, say, a seventh-century manuscript (all things being equal). In reconstructing word by word these secondary NT documents, textual critics must identify both *accidental* errors of translation and *intentional* changes made within later manuscripts. As they detect these errors and changes, the critics move closer to identifying the text of the original documents.

While some of these changes may have been minor or inconsequential, any modification of these early texts could significantly alter their meaning and dramatically affect our understanding of the Christian faith. The Gospel of Mark provides a serious instance where the later copied editions do not square with the earlier editions. That is, the later versions of Mark have been tampered with and revised by human hands.

Scholars believe, for example, that in the original version of Mark, no Resurrection appearances existed. Virtually all critics agree that they were added to Mark's account in the late second century. Their judgment is based on the fact that the oldest biblical manuscripts, including the *Codex Vaticanus* and the *Codex Sinaiticus* (two of our most reliable sources), finish Mark's Gospel at 16:8 and do not have the expanded version (16:9-20) of the Resurrection. Thus, when the Revised Standard Version (RSV) of the Bible first appeared in 1952, the Resurrection (Mark 16:9-20) had been removed from the main text and reduced to footnotes.

One of the most significant corruptions of a NT passage is in the text of 1 John 5:7-8, in which the early manuscripts were rewritten in such a way as to explicitly define the concept of the Trinity. Here is how it happened.

In A.D. 400 a Latin translation of the Bible called the Vulgate was produced by Jerome.* An estimated 8,000 copies were eventually made and circulated over many years. In the *early* copies of the Vulgate, the scriptural passage in question (1 John 5:7-8) reads:

> There are three which bear witness, the spirit and the water and the blood, and the three are one.

In the *later* editions of the Vulgate, the passage was changed to read:

> There are three which bear witness on Earth, the spirit and the water and the blood, and these three are one in Christ Jesus: and there are three who bear witness in heaven, the Father, the Word, and the Spirit, and these three are one.[6]

---

* *St. Jerome (A.D. 347-420), a biblical scholar, was one of the first theologians to be called a Doctor of the Christian church.*

Here, then, is a new interpretation and expansion of the earlier text to include the concept of the Trinity. This rendering could not have been part of the original text of 1 John because the Greek manuscripts and versions *preceding* the Vulgate do not include it, nor do the writings of Jerome, Augustine, and other church notables. According to the world-famous scholar Bruce Metzger,* this expanded version of the Trinity was concocted, as it did not appear in manuscripts of the Latin Vulgate before about A.D 800.[7] Since not even the early versions of the Vulgate have this embellished rendition, and it is only in the later editions that the Trinitarian concept suddenly appears, it is clearly an addition to, and an alteration of, the earlier versions. (My personal theory is that this Trinitarian rewrite is the result of what transpired at the Council of Chalcedon when, in A.D. 451, the Church officially finalized the doctrine of the Trinity. The corruption of 1 John occurred after that event and is, perhaps, the work of an overly zealous monk who sought to bring this scripture into line with the newly proclaimed doctrine.)

Unfortunately, this seriously altered passage is but one of many that made its way into the popular 1611 King James Version (KJV) of the Bible.† which for almost four centuries has been regarded as the infallible word of God. Despite its perennial popularity, the KJV contains numerous inaccuracies, as it is based on the work of the famed scholar Erasmus.‡ He relied upon the Latin Vulgate, translating this text into Greek in 1518. His version contains readings which have never been found in any known Greek manuscript. Although subsequent editors made corrective alterations in Erasmus' text, it nevertheless remained flawed. This blemished rendition became the popular and enduring version of

---

Bruce Metzger is Professor of NT Language and Literature at Princeton Theological Seminary. In his 1992 publication The Text of the New Testament (Its Transmission, Corruption, and Restoration), *Metzger provides an excellent account of the transcribing and transmission of the NT, and also provides information concerning recent advances in NT studies.*

†*In this translation the verses are reversed and slightly modified from what we read in the Vulgate, but the overblown description of the Trinity remains obvious.*

‡*Desiderius Erasmus (1466-1536) was a Dutch Roman Catholic humanist who was ordained in 1492.*

the Greek Testament. It came to be known as the *Textus Receptus of the NT and was the basis for the later King James Version.*[8]

The KJV had no serious rival until the 1952 publication of the RSV which was based on earlier and more accurate texts than the *Textus Receptus.* The RSV corrected, for example, the overblown Trinitarian passage of 1 John. For centuries, this passage and many others were passed off as unquestionable truth with the claim that the Bible is inerrant. Only through analytical study, such as textual criticism, can such corruptions be detected.

This is not to suggest that such alterations or additions have no value, but they were certainly *not* what the authors of the original NT wrote. While textual criticism cannot determine the precise authenticity of all biblical writing, through careful comparative analysis it can verify some content as genuine and reveal other content as altered or added later.

In recent times, both the KJV and the RSV have been revised. In 1979 the *New* King James Version (NKJV) was upgraded through the efforts of more than 130 biblical scholars representing a broad cross section of *evangelical* Christendom. In 1989 the *New* Revised Standard Version (NRSV) made its appearance through the *ecumenical* efforts of scholars affiliated with various Protestant denominations, several Roman Catholic members, an Eastern Orthodox member, and a Jewish member who served in the OT section.

These two translations once again illustrate the differing attitudes toward biblical criticism. It is apparent that fundamentalist scholars continue to undermine the basic principles of objective inquiry by allowing their religious presuppositions to influence their investigative procedures. Evidence the fact that scholars working on the NKJV were required to sign a statement of faith declaring their belief that the Scriptures in their entirety are the uniquely inspired word of God, free from error in their original form! And, in order to avoid any disharmony between past and present biblical revision, they again have relied on the inaccurate Greek text *Textus Receptus.* Thus, the NKJV has retained the exaggerated version of the Trinity already examined in 1 John 5:7-8.

In contrast, the ecumenical group of scholars working on the NRSV improved their translation based on significant advances from the discovery and interpretation of documents in the Semitic languages, information from the Dead Sea text of Isaiah and Habakkuk and other Hebrew Scriptures and earlier Greek manuscripts of the NT. As a consequence, they once again had no choice but to footnote the Trinitarian concept described in 1 John. To do otherwise would fly in the face of their investigative findings.

The RSV/NRSV also deleted from the main text (and put in a footnote) the long-familiar story in which Jesus chided the persecutors of a woman charged with adultery: "He that is without sin among you, let him cast a stone at her" (John 8:1-11). The story was extracted because it is not found in any NT manuscripts prior to those produced at the end of the fourth century, and no Church father before this time refers to it. The account apparently was added to the Scriptures about 300 years after the Gospel of John was written; therefore, it does not appear to be an authentic part of the original text.[9]

In spite of these valiant efforts to produce a sharper rendition of the original writings, however, the editors of the NRSV did not emerge untarnished. Their new version reinstated the Resurrection story (Mark 16:9-20) which, as you will remember, had been deleted in the 1952 version. At least they managed to footnote the doubtful credibility of the Resurrection account. But if the account is doubtful, why was it reinstated into the main text? This editorial swing is probably an attempt to placate disgruntled Christians who have consistently criticized the RSV's numerous changes.

The Five Gospels—The Scholars Version (SV). In 1985 the Jesus Seminar, a distinguished group of biblical scholars, reassessed the gospels, including the recently discovered Gospel of Thomas. They used their collective expertise to determine the authenticity of more than 1,500 sayings attributed to Jesus. Unlike other English translations, the Scholars Version (published 1993) is free of ecclesiastical and religious control. The SV is authorized by scholars. According to the Seminar, no more than 20 percent of the sayings attributed to Jesus were spoken by him. A color-coded system is used to help the reader distinguish between what Jesus probably said as opposed to the sayings that have been embellished or created by his followers, or borrowed from common lore. The work rigorously explores the historical and literary factors behind the Seminar's findings.

The work is interesting and refreshing. A good friend of mine, however, brought to my attention the negative aspect of such an endeavor. He argues vigorously that such a stilted portrayal of the historical words of Jesus places too much emphasis on history. As he and others have correctly pointed out, the Bible is not solely a historical document—it is more than history. It seeks to convey truth that goes beyond factual proofs.

I concur with this criticism; such thinking conforms to what I have already demonstrated in the Resurrection story. Nevertheless, if Christians are to move beyond their traditional understanding of Scripture, such graphic (although perhaps sterile) disclosures are necessary. The key must be in balancing the cold realities of scholarship with the spiritual realities of faith.

Form Criticism

An important development in biblical research called form criticism emerged in Germany after World War I. The Gospels as we know them developed from earlier written sources, but form critics contend that even before these written sources there must have been an oral tradition about Jesus' life and ministry. Form criticism explores this oral tradition behind the Gospels and the system for transmitting the stories about Jesus from person to person and generation to generation. These oral transmissions are of primary interest to form scholars since they preserved and perpetuated the story of Jesus, his life, and ministry until translated into written form. When Christianity began, the first verbal accounts of Jesus circulated as independent units, but they were not transmitted in a chronological order (the sole exception being the Passion narrative, Christ's suffering and death). Mark was the first to place these early accounts of Jesus into a logical sequence.

The first concern of form critics is the distinctive forms taken by these early verbal accounts of Jesus prior to the writing of Gospels. Some of these forms were: (1) the *pronouncement story,* a brief narrative describing an encounter between Jesus and one or more persons which typically ends with an inspired saying or sayings; (2) the *miracle story,* which has as its principal point a miraculous act of Jesus; and (3) the *parable,* a short fictitious story, using characters or events seemingly drawn from real life, that demonstrates a moral attitude or religious principle.

A more important concern of form critics is the *history* of these spoken accounts of Jesus—how they originated, developed, and evolved during early Christianity. In the words of Norman Perrin:

> Form critics have been able to show that the sayings and stories in the synoptic Gospels have a long history of transmission in the tradition of the Church, during which they have been changed and developed in all kinds of ways.[10]

Examples of this kind of change are the parables of Jesus. Before they were written, the parables were arranged by the primitive Church under specific headings with invented settings. In other words, the "historical" backdrops into which the parable was placed were modified, expanded, and always related to concrete situations in which the Church found itself. Joachim Jeremias* notes that the Book of Luke, for example, preserves the original historical setting in which Jesus presented the parable of the lost sheep. According to the parable, a shepherd discovers that one of his 100 sheep has gone astray and promptly leaves the other 99 to seek out the lost one; he rejoices when he finds it. In Luke's portrayal, Jesus tells this parable as a defense against the charges made by his opponents, the Pharisees, who accused him of mingling and eating with sinners. By these words, Jesus justified his involvement with sinners (Luke 15:1-7).

In contrast, in Matthew 18 this parable is presented in a far different framework. The disciples of Jesus are asking who will be the greatest in the kingdom of heaven. Jesus, in response, speaks about the humility of a child. He illustrates to his disciples the need for such humility as the prerequisite for entering the kingdom of heaven. Jesus then emphasizes the importance of children and turns to warnings about deceiving children. To finalize the importance of this teaching, Jesus goes on to tell the parable, this time portraying the lost sheep not as a lost sinner but as a lost child.

Here we can see that the setting and the focus of the parable has changed. The parable as presented by Matthew is now couched in a different framework than that of Luke; the historical backdrop and meaning of the parable have been modified to meet the immediate needs of the author, the Church, or both.[11]

Many realized soon after its inception in the early 1920s that form criticism could shake the very foundations of NT beliefs. As the findings of form criticism were revealed, it became apparent that the possibility of knowing Jesus historically was suddenly open to question. What did Jesus actually say or do? The reliability of Scripture would be in doubt if the early Church not only *interpreted* the traditional accounts of Jesus but *created* them.

Joachim Jeremias (1900-) is a German scholar, former professor of NT at Gottingen University in West Germany. He received the medal award for Biblical Studies, British Academy, 1958.

Such was the belief of the two most influential form critics, Martin Dibelius* and Rudolph Bultmann.† These scholars concur that the NT accounts of miracles performed by Jesus were largely imaginative notions conceived by the Gentile churches. Both similarly identified most of the Scriptural stories about Jesus as myths, legends, or tales, and believed they were created by the early church, in some instances, to credit the origin of later beliefs and practices to Jesus' ministry. These two investigators were also skeptical about the authenticity of many of the statements made by Jesus in the Scriptures, as well as about the parables.[12]

Many Christians charge that form criticism fails to take into account the effect of Jesus' words and deeds on those followers, who, after his death, formed the nucleus of the early Christian community. They contend that these eyewitnesses surely would have preserved and corrected important information about Jesus during the formative years when his teachings were being transmitted, interpreted, and committed to record. Some attacks on form criticism were made to keep the teachings of Jesus from being obscured by the dust of scholarship.

Nevertheless, form criticism raises a number of valid points, and many serious questions remain unanswered. As W.D. Davies‡ reflects, the findings of form critics raised some skepticism about the historical validity of much of the NT. Still, their research significantly made clear how the early Christian churches, because of their beliefs and circumstances, modified some of the stories and sayings now recorded in the Gospels.[13] The 1993 publication of *The Five Gospels* (SV), supports this line of thinking.

Redaction Criticism

Following World War II, a new research procedure known as *redaction criticism*, from the word *redactor* (editor), was developed.

Martin Dibelius (1883-1947) was Professor of NT Theology at Heidelberg University (Germany). His work greatly advanced the study of form criticism.
† Rudolf Karl Bultmann (1884-1976) was a German theologian who advocated demythologizing the New Testament.
‡ William David Davies (1911-) was Professor of Biblical Theology at Duke University, 1950-1955; professor of religion at Princeton University, 1955-1959; and Edward Robinson Professor of Biblical Theology at Union Theological Seminary, N.Y., 1959-1966.

Redaction criticism distinguishes between the traditional written source materials of the Gospel writer and the author's redaction (editing, rewriting) of that material. It also seeks to determine the author's religious views as implied by his redaction.

One way to achieve this goal is to compare the ways in which the Gospel writers treated the same source material. If, for example, the author of Matthew based his writing on the earlier Book of Mark, what changes, revisions, additions, and omissions did he make when putting together his Gospel, and why? Why did he rearrange the writings of Mark or put them into a different historical setting? Why did the writer expand a passage or change the sequence of events? How are the author's personal beliefs about Jesus reflected in the way he presents the material? To illustrate the methods and findings of redaction criticism, let's focus on the last question: Matthew's personal beliefs about Jesus and how they affected his writing.

We know that 51 percent of Mark was reproduced in Matthew. Is there anything conspicuous about what Matthew chose not to recopy from Mark's Gospel? Prominently apparent is Matthew's editorial eagerness to safeguard Jesus' character. He portrays Jesus as perfect goodness and divine power, and declines to include any verses from Mark which might detract from this image. To that end, Matthew excluded references to Jesus' harshness toward the leper (Mark 1:43); to Jesus' anger (Mark 3:5; 10:14); to Jesus' recognition by evil spirits and demons, probably on the grounds he was accused of being in league with the Devil (Mark 1:24; 3:11); to the charge of insanity against Jesus (Mark 3:21); and to Jesus' effort to walk past his disciples who were distressed on the sea (Mark 6:48).[14]

As further example, Matthew was also concerned about associating Jesus with the *magical* aspects of Mark's story regarding the woman with the hemorrhage (Mark 5:25-34). Mark tells us that the woman was healed immediately after touching Jesus' garments. Matthew, however, changes the story to have the actual healing occur, not upon her touch of his garment, but upon his verbal approval of her (Matt. 9:20-22). As the German scholar E. Kasemann observes:

> The idea that the garments of the miracle worker communicate divine power, which leaps forth and is capable of healing, is a vulgar Hellenistic notion that appears in exactly this way in the account of Peter's

healing shadow and Paul's miraculous handkerchief (Acts 5:15; 19:12) and later shapes the cult of relics. Matthew corrects this crudely magical view by making the cure take place no longer through the touching of the garment . . . but through Jesus' word of power.[15]

Matthew is unique not only in how he handled Mark's material, but what he brought to his writing concerning Jesus. One of his editorial goals is to show Jesus in harmony with the OT as part of the divine plan. He seems bent on convincing the Jews that Jesus is the Messiah. Since most Jews had a high regard for OT prophecy, Matthew sought to bring Jesus in line with it at every opportune point—sixteen times in all.

Unfortunately, in his exuberance to depict Jesus as the fulfillment of OT prophecy, he found prophecies where *no* prophecies were intended. The flight to Egypt story (Matt. 2:13-15) is a good example. Joseph took Mary and the infant Jesus and fled to Egypt to escape the wrath of King Herod, who was seeking to destroy the child. They remained in Egypt until Herod's death, then returned to Israel. "This," said the author of Matthew, "was to fulfill what the Lord [God] had spoken by the prophet, 'Out of Egypt have I called my son.'" But the OT quotation cited here which Matthew drew from Hosea 11:1 actually reads:

> When Israel was a child, I loved him, and out of Egypt
> I called my son.

This association of Israel as the son of God is also found in Exodus 4:22-23, where God instructs Moses:

> And you shall say to Pharaoh, "Thus says the Lord,
> Israel is my first born son . . . let my son go . . ."

Obviously, these OT verses are not prophecies and have nothing to do with Jesus or his flight to Egypt. They merely describe how God delivered Israel from the bondage of the Egyptian pharaoh.

Another example of how Matthew alludes to prophecy where none exists is seen in this same chapter (Matt. 2:16-18) when Herod, in an effort to assassinate Jesus, orders the slaughter of all male children aged two and under in Bethlehem and surrounding regions. Matthew states:

Then was fulfilled what was spoken by the prophet Jeremiah: "A voice was heard in Ramah, wailing and loud lamentation, Rachel weeping for her children, she refused to be consoled, because they were no more."

This verse from Jeremiah that Matthew quoted was not a prophecy, nor was it in any way related to Herod's slaying of the children. Jeremiah's words simply describe the mood of the people of Jerusalem as they were led away to captivity by the Babylonians. As they moved sadly toward an alien land, they passed Ramah, the place where Rachel lay buried (1 Sam. 10:2). The verse portrayed Rachel as weeping, even in the tomb, over the fate that had befallen her people. Clearly, Matthew served his own purpose by taking an unrelated text in the OT and calling it a prophecy where no prophecy was intended.

This overriding desire to persuade readers, principally Jewish readers, that Jesus was the Anointed One of God, would also explain why Matthew catered to the Jewish reverence for law. The following quote, attributed to Jesus, is unique to Matthew (5:17); it is not found in the other Gospels:

Think not that I have come to abolish the law and the prophets; I have come not to abolish them but to fulfill them.

Did Matthew attribute these words to Jesus in order to link him to this most crucial element of Jewish life (as many scholars believe) or did Jesus actually make this opportune statement? Also, in Matthew 12:5-7, the author injected a statement not found in Mark. He justified Jesus' breaking the Sabbath by bringing it back in line with Jewish law.[16]

Further Reflection

In the wake of biblical criticism, scholars found it impossible to believe that the Bible was ever intended to convey infallibility. And how can we now accept the Bible as definitive when every type of scholarly inquest verifies that our Bible has undergone significant changes from its inception? Even if we were fortunate enough to possess the original Gospels, they could not convey the actual words of Jesus since there is little doubt he taught in Aramaic. The original Gospels were written in Greek, the international language of the day—a translation from the very beginning. And even before the authors of the NT received the stories about Jesus, there is strong evidence to indicate that such materials were altered and even possibly invented by early Christians. Further compounding the issue of transmission are the Gospel writers themselves, who took this material and retained, omitted, revised, and rearranged what they chose. All of this, of course, was followed by centuries of copied editions which were translated and retranslated, copied and recopied by different people in different places at different times throughout the world. Saint Jerome complained that some translations were not versions, but perversions.

Moreover, we can no longer assume that biblical language and concepts such as the Virgin Birth, the Lord's Supper, or the Resurrection are unique to Christian thought. It appears that some of these ideas have been directly borrowed from the culture and religions of that time.

To compensate for the glaring discrepancy between traditional trust in the Bible's absolute authority and the findings of biblical criticism, some scholars sought refuge behind irrational theories. One such theory, still popular today, is that although the Bible in hand is no longer inerrant, we can rest assured that the original writings (which conveniently no one possesses) were inerrant! Herein is another pseudo-intellectual loophole of convenience. This line of thinking serves only to dupe the unsuspecting masses and to help sustain the wishful thinking of Christians who are unable or unwilling to face the reality of the situation.

Still other Christians will acknowledge that the Bible has been on the bumpy road to change, but they see these changes as reflecting only what God really intended: "The way our Bible is now is *correct,* or God wouldn't have let it be the way it is now." I have heard this illogic before. Isn't this argument identical to what Christians have always believed about their Bible anyway? Pick a century! Pick a time! Pick a Bible! Which version? Which verse? Which words? When was the Bible, any Bible, not considered the ultimate word of God by its followers?

Reflect on the consequences of such an assumption. We've tortured because we believed every word; we've killed because we believed every word; we've put people into chains (literally and emotionally) because we believed every word; we've stood against knowledge and promoted ignorance because we believed every word; we've alienated friends and family because we believed every word. And now all we know for certain is that it is wrong to blindly follow the Bible because, ironically, we now know that the Bible's message on certain matters is less than acceptable, if not repugnant.

Adding to the confusion is that today we don't even have a consensus on what truly constitutes the Bible *as a whole*. Without detouring into the history of biblical development, we must ponder the fact that each religious body has its own canon (the official list of books of the Bible accepted by the "church" as genuine and sacred). The Catholic Bible, for example, has twelve additional books (known as the Apocrypha) not presently considered as part of the Protestant Bible (canon). This discrepancy occurred during the Protestant Reformation when it was decided that the Apocrypha did not measure up in spiritual value to other biblical literature. For centuries these books were considered to be God's word (and still are for the Catholic Church) but since the sixteenth century, at least for Protestants, they simply have become an unimportant and ignored group of also-rans.* Thus, for what has turned out to be almost half of Christendom, these once-sacred books slid into oblivion! In short, we have two Bibles: one with and one without the Apocrypha. Which one reflects God's intention?

Not only do Catholics and Protestants (which make up the Western church) disagree on what constitutes the canon, but the Greek, Russian, Armenian, Coptic, Ethiopian, and Syrian groups (which make up the Eastern church) also disagree on this issue. In fact, hardly any of these groups agree with one another on what should comprise the canon as a whole. Moreover, the Ethiopian Orthodox Church also includes in its canon 1 Enoch and Jubilees, writings considered as pseudepigraphal (not regarded canonical, inspired, or worthy of a place in religious use) by other religious institutions.[17] Now, which of these biblical variations reflects God's intention? Which is the "real" canon?

Of course, aside from the Apocrypha and the additional books of the Ethiopian church, there is widespread agreement on the NT canon and remaining books of the OT canon. This will mislead Protestants into thinking there is really no problem here since what they consider to be the canon is already included in other expanded canons. But let's not miss the point: Whatever Bible

---

* *In recent years some Protestant Bibles have included the Apocrypha, but only as a non-biblical supplement.*

we follow or don't follow does not tell us which Bible we should follow. We generally accept the Bible of our tradition and then view it as an unquestionable authority, not caring or even knowing that one Christian's sacred writing is not necessarily another Christian's sacred writing!

Appendix 2
Biblical Fallibility

The following information gives a quick scan of the issue of biblical fallibility. The truth is, however, an entire book could be written on this subject alone.

In the OT there is evidence of superstition and legend, such as the popular fable in which God is said to open the mouth of Balaam's ass (the world's first talking donkey). Thereafter, the two are shown having a conversation (Num. 22:28).

The Bible also contains what might be called morally unworthy passages.* In one of these, the prophet Samuel, who purportedly speaks to and for God, orders King Saul to destroy the Amalekites, saying ". . . do not spare them, but kill both man and woman, infant and suckling, ox and sheep, camel and ass" (1 Sam. 15:3). King Saul obeyed but spared Agag, the king of the Amalekites, and some of the animals. According to the passage God grew angry with Saul since he disobeyed the command to commit genocide and declared, through Samuel, that the Kingdom of Israel would be torn away from Saul. Meanwhile, Samuel obediently takes a sword and hacks Agag to death (1 Sam. 15:33).

The Bible's fallibility also is revealed by its antiquated world view. Various concepts portray a flat Earth, the sun revolving around the Earth and a three-story universe in which the Earth is between heaven and hell. Of course, these beliefs simply reflect the scientific limitations of the day.

Comparison of biblical material with other historical sources also reveals some possible discrepancies in the Scripture. An example is the statement by Luke (2:1) that Quirinius, governor of Syria, conducted a census when Jesus was born prior to Herod's

---

* Such passages are "morally unworthy" only in the context of our present understanding of morality, of course. When originally written, such concepts merely reflected the accepted values and belief systems of their time.

death. The noted Jewish historian Josephus,* states that this census was conducted several years after Herod's death.[1]

Contradictions within the four Gospels in relating the same account also undermine the claim for biblical inerrancy. A careful cross-analysis of the Gospels reveals considerable harmony of thought, but also a lack of agreement among the authors as to the order in which Jesus said and did what is reported of him. While in Matthew (8:1-4) the healing of a leper is followed by the healings of Peter's mother-in-law and a crowd of people (Matt. 8:14-17), the order of these three events is reversed in Mark (1:40-45, 29-34). Similarly, in Matthew (8:23-27), the crossing of the lake and the stilling of the storm occur long before the teaching in parables, but in Mark, the teaching in parables takes place just before the crossing of the lake.[2] In addition to these discrepancies, certain parallel accounts of the same incident vary significantly from Gospel to Gospel. For example, Matthew and Luke contain conflicting genealogies for Jesus. In Matthew (1:16), Joseph is reported to be the son of Jacob, while in Luke (3:23) Joseph is called the son of Heli. These variations between the Gospels become more apparent when we examine the Resurrection accounts.

Resurrection Conflicts

The contradictions in the Gospel accounts of the Resurrection of Jesus first drew serious attention through the publication in 1777 of *Fragments from Wolfenbuttel*, edited by Gotthold Ephraim Lessing.† These excerpts, taken from a larger work written by noted Hebrew scholar Herman Samuel Reimarus (1694-1768) are described here as presented in *New Testament Disunity* by John Charlot.

Contradictions in the accounts of the Resurrection were evident to early biblical scholars. In Luke, for example, the women buy spices on the eve of the feast day to prepare Jesus' body for entombment. But in Mark, they buy the spices after the feast day.

Flavius Josephus (A.D. 37-95?) was a renowned historian of the Jews. He wrote several works including the famous Antiquities of the Jews, a history of the race from creation to the war with Rome.

† *Gotthold Ephraim Lessing (1729-1781) was a philosopher and theologian. He published fragments from a book by the free-thinking H.S. Reimarus.*

Contradicting both of these accounts is the Book of John, which says Nicodemus brought 100 pounds of spices and, with the help of Joseph of Arimathea, prepared Jesus' body for immediate entombment in accordance with Jewish law.

The descriptions of the tomb's opening also conflict. In Mark, Luke, and John, the women find the tomb open. Matthew, however, states that when the women reached the tomb it was closed and an angel appeared and opened it. In Mark and Matthew only one angel appeared; in Luke and John, two angels appeared. In each of these Gospels the angels make different statements and perform different acts, and the women's actions differ. In Matthew, Mary Magdalene is not confronted by Jesus at the tomb. But in John's account, Jesus appears to her outside the tomb. Also, in Matthew, Mary is frightened by the Resurrection phenomenon and says nothing to anyone. In John, she runs to tell the disciples. Says Herman Reimarus of the witnesses of the events, ". . . they claim to be . . . directed by the Holy Spirit, who leads them into all truth. How then can such contradictions arise among them—one that, even . . . by the most careless observation of the circumstances, would not easily be committed?"[3]

Gospel accounts of the locations where Jesus appeared after his Resurrection also conflict. Certain accounts report these appearances in Jerusalem, others in Galilee (a region of northern Israel). The number of these appearances, their order, and the persons to whom Jesus appeared also vary sharply among the Gospels. According to Reimarus, ". . . they themselves, in this way, destroy from both sides the credibility of their witness."[4]

While some of these discrepancies can be brushed aside, this disunity does not lend credence to an infallible Bible—certainly not as traditionally held.

Appendix 3

The Historical Jesus

Given the findings of biblical criticism, it was inevitable that scholars became concerned with the "historical Jesus"; that is, can the real Jesus be discerned from the Gospels? The consensus today is that the historical Jesus—the words and actions of Jesus and the real events surrounding his life—cannot be determined with precision. While we know how the author of a Gospel regarded Jesus by what he reported (and how he reported it), it is not always possible to penetrate beyond the Gospel portrayals of Jesus to Jesus himself. We cannot determine with certainty what Gospel statements about his life and career are genuine.[1]

For anyone in search of "what Jesus was really like," it may be disconcerting to learn that a bull's-eye portrait of his life is impossible. Nevertheless, we are well-informed on the nature of his ministry and the content of his teachings, even allowing for the modifications these narratives underwent before, during, and after the writing of the Gospels. The general impression of Jesus, conveyed repeatedly in the Gospels, is quite independent of historical verification of any specific words or actions. "The four Gospels," Edward Schillebeeckx* says, ". . . contain sufficient basic information about Jesus and recollections of Him in respect of his message, his attitude to life and his conduct as a whole."[2] Clearly, the ethic of Jesus demands absolute obedience to the will of God, without qualification or exception.[3] His emphasis on love, mercy, justice, compassion, and other caring attitudes is obvious. In spite of biblical imperfection, the nature of his life and ministry remain unmistakable.

There are, of course, certain Gospel portions with a high probability of historical accuracy. Critics have indicated that the

---

* *Edward Schillebeeckx (1914-) is a highly regarded Roman Catholic theologian and writer.*

Aramaic structure and expression in certain statements ascribed to Jesus greatly increases the probability of their genuineness. Historical reliability is further increased when we eliminate from the statements attributed to Jesus in the Gospels those elements reflecting the Church's post-Resurrection thinking.[4]

One final note on the historical Jesus. The treatment given herein on this very complex subject can be described as nothing less than incomplete. Numerous books and articles, by eminent scholars are available; the reader is encouraged to pursue the quest.

Appendix 4
Catholicism and the Astrolabe Mind

During the Enlightenment the Catholic Church set forth decrees forbidding the historical study of the Scriptures, the Church, and doctrines as practiced by Protestant scholars. Catholics had long been required by Church teachings to accept the inerrancy of Scripture. No Catholic would dare to suggest that Paul was not the author of Hebrews, that Matthew was not the first of the four Gospels to be written, or that the Genesis story of creation was anything but a literal, historical account. Even so, some Catholic theologians seriously questioned these presuppositions.

The Church responded in predictable fashion. In 1864 Pope Pius IX condemned modern thought in his *Syllabus of Errors.* Following him, Pope Leo XIII set forth a rigidly traditional view of biblical inspiration which denounced "liberal" theology. In 1903 he created the Pontifical Biblical Commission to monitor Catholic Bible scholarship. According to the *New Catholic Encyclopedia* (Vol. XI, p. 551) the Commission's basic purpose was, and still is, to safeguard the authority of Scripture and oversee its proper interpretation. His Successor, Pope Pius X, issued in 1907 the famous encyclical *Pascendi Dominici Gregis,* in which he condemned the entire investigative process[1] and denounced modernism as a "synthesis of all heresies."[2] Thus, through papal declarations and official pronouncements of the Pontifical Biblical Commissions, the Catholic Church stubbornly maintained that the Bible was without error. Their proclamations encouraged Catholics to ignore the findings of biblical scholars since *the Pope* was the final authority in all matters of interpretation. Not until 1943 when Pope Pius XII tendered his encyclical on biblical studies, *Divino Affante Spirit,* and with the encouraging reply of the Pontifical Biblical Commission to Cardinal Suhard in 1948, did Catholic leadership openly acknowledge the value of biblical criticism.[3]

Unfortunately, these positive gestures have even today not resulted in further freedom of expression. Scholars, priests, teachers, and writers continue to be muzzled by the Catholic hierarchy. Specifically, the Pontifical Biblical Commission and the Congregation for the Doctrine of the Faith* have prosecuted some of the most eminent Catholic scholars today. In 1979 and 1983, Father Edward Schillebeeckx of the University of Nijmegen in Holland was brought before a tribunal of the Congregation of the Doctrine of the Faith where one of his judges publicly accused him of heresy. Based on two of his controversial books—*Jesus: An Experiment in Christology,* and *Ministry: A Case for Change*—he was charged with questioning the *literal* truth of such beliefs as the Resurrection and the Virgin Birth. He also questioned the Church's position on celibacy and their stance against the ordination of women.

Another example of such persecution is that of Charles E. Curran, well-known Catholic theologian and writer. In 1986 he was ordered by the Vatican to recant his views on birth control and other sexual issues. Refusing to do so, he was dismissed in 1987 from the faculty of Catholic University of America in Washington.

The most telling moment of smothering freedom of thought and debate within the Catholic Church occurred in 1979 when it condemned one of its most eminent theologians, Hans Kung, for raising questions—first published in his controversial book *Infallible?*—concerning the doctrines of the Virgin Birth, the inerrancy of Scripture and papal infallibility. The Pope, acting on the formal recommendation of the Congregation, discharged Kung from his teaching post as head of the Department of Theology at the University of Tübingin, one of Germany's most respected schools. He was also informed that he was no longer a Catholic theologian, was not qualified to teach Catholic doctrine, and was forbidden to teach, write, or publish further.

---

* *The Congregation for the Doctrine of the Faith was originally known as the Holy Inquisition (13th century) and then termed the Holy Office in 1542. In 1965, it was renamed the Congregation for the Doctrine of Faith. The reigning Pope always resides as its official head.*

Appendix 5

The Immaculate Conception

To many, the Immaculate Conception is a marked advance for Christianity since it elevates Mary, a woman, to a high level of honor and esteem. But does this indicate new, greater respect for women by the Church? Not really. If anything, this special honor resulted from the Church's unwillingness to regard women as equals and its desire to circumvent the concept of "inherent sin." It was paramount that Mary surpass the rest of her gender since all daughters of Eve were held to be inferior to men. Their loss of virginity and conceiving/bearing children were not simply natural processes, but painful symbols of their degraded status.[1] It would not be proper for Mary, the mother of Jesus, to occupy such an inferior position.

Conveniently, then, the doctrine of the Immaculate Conception served more to protect Jesus' image than to honor Mary. Jesus had to be free from the taint of a normal two-parent procreation (hence, the Virgin Birth). Now, via the Immaculate Conception, it was possible for him to be free of sin even with one parent. Mary could conceive in purity since this doctrine declared her to be without blemish. For this reason, the Immaculate Conception was supported by numerous theologians and pious believers centuries before it became Church dogma.[2] This doctrine also explained why a woman, who under normal circumstances was considered inferior, played such a prominent role in the coming of God's only son.

The downside of this doctrine was that it led Church leaders to emphasize the importance of virginity. In time, it was suggested that a woman could escape her "inferiority" and somehow make amends for her second-class nature by accepting the virginal life, possibly becoming a nun. This was the highest level she could attain in the eyes of the Church. What greater example of self-fulfillment and esteem could there be? By remaining virgins, women would be following in Mary's footsteps. They would no longer tempt men to sin or suffer the pain of losing their virginity and bearing children.

Many women, believing, as the Bible and Church taught, that they were evil and inferior, accepted virginity as the means to deliverance. But the promise that women could gain more grace in the eyes of God by remaining chaste was an empty illusion and doomed by the very system that gave it life. For even though a woman denied her sensuality in embracing virginity, she could never overcome the Church's belief that she was a threat to men—a source of sinful contamination and a constant temptation to men. For example, heavy concealing curtains were draped around the bed of a dying nun to prevent the priest who administered the last rites from gazing upon her. Similarly, in monasteries housing nuns and priests, the sisters were not permitted to sing, lest the sound of their voices, like those of the mythical Sirens, arouse passion in the men.[3]

In short, there were three basic reasons why women, until recently, were unable to make any significant strides against the humiliating stigma assigned them by the Church. First was the pressing weight of biblical thought which, more often than not, fostered negative impressions about women, sex, and even marriage.

Second was the continuing belief of the early Church fathers and those who followed that women were biologically inferior, even those who remained virgins. This popular belief was later solidified through the writings of Thomas Aquinas.

Finally to blame was the doctrine of the Immaculate Conception. Although women attempted to emulate Mary, they could hardly succeed because she had been elevated to a position reserved only for her. Mary, at her inception, was considered free from original sin by the grace granted only to her by God.[4] She was, therefore, the world's only sinless virgin, while all other women (including virgins) were contaminated by the stigma of original sin. Men found it easy to praise Mary since she was uniquely blessed—the only woman of her kind. In contrast, they found it easy to denigrate other women since they couldn't measure up to Mary even if they remained chaste. In other words, Mary was the unstained and Holy Virgin. All other women, regardless of their sexual status, were considered normal and, therefore, inferior.

Appendix 6
Fundamentalism/Evangelicalism

Fundamentalists are Christians with a unique set of very conservative religious views and attitudes that other Christians do not have. These ultra-conservative attitudes are the product of opposition to biblical criticism, and any Christian that adheres to them, regardless of denomination, is a fundamentalist. In other words, fundamentalism is not restricted to any specific religious body. For example, we may say that the United Methodist Church is non-fundamental only because the majority of its members are not fundamentalists, but this does not mean that fundamentalists are not present within the United Methodist structure. On the contrary, they are present in significant numbers although they are not yet representative of the majority as they are, for example, in the Baptist denomination.

Following the notorious Scopes ("monkey") trial of 1925 in which a Tennessee school teacher was convicted for expounding the theory of evolution, fundamentalists were perceived by the public as too conservative and religiously unbalanced. Consequently, during the '30s and '40s the fundamentalist movement disappeared from public view and spent its time building its own institutions.

Fundamentalism re-emerged in the late 1940s, adopting the "evangelical" label—a progressive wing of the old fundamentalism that was more open to the world and church tradition. According to *The Perennial Dictionary of World Religions* (p. 244), Carl F.H. Henry signaled the beginning of this neo-evangelicalism with the publication of *Uneasy Conscience of Modern Fundamentalism* in 1947. E.J. Carnell (1919-67) was an early theologian of this new type of conservative faith.

Since the late 1940s, factions and distinctions of this division have only added to the confusion of how this movement should be defined. We now have what is called (1) the old fundamentalism (represented most visibly by South Carolina's Bob Jones University which did not admit blacks until 1971 and still forbids interracial dating), (2) the new fundamentalism (strongly led by such leaders as the Rev. Jerry Falwell, the Rev. Pat Robertson, and the Rev. Kenneth Copeland) which seeks to shed the old reputation of bigotry and cultural narrowness, and (3) evangelicals (influenced by the Rev. Billy Graham and positioned to the left of both the old and new fundamentalists).

Obviously, these conservative groups overlap in numerous ways. Consequently, almost everyone uses these terms interchangeably since they continue to be in flux and because fundamentalists and evangelicals share very similar beliefs and values. Even leaders and followers of these groups become confused when trying to categorize themselves and others in this movement (helping to explain the confusion that is also in media reports). Even so, as we have seen, distinctions to exist between these groups. It is, however, a matter more of attitude than of theology. They universally affirm, for example, the doctrine of inerrancy although different shades of meaning will exist between these religious bodies. In any case, the evangelicals (as defined herein) are more apt to tolerate a somewhat broader range of biblical interpretation and are often willing to coexist with the more moderate/liberal mainline denominations.

Notes

CHAPTER I   Absolute Authority—Tyrannical Religion

1. C. Richardson, *The Early Christian Fathers*, 119.
2. Hardie, *Christology of the Later Fathers*, 173.
3. Kahl, *The Misery of Christianity*, 33.
4. Furnish, *Theology and Ethics in Paul*, 212.
5. Evans and Hagner, *Anti-Semitism and Early Christianity*, 2; Buttrick, *The Interpreter's Bible*, 598.
6. Efroymson, Fisher, and Klenicki, *Within Context*, 6-8; Chrysostom, *The Fathers of the Church*, 68: xxxviii.
7. Grayzel, *A History of the Jews*, 269.
8. Seiferth, *Synagogue and Church in the Middle Ages*, 48.
9. Kahl, *The Misery of Christianity*, 55.
10. Ibid., 56; Grayzel, *A History of the Jews*, 273.
11. Vogt, *The Jews: A Chronicle for Christian Conscience*, 80.
12. Grayzel, *A History of the Jews*, 305.
13. Vogt, *The Jews*, 58.
14. Grayzel, *A History of the Jews*, 306.
15. P. Johnson, *A History of Christianity*, 246.
16. Seiferth, *Synagogue and Church*, 70.
17. Grayzel, *A History of the Jews*, 312.
18. Kahl, *The Misery of Christianity*, 56-57.
19. Synan, *The Popes and the Jews in the Middle Ages*, 129.
20. Grayzel, *A History of the Jews*, 345.
21. Lea, *A History of the Inquisition of the Middle Ages*, III: 379.
22. Grayzel, *A History of the Jews*, 345.
23. Gail, *The Three Popes*, 186-87.
24. Kahl, *The Misery of Christianity*, 58.
25. Ibid., 59.
26. Dawidowicz, *The War Against the Jews 1933-1945*, 23.
27. P. Johnson, *A History of Christianity*, 490.
28. Dawidowicz, *The War Against the Jews*, 23.
29. Myers, *History of Bigotry in the United States*, 388-89.
30. Kahl, *The Misery of Christianity*, 60-61.
31. Spotts, *The Churches and Politics in Germany*, 9. Statistics from this source provided by Pastor Wilhelm Niemoller and Professor Karl Kupisch.

32. Helmreich, *The German Churches Under Hitler*, 344-45.
33. Bronowski, *The Ascent of Man*, 374.
34. Lea, *A History of the Inquisition*, I: 213.
35. Ibid., 215.
36. Walker, *A History of the Christian Church*, 231.
37. Ibid., 232.
38. Bronowski, *The Ascent of Man*, 216.
39. Kamen, *The Spanish Inquisition*, 185-86.
40. O'Brien, *The Inquisition*, 102-03.
41. Nigg, *The Heretics*, 222.
42. Ibid., 236.
43. Lea, *A History of the Inquisition*, I: 235.
44. Nigg, *The Heretics*, 207.
45. Kahl, *The Misery of Christianity*, 68.

CHAPTER II   Absolute Authority—Continued Chaos

1. P. Johnson, *A History of Christianity*, 75.
2. Furnish, *Theology and Ethics*, 51-55.
3. Ruether, *Religion and Sexism*, 137.
4. Ibid., 123.
5. C. Richardson, *The Early Christian Fathers*, I: 118.
6. P. Johnson, *A History of Christianity*, 49.
7. Kahl, *The Misery of Christianity*, 77.
8. C. Richardson, *The Early Christian Fathers*, I: 436.
9. Bainton, *Women of the Reformation*, 12
10. Kahl, *The Misery of Christianity*, 79-81.
11. Ruether, *Religion and Sexism*, 217.
12. Tappert, *Table Talk*, 54: 8, 174-75.
13. Ibid., 160.
14. Ibid., 171.
15. Scarre, *Witchcraft and Magic in Sixteenth and Seventeenth Century Europe*, 25; O'Brien, *The Inquisition*, 112-13.
16. Kelly, *The Devil, Demonology and Witchcraft*, 25.
17. Ibid., 29.
18. C. Richardson, *The Early Christian Fathers*, I: 327, 360.
19. Kelly, *The Devil, Demonology and Witchcraft*, 37.
20. O'Brien, *The Inquisition*, 137-38.
21. Ibid., 119-22.
22. Lea, *A History of the Inquisition*, III: 549.
23. Ibid.
24. P. Johnson, *A History of Christianity*, 309.
25. O'Brien, *The Inquisition*, 122.
26. Kamen, *Spanish Inquisition*, 204.

27. P. Johnson, *A History of Christianity*, 309.
28. Parker, *John Calvin: A Biography*, 59.
29. O'Brien, *The Inquisition*, 117-18.
30. Ibid., 101, 103.
31. Kamen, *Spanish Inquisition*, 176.
32. Solzhenitsyn, *The Gulag Archipelago*, Part I-II, 12-13.
33. Nigg, *Das Buch der Ketzer*, 271.

CHAPTER III   Ongoing Bibliolatry

1. Rochman, Tippit, and Peterzell, "Apologists for Murder," 39.
2. "AIDS Ruckus in the Vatican," 58.
3. "Creationists Lose First Round of a Long Fight," 34. See also articles by John Skow, Allen Hammond, and Lynn Margulis in *Science 81* 2 (December 1981), no. 10: 53-60; "Enigmas of Evolution," *Newsweek* 99 (March 29, 1982), no. 13: 44-49; Fosdick, Harry Emerson, "Shall the Fundamentalists Win?" *The Christian Work* 102 (June 10, 1922), 716-19, 722; *Lubbock Avalanche Journal* 58 (January 15, 1984), no. 19: A-17.
4. Berra, *Evolution and the Myth of Creationism*, 126-132.

CHAPTER IV   The Astrolabe Mind

1. Van Doren, *A History of Knowledge*, 199-203; Bronowski, *The Ascent of Man*, 216.
2. Schafter, "Moon Science," 90.
3. Smart, *The Strange Silence of the Bible in the Church*, 64.
4. Feuillet, *Introduction to the New Testament*, 143.
5. Paine, *The Age of Reason*.
6. Bedell, Sandon, and Wellborn, *Religion in America*, 255.
7. Farley, "Can Church Education Be Theological Education?" 164-65.
8. Smart, *The Strange Silence*, 66-67.
9. Crim, *The Perennial Dictionary of World Religions*, 269. Also see: Perrin, Norman, *The New Testament: an Introduction*, 163.

CHAPTER V   New Testament Mythology

1. Perrin, *The New Testament*, 21-22.
2. Hick, *The Myth of God Incarnate*, 154.
3. Frei, *Theology and Narrative*, 47-48; Doty, *Contemporary New Testament Interpretation*, 90.
4. Metzger, *Historical and Literary Studies*, 19.
5. Ibid.
6. Metzger, *Historical and Literary Studies*, 19.

7. Ibid., 18.
8. Charlesworth, *Jesus' Jewishness*, 64.
9. Baigent and Leigh, *The Dead Sea Scrolls Deception*, 130-31.
10. Campbell, *Myths to Live By*, 221-22.
11. Hick, *The Myth of God Incarnate*, 152.
12. Spong, *Rescuing the Bible From Fundamentalism*, 232.
13. Campbell, *Myths to Live By*, 220.
14. Gewitz, *Looking at Ourselves*, 269.

CHAPTER VI   Christology

1. Kee, Young, and Froehlich, *Understanding the New Testament*, 35.
2. A. Richardson, *A Theological Word Book of the Bible*, 45.
3. Ibid.
4. Kee, Young, and Froehlich, *Understanding the New Testament*, 35.
5. Tenney, *New Testament Survey*, 15. See also: Perrin, *The New Testament*, 48.
6. Feuillet, *Introduction to the New Testament*, 15.
7. Ibid., 31, 20.
8. Conzelmann and Lindemann, *Interpreting the New Testament*, 143.
9. Feuillet, *Introduction to the New Testament*, 98.
10. Hick, *The Myth of God*, 96, 204.
11. Perrin, *The New Testament*, 48.
12. Ibid., 42-54.
13. Borg, *Meeting Jesus Again for the First Time*, 9; Fosdick, *A Guide to Understanding the Bible*, 44.
14. Norris, *The Christological Controversy*, 2.
15. Perrin, *The New Testament*, 49-50.
16. A. Richardson, *Theological Word Book*, 46.
17. Ibid., 131.
18. Kee, Young, and Froehlich, *Understanding the New Testament*, 201.
19. Ibid.
20. Fosdick, *A Guide to Understanding the Bible*, 45.
21. Charlot, *New Testament Disunity*, 84.
22. A. Richardson, *An Introduction to the Theology of the New Testament*, 147-48.
23. Charlot, *New Testament Disunity*, 84.
24. Perrin, *The New Testament*, 52-53; 2d edition, 84.
25. Perrin, *The New Testament*, 2d edition, 94-95, 101-02.
26. Kee, Young, and Froehlich, *Understanding the New Testament*, 330-31.

27. Perrin, *The New Testament*, 249.
28. Fosdick, *Understanding the Bible*, 46.
29. Spong, *Resurrection*, 75-77; Perrin, *The New Testament*, 6-8, 41, 138.
30. Hengel, *Judaism and Hellenism*, I: 58-78, 83ff. See also: Spivey and Smith, *Anatomy of the New Testament*, 52.
31. Hick, *The Myth of God*, 112.

CHAPTER VII   Progressive Revelation

1. Fosdick, *Understanding the Bible*, 54.
2. Weatherhead, *The Christian Agnostic*, 63.
3. Dunn, *Unity and Diversity in the New Testament*, 97-98.
4. Barclay, *The Gospel of Matthew*, I: 160.
5. Ibid., 175.
6. Dunn, *Unity and Diversity*, 63.
7. Fosdick, *Understanding the Bible*, 40.
8. Dunne, *The Way of All the Earth*, 48-49.
9. Wilkens, *The Myth of Christian Beginnings*, 158-60.
10. Niebuhr, *The Meaning of Revelation*, 5.
11. Bronowski, *The Ascent of Man*, 353.

CHAPTER VIII   Obstacles to Maturity

1. Edwards, *The New Dictionary of Thoughts*, 554.
2. Bronowski, *The Ascent of Man*, 437.
3. Barrett, *Irrational Man*, 92.
4. Fromm, *Psychoanalysis and Religion*, 57.
5. Fromm, *The Anatomy of Human Destructiveness*, 230.
6. Campbell, *Myths to Live By*, 218.
7. Ibid., 44-45.
8. Ibid.
9. Ibid., 220.
10. Edwards, *The New Dictionary of Thoughts*.
11. Ibid.
12. Lewis, *Christian Reflections*, 159.
13. Lewis, *Mere Christianity*, 55-56.
14. Barclay, *The Gospel of Matthew*, I: 131.
15. Barr, *Fundamentalism*, 207.

CHAPTER IX   What is Truth?

1. Adler, *Six Great Ideas*, 34.
2. Ibid., 41.
3. Ibid., 43.

4. Copi, *Introduction to Logic*.
5. Adler, *Six Great Ideas*, 49-50.

CHAPTER X   Possible Solutions

1. Hick, *The Myth of God*, 9.

EPILOGUE

1. From the unpublished writings of poet Elaine Kathryn Inman (1976-   ).
2. Dunne, *The Way of All the Earth*, 114.
3. Rogers, *On Becoming a Person*, 27.

APPENDIX 1   Biblical Criticism

1. Perrin, *The New Testament*, 8.
2. Barclay, *The Gospel of Matthew*, xviii.
3. Aland and Aland, *The Text of the New Testament*, 77; Metzger, *The Text of the New Testament*, 262. See also: Harrison, *Introduction to the New Testament*, 64.
4. McNeile, *An Introduction to the Study of the New Testament*, 373.
5. Ibid.
6. Grant, *A Historical Introduction to the New Testament*, 47.
7. Metzger, *The Text of the New Testament*, 101-02.
8. Ladd, *The New Testament and Criticism*, 59-60. See also: Metzger, *The Text of the New Testament*, 100-103.
9. Grant, *A Historical Introduction to the New Testament*, 42-43.
10. Perrin, *The New Testament*, 12.
11. Jeremias, *Rediscovering the Parables*, 32.
12. Kee, Young, and Froehlich, *Understanding the New Testament*, 90-91.
13. Davies, *Invitation to the New Testament*, 84.
14. S. Johnson, *The Interpreter's Bible*, 7: 234.
15. Kung, *Theology for the Third Millennium*, 287.
16. S. Johnson, *The Interpreter's Bible*, 7: 236.
17. *Religious Encyclopedia*, 174.

APPENDIX 2   Biblical Fallibility

1. Marshall, *New Testament Interpretation*, 128.
2. Ibid., 127-28.
3. Charlot, *New Testament Disunity*, 80-81.
4. Ibid., 81.

APPENDIX 3 The Historical Jesus

1. Sandmel, *A Jewish Understanding of the New Testament*, 207.
2. Schillebeeckx, *Jesus: an Experiment in Christology*, 72.
3. Fuller, *The New Testament in Current Study*, 35.
4. Ibid., 33.

APPENDIX 4 Catholicism and the Astrolabe Mind

1. Bedell, *Religion in America*, 270.
2. Pelikan, *The Riddle of Roman Catholicism*, 70.
3. Brown et al, *The Jerome Biblical Commentary*, 603.

APPENDIX 5 The Immaculate Conception

1. Ruether, *Religion and Sexism*, 223.
2. Pelikan, *The Riddle of Roman Catholicism*, 331-32.
3. Ruether, *Religion and Sexism*, 244.
4. Pelikan, *The Riddle of Roman Catholicism*, 131.

Bibliography

Adler, Mortimer J. *Six Great Ideas*. New York: Macmillan Publishing Co., 1981.

"AIDS Ruckus in the Vatican," *Time*, 134 (Nov. 27, 1989): 58.

Aland, Kurt, and Barbara Aland. *The Text of the New Testament (An Introduction to the Critical Editions and to the Theory and Practice of Modern Textual Criticism*, translated by Errol F. Rhodes. Grand Rapids: William B. Eerdmans, 1987; revised edition, 1989.

Baigent, Michael, and Richard Leigh. *The Dead Sea Scrolls Deception*. New York: Summit Books, 1991.

Bainton, Roland H. *Women of the Reformation in Germany and Italy*. Minneapolis: Augsburg Publishing House, 1971.

Barclay, William. *The Gospel of Matthew*, Vol. I, 2d ed. Philadelphia: The Westminster Press, 1958.

Barr, James. *Fundamentalism*. Philadelphia: Westminster Press, 1978.

Barrett, William. *Irrational Man*. Garden City, NY: Doubleday Anchor Books, 1962.

Bedell, George C., Leo Sandon, and Charles T. Wellborn. *Religion in America*, 2d Edition. New York: Macmillan, 1982.

Berra, Tim M. *Evolution and the Myth of Creationism: A Basic Guide to the Facts in the Evolution Debate*. Stanford, CA: Stanford University Press, 1990.

Boberg, Dorothy Kurth. *Evolution and Reason—Beyond Darwin*. North Hollywood, CA: Clarion Pacific Publishers, 1993.

Borg, Marcus J. *Meeting Jesus Again for the First Time (The Historical Jesus and the Heart of Contemporary Faith)*. New York: HarperSanFrancisco, 1994.

Bronowski, J. *The Ascent of Man*. Boston: Little Brown and Co., 1973.

Brown, Raymond E., *et al*, Eds. *The Jerome Biblical Commentary*. Englewood Cliffs, NJ: Prentice Hall, 1968.

Buttrick, George Arthur. *The Interpreter's Bible*, Vol. VII, edited by Nolan B. Harmon. New York: Abingdon, 1951.

Campbell, Joseph. *Myths to Live By*. New York: Bantam, 1973.

Charlesworth, James H. *Jesus' Jewishness (Exploring the Place of Jesus within Early Judaism)*. New York: Crossroad Publishing Co., 1991.

Charlot, John. *New Testament Disunity.* New York: E.P. Dutton, 1970.

Chrysostom, Saint John. *The Fathers of the Church*, Vol. 68, translated by Paul W. Harkins. Washington: The Catholic University of America Press, 1979.

Coleman, Richard J. *Issues of Theological Warfare: Evangelicals and Liberals.* Grand Rapids: William B. Eerdmans, 1972.

The Columbia Encyclopedia, 3rd Edition (1968) s.v. "tammuz."

Conzelmann, Hans, and Andreas Lindemann. Interpreting the *New Testament: An Introduction to the Principles and Methods of New Testament Exegesis*, translated by Siegfried S. Schatzmann, from the 8th rev. German edition. Peabody, Mass: Hendrickson Publishing, 1985.

Copi, Irvine, J. *Introduction to Logic*, 4th ed. New York: Macmillan, 1972.

"Creationists Lose First Round of a Long Fight," *U.S. News & World Report* 92, no. 2 (Jan. 18, 1982): 34.

Crim, Keith, General Editor. *The Perennial Dictionary of World Religions.* San Francisco: HarperCollins, 1989. Originally from Abingdon Press, 1981.

Davies, W.D. *Invitation to the New Testament.* Garden City, NY: Doubleday and Co., 1966.

Dawidowicz, Lucy S. *The War Against the Jews 1933-1945.* New York: Holt Rinehart and Winston, 1975.

Doren, Charles Van. *A History of Knowledge.* New York: Ballantine Books, 1991.

Doty, William G. *Contemporary New Testament Interpretation.* Englewood Cliffs, New Jersey: Prentice-Hall, 1972.

Dunn, James D.G. *Unity and Diversity in the New Testament.* Philadelphia: The Westminster Press, 1977.

Dunne, John S. *The Way of All the Earth.* New York: Macmillan Publishing Co., 1972.

Edwards, Tryon. *The New Dictionary of Thoughts*, rev. and enl. by C.N. Catrevas, Jonathan Edwards, and Ralph Emerson Browns. New York: Standard Book Co., 1960.

Efroymson, David P., Eurgen J. Fisher, and Leon Klenicki, Eds. *Within Context: Essays on Jews and Judaism in the New Testament.* Collegeville, MN: The Liturgical Press, 1993.

"Enigmas of Evolution," *Newsweek* 99, no. 13 (March 29, 1982): 44-49.

Evans, Craig A., and Donald A. Hagner, Eds. *Anti-Semitism and Early Christianity (Issues of Polemic and Faith).* Minneapolis: Fortress Press, 1993.

Farley, Edward. "Can Church Education Be Theological Education?" *Theology Today* (Princeton University Journal) 42 (July 1985): 164-65.

Feuillet, Robert A. *Introduction to the New Testament.* New York: Desclee Co., 1965.

Fosdick, Harry Emerson. *A Guide to Understanding the Bible.* New York: Harper Chapel Books, 1965.

Fosdick, Harry Emerson. "Shall the Fundamentalists Win?" *The Christian Work* 102 (June 10, 1922): 716-19, 722.

Frei, Hans W. *Theology and Narrative (Selected Essays),* Edited by George Hunsinger and William C. Placher. Oxford: Oxford University Press, 1993.

Fromm, Erich. *The Anatomy of Human Destructiveness.* Greenwich, CT: Fawcett Publications, 1973.

Fromm, Erich. *Psychoanalysis and Religion.* New York: Bantam Books, 1967.

Fuller, Reginald H. *The Formation of the Ressurrection Narratives.* New York: The Macmillan Company, 1972.

Fuller, Reginald H. *The New Testament in Current Study.* New York: Charles Scribners Sons, 1962.

Funk, Robert W., Roy W. Hoover, and the Jesus Seminar, Translators and Commentators. *The Five Gospels (The Search for the Authentic Jesus).* New York: Macmillan Publishing Co., 1993.

Furnish, Victor P. *Theology and Ethics in Paul.* Nashville: Abingdon Press, 1968.

Gail, Marzeih. *The Three Popes.* New York: Simon and Schuster, 1969.

Gewitz, James. *Looking at Ourselves.* Boston: Little, Brown and Co., 1976.

Gillis, Anna Maria. "Keeping Creationism Out of the Classroom: Grassroots Efforts and the Constitution Hold Their Own Against Religious Extremism," *Bioscience* 44, no. 10 (November 1994).

Grant, Robert M. *A Historical Introduction to the New Testament.* New York: Harper and Row, 1963.

Grayzel, Solomon. *A History of the Jews,* Revised Edition. New York: A Mentor Book from New American Library, 1968.

Hardie, Edward Rochie. *Christology of the Later Fathers,* Vol. 1 of *The Library of Christian Classics* (26 vols.), edited by John Baillie. Philadelphia: Westminster Press, 1954.

Harrison, Everett F. *Introduction to the New Testament,* Revised Edition. Grand Rapids: William B. Eerdmans, 1971.

Hawking, Stephen W. *A Brief History of Time.* New York: Bantam, 1988.

Helmreich, Ernst Christian. *The German Churches Under Hitler.*

Detroit: Wayne St. University Press, 1979.

Hengel, Martin. *Judaism and Hellenism (Studies in their Encounter in Palestine during the Early Hellenistic Period)*. Philadelphia: Fortress Press, 1974.

Hick, John, Editor. *The Myth of God Incarnate*. Great Britain: SCM Press, 1977.

Jeremias, Joachim. *Rediscovering the Parables*. New York: Charles Scribners Sons, SCM Press, 1966.

Johnson, Paul. *A History of Christianity*. New York: Atheneum, 1976.

Johnson, Sherman E. *The Interpreter's Bible*, Vol. 7.

Kahl, Joachim. *The Misery of Christianity*, translated by N.D. Smith. Middlesex, England: Penguin Books, 1971.

Kamen, Henry. *The Spanish Inquisition*. New York: New American Library, 1965.

Kee, Howard Clark, Franklin W. Young, and Karlfried Froehlich. *Understanding the New Testament*, 2d Edition. Englewood Cliffs, NJ: Prentice-Hall, 1965.

Kelly, Henry Ansgar. *The Devil, Demonology and Witchcraft*, Revised Edition. Garden City, NY: Doubleday, 1974.

Kung, Hans. *Theology for the Third Millennium*. New York: Doubleday, 1988.

Ladd, George Eldon. *The New Testament and Criticism*. Grand Rapids: William B. Eerdmans, 1967.

Lea, Charles Henry. *A History of the Inquisition of the Middle Ages*, 3 vols. New York: S.A. Russell Publishers, 1955.

Lewis, C.S. *Christian Reflections*, Edited by Walter Hooper. Grand Rapids: William B. Eerdmans, 1967.

Lewis, C.S. *Mere Christianity*, rev. and enl. ed. New York: The Macmillan Publishing Co., 1960.

Lubbock Avalanche Journal 58, no. 19 (January 15, 1984): A-17.

Marshall, I. Howard, Ed. *New Testament Interpretation*. Grand Rapids: William B. Eerdmans, 1977.

McNeile, A.H. *An Introduction to the Study of the New Testament*, 2d Edition, Revised by CSC Williams. London: Oxford University Press, Amen House, 1953.

Metzger, Bruce M. *Historical and Literary Studies*. Leiden, Netherlands: E.J. Brill, 1968.

Metzger, Bruce M. *The Text of the New Testament*. New York: Oxford University Press, 1992.

Morris, James. *The Preachers*. New York: St. Martin's Press, 1973.

Myers, Gustavus. *History of Bigotry in the United States*. New York: Random House, 1943.

Niebuhr, H. Richard. *The Meaning of Revelation*. New York: Macmillan, 1960.

Nigg, Walter. *Das Buch der Ketzer*, 4th Edition. Zurich and Stuttgart, 1962.

Nigg, Walter. *The Heretics*, edited and translated by Richard and Clara Winston. New York: Alfred A. Knopf, 1962.

Norris, Richard A. *The Christological Controversy*. Philadelphia: Fortress Press, 1980.

O'Brien, John A. *The Inquisition*. New York: Macmillan, 1973.

Pache, Rene. *The Inspiration and Authority of Scripture*, trans. by Helen I. Needham. Chicago: Moody Press, 1969.

Paine, Thomas. *The Age of Reason*, Pt. I, 2d Rev. Ed., edited with an intro. by Alburey Castell. Indianapolis: Bobbs-Merrill, 1957.

Parker, T.H.L. *John Calvin: A Biography*. Philadelphia: Westminster Press, 1975.

Pelikan, Jaroslav. *The Riddle of Roman Catholicism*. Nashville: Abingdon, 1959.

Perrin, Norman. *The New Testament: an Introduction*. New York: Harcourt Brace Jovanovich, 1974. Also, 2d edition under the general editorship of Robert Fern. New York: Harcourt Brace Jovanovich, Inc., 1982.

Peters, Edward. *Inquisition*. New York: The Free Press—Collier Macmillan Publishers, 1988.

Religious Encyclopedia, 174.

Richardson, Alan. *An Introduction to the Theology of the New Testament*. New York: Harper and Row, 1958.

Richardson, Alan, Editor. *A Theological Word Book of the Bible*. New York: The Macmillan Publishing Co., 1950.

Richardson, Cyril Charles. *The Early Christian Fathers*, Vol. 1 of *The Library of Christian Classics* (26 vols.), edited by John Baillie. Philadelphia: Westminster Press, 1953.

Rochman, Bonnie, Sarah Tippit, and Jay Peterzell. "Apologists for Murder," *Time* 144, no. 7 (August 15, 1994).

Rogers, Carl R. *On Becoming a Person*. Boston: Houghton Mifflin Co., 1961.

Ruether, Rosemary Radford. *Religion and Sexism*. New York: Simon and Schuster, 1974.

Sandmel, Samuel. *A Jewish Understanding of the New Testament*. New York: KYAV Publishing House, 1956.

Scarre, Geoffrey. *Witchcraft and Magic in Sixteenth and Seventeenth Century Europe*. London: Macmillan Education LTD, 1987.

Schafter, James. "Moon Science," *Popular Science*, October 1978, 90.

Schillebeeckx, Edwards. *Jesus: an Experiment in Christology.* New York: Crossroads, 1981.

Seiferth, Wolfgang S. *Synagogue and Church in the Middle Ages.* New York: Frederick Ungar Publishing Co., 1970.

Smart, James D. *The Interpretation of Scripture.* Philadelphia: Westminster Press, 1961.

Smart, James D. *The Strange Silence of the Bible in the Church.* Philadelphia: Westminster Press, 1970.

Solzhenitsyn, Aleksandr. *The Gulag Archipelago,* Parts I-II, translated by Thomas P. Whitney. New York: Harper and Row, 1973.

Spivey, Robert A., and D. Moody Smith. *Anatomy of the New Testament.* New York: Macmillan Publishing Co., 1982.

Spong, John Shelby. *Rescuing the Bible From Fundamentalism.* New York: HarperSanFrancisco, 1991.

Spong, John Shelby. *Resurrection: Myth or Reality?* New York: HarperSanFrancisco, 1994.

Spotts, Frederic. *The Churches and Politics in Germany.* Middletown, CT: Wesleyan University Press, 1973.

Synan, Edward A. *The Popes and the Jews in the Middle Ages.* New York: Macmillan Publishing Co., 1965.

Tappert, Theodore G. *Table Talk,* in *Luther's Works,* Vol. 54, edited by Jaroslav Pelikan (vols. 1-30) and Helmut T. Lehmann (vols. 31-55). Philadelphia: Fortress Press, 1967.

Tedeschi, John. *The Prosecution of Heresy (Collected Studies of the Inquisition in Early Italy).* Binghampton: State University of New York, 1991.

Tenney, Merrill C. *New Testament Survey,* revised by Walter M. Dunnet. Grand Rapids, MI: William B. Eerdmans, 1985.

Van Doren, Charles. *A History of Knowledge.* New York: Ballantine Books, 1991.

Vogt, Hannah. *The Jews: A Chronicle for Christian Conscience,* with two chapters by Robert H. Roberts. New York: Association Press, 1967.

Walker, Williston. *A History of the Christian Church,* revised by Cyril C. Richardson. New York: Scribners, 1959.

Weatherhead, Leslie D. *The Christian Agnostic.* New York: Abingdon Press, 1965.

Wilkens, Robert L. *The Myth of Christian Beginnings.* New York: Doubleday & Co., 1971.

The World Book Encyclopedia, 1992, s.v. "bubonic plague."

World Christian Encyclopedia, ed. by David B. Barrett. New York: Oxford University Press, 1982.

Index

About the Author

Ernie Bringas was born in San Diego, California, in 1939. He obtained his B.A. at the California State University, Long Beach. His graduate study led to an M.Div. (Master of Divinity) degree at United Theological Seminary, Dayton, Ohio, in 1966. Further religious studies were briefly pursued at Fuller Theological Seminary (Pasadena, California) and at the Pacific School of Religion (Berkeley, California).

During the early '60s, while pursuing his university and seminary studies, Ernie and his partner Phil Stewart founded a rock group which came to be known as THE RIPCHORDS. The group, recording for Columbia Records, placed five hit singles on the Billboard/Cashbox Top 100 charts (1963-66).

After obtaining his M.Div., Ernie was ordained as a minister of the United Methodist Church and served various Methodist churches, primarily in California but also in Texas. One of the highlights of his ministry centered at the Good Samaritan United Methodist Church in Cupertino, California, where, as Minister of Youth from 1969 to 1975, he developed the most successful high school youth program in the history of the California Conference (the youth group registered a record high attendance of 346, with an average weekly attendance of over 200). Ernie also served (1983-86) as one of four ministers of the First United Methodist Church in Lubbock, Texas, a 6000-member church which ranks as the 9th largest UMC in the world.

At the present time, Ernie is on leave of absence from the church. Although he serves churches on a volunteer basis, much of his time and energy are now directed toward his writing endeavors.

Hampton Roads Publishing Company
concentrates on three related areas of interest:
Metaphysics,
Alternative medicine
Visionary fiction.
For a copy of our latest catalog, call toll-free,
(800) 766-8009, or send your name and address to:

Hampton Roads Publishing Company, Inc.
134 Burgess Lane
Charlottesville, VA 22902